MONTY

"a little man on the make"

TOWARDS ALAMEIN

by David S Britton

2nd edition
Published in 2016 by FeedARead Publishing
Copyright David S Britton

FOREWORD

This book is a piece of historical fiction about Field Marshall Montgomery (Monty), and the many battles he had to fight with himself, and the army hierarchy, to get to the battlefield of Alamein. It is a well-researched piece drawing on many existing histories, especially the brilliant trilogy by Nigel Hamilton, as well as some documents in the Imperial War Museum.

From one angle, my story is a pacifist's tribute to a humane military man. Or, I should say, an ex-pacifist's tribute – though it was a considerable time after changing my mind on issues of peace and war that I became focussed on Montgomery. You could not grow up in the 1940's and 50's without hearing about him, and seeing his face in various contexts – most frequently, he and Churchill together. Peter Ustinov and Peter Jones lampooned most of the British 2nd World War Generals in 1955, in their wonderful radio programme 'In All Directions', and The Goons took a dig at the multiple memoirs then being serialised in the Sunday papers. My Prologue picks up on that time and that atmosphere.

Why and when did Monty cease to be a figure of fun in my eyes, and become a figure of intense interest? First, when I learnt of him as a brilliant teacher, holding his audience for hours, and able to make the most complex things clear even in battle situations. Every man was to know the overall plan, and what his own role was. Having had a roving education myself, following my father's army postings, and two years of National Service in the Army Education Corps, without getting much of an overall plan, followed by three years doing history at Oxford, where the fog only thickened, Monty's brand of clear explanation, coupled with caution and a determination not to throw away lives, attracted and interested me.

But beyond that, it was the impact on his life and career of two major relationships that made me want to write about him. The influence of his beloved wife, a bohemian painter, who changed him from a narrowly military mindset, riding over an unloved and wretched childhood, to the man of wide sympathies and capacity for reaching out to others which made him so great a leader of men: and with Churchill, who couldn't stand him, and who Monty needed, to get his chance to take his country to victory at Alamein. Slowly, slowly Monty won him over. Monty, who could sleep like a baby, and keep calm through bombardment and battle, gave Churchill, on the verge of a nervous breakdown, sun, sea, and a chance to paint.

This story is based on a great deal of real detail, but carried forward mainly by imagined dialogue, which brings out both Monty's vanity, and his capacity for unusual empathy and humour. The reader is invited to 'see' the action as if watching a film, or there as it happens. Everything is in the present tense, is happening now.

Always sure he is right, totally tactless to those he cannot respect, and in no way a public-school gentleman, Monty could never be popular with the top brass (or conventional military historians - Nigel Hamilton's volumes give a much more positive picture).

I earned my living teaching history in secondary schools, and selling paintings, till I retired from teaching, (and then lost most of my sight a year ago, which impedes but does not stop the painting).

I think that this story could be enjoyed by many of the people who still know Monty's name, and watch the recent TV programmes about him and the war, but who would not read traditional histories. It gives a true picture of the man and his achievement, in the setting of his times.

TABLE OF CONTENTS

PROLOGUE

Early September 1955, a mellow evening. A long-legged handsome man in his late 30's walks across the big lawns of the old Mill-house, rings a perfunctory bell, and walks in quietly. So quietly in fact, and after such a feeble ring, that he is sure he hasn't been heard by the guests at table in a far room, or by Monty himself, who is at the head of the table – and who appears to be holding forth in a manner only too familiar to the visitor, his stepson.

The stepson, Richard Carver by name, moves aside quickly, hiding behind a coat-rack, and listens and watches carefully for a minute or two. Nobody speaks except Monty, and it is Monty in his most vainglorious mode, with no humour except the laboured jokes one is obliged to laugh at; no gaps in his armour, and little in the way of pauses in which his guests might contrive to put in their pennyworth. Consequently there is the cut-glass propriety and exhausting silence, in which the slightest tummy-rumble is heard by its perpetrator. Everyone present registers even the politest clearing of the throat, a starched cuff re-arranged, or a collar loosened. These create the faintest of echoes, and are sensed as possibly rude.

The four guests are of the starched variety, certainly. Two middle-aged men in evening dress, presumably military, though the stepson in hiding does not recognise them, and their wives, evening-dressed and polished and coifed and scented in the appropriate manner. Monty is gathering yet another little group of the next generation of promising officers. He himself is approaching seventy ... and is endeavouring to press on them his former glory and his enduring greatness, together with certain crucial lessons and sound principles, gathered both from his teaching days and from his considerable battle experience.

At this precise moment Monty is saying, ' So I said to General Lumsden, one of the Tank Commanders, after the battle of Alamein was over ... I said " You fool, Lumsden! Had you got your tanks forward, as I ordered you to do, you would have shared in the glory of that victory in the wonderful breakout phase. But there you were, lagging behind as usual. And <u>why</u>, Lumsden, I ask you, why?" And Lumsden said "The tanks were just not up to the job, sir!" And I said " Not up to the job, Lumsden! No, it's you who are not up to the job, Lumsden, and that's why I'm relieving you of your command." And he just said "Thank you sir." That's all he said,. "Thank you sir." He had nothing else to say. Just not up to the job, I'm afraid. Still, the poor man is dead now, killed in the last year of the war, so I shouldn't rub this particular lesson in too hard … But, the correct use of Armour is of huge importance in battle, and I pride myself on having had the keenest appreciation of that in the entire British, and indeed the entire Allied Army at the time.

'However, I don't want to bore you with tanks and all that. Let's talk about the Infantry, a matter on which I am possibly the world's leading expert. Now first of all … Oh, here is my stepson Richard, a most excellent fellow.'

So Richard makes his welcome entrance at that point of the evening when the guests were saying to themselves, in the depths of their chests, 'Home, and absolute bliss, in just one hour from now!' Richard makes for the far end of the table. Everyone is introduced, and Richard sits down.

'As I was saying,' says Monty, 'a fine fellow, with the virtues of both splendid parents embodied in his person!' Richard bows as gracefully as it is possible to do from a seated position, as Monty then says, 'Though why he should want to skulk behind the hat-stand for a full two minutes before entering the room only he can tell us!'

There is a little explosion and almost laughter all round, and a pained splutter from Richard.

'I was only listening to hear if I knew any of the guests by their voices, Monty. Preparing myself, as it were.'

'Rubbish, my boy. You were listening to find out if this was one of my boring monologue evenings, so that you could learn how to play it.'

'Oh honestly, Monty!' says Richard, embarrassed, as the guests actually deign to laugh, and begin to feel relaxed.

'Oh honestly, Oh honestly, Richard,' Monty mimics.

Richard has just met yet another of his 'you can't ever fool Monty' events ... from personal experience, and from tales handed down and going back some thirty years ... nearly all of his own life-time, in fact.

'Oh, but we weren't bored!' says one of the wives, gushingly, and with the relief of some animation in her frame and psyche.

'Nonsense, of <u>course</u> you were bored!' says Monty. 'I always bore people on these occasions. I do not intend to bore them. I always hope that by some magic in the atmosphere, by what I bring, or what my audience may happen to bring along, the occasion will light up, and I will sparkle, and the guests will never want to go home!' Monty pauses, and there is a slightly embarrassed silence while the guests hope and pray that Monty will desist from exploring this aspect of his theme. But Monty is merciless, 'Whereas, what do we have here,' he says 'but four polite guests absolutely longing to get home ...'

There is a subdued protest.

'... Absolutely longing to get home,' he repeats. 'And absolutely stifled, both in their minds and in their evening dress.'

'But it is really very interesting,' says the other elegant lady. 'And I'm sure very instructive for all the officers who come here.'

'Yes, it could be ... it could be ...' says Monty, 'But unfortunately, it usually isn't.'

A longish silence.

'All my own fault of course,' he ventures at last. 'My own ego and vanity getting in the way, usually.'

Another silence.

'Nothing much I can do about it, usually, unfortunately, ' says Monty, 'for once I am <u>launched</u>, once I am <u>sailing</u> ... once I have got the bit between my teeth ... and so on ...' He stops.

There is a silence now which allows the truth. The ladies cease to protest, and the gentlemen hold their peace.

'I need a mentor, you see,' Monty begins again, 'I need a disciplinarian around. Someone to keep me in check. Someone I can <u>respect,</u>' he says emphatically. 'Unfortunately, there have been very few military men, either at my own level, or above it, I've been able to respect. Alanbrooke I've always respected ... a great and good man ... and Alanbrooke has been my mentor through much of my military career. A man able to tell me off for my faults in a most persuasive way. Him I always obey, because he is always right where I am concerned, and where most military things are concerned.'

But what about the staff team you worked with ... at Alamein, and in Normandy?' says Richard, 'What about good old Freddie de Guingand, and Bill Williams, and Richardson ... and Kit Dawnay ... and Johnny Henderson ... and...'

'Yes, yes, yes!' says Monty, 'all fine men, who spoke their minds to me on military issues, as I encouraged them to do ... but not mentors in general, I'm afraid. Being younger than me, they could hardly perform that task.'

'If you listened to Alanbrooke,' says Richard, 'couldn't you then apply his catechism at all times, Monty? That's what puzzles people.'

'Not when my own need for glory is in full flow,' says Monty. 'A runaway horse. And always the stupid self-justification that in fact, this person, or that person, or this or that group of persons, haven't actually heard me before, and wouldn't necessarily know my full greatness as a military leader ...'

'But you were a public figure for years,' Richard says. 'Everyone knew about Alamein, and about D-Day.'

'But it is peacetime now,' says Monty, 'and people soon forget. I keep needing to remind them ... it's not pleasant to find yourself being gradually forgotten, when at one time you've been in the news every other day, and a hero to millions.'

'Something of a drug, then, fame?' asks one of the officers, 'Hard to get off it, I suppose.'

'Yes,' says Monty, 'and especially when you've spent so many years building towards it ... difficult years, with most of the military establishment against you ... stuffy people, people without a sense of urgency, not seeing the dangers ahead. I saw the dangers, spoke up ... and was vindicated in the end.'

'Good for you, Monty,' says the other officer. 'In fact, quite like Churchill!'

'Nice to be compared to Churchill,' says Richard, 'That should have been enough, one would think … but does Churchill keep on crowing about it?'

'No, he doesn't. Though he's vain enough, by God!' says Monty 'Even in areas where he's got plenty to be modest about! But Churchill is pretty quiet now. And probably a bit lonely, like me,' says Monty. 'And I understand he is actually depressed. I mean, having been Prime Minister, and a war-hero, and now a National Monument, does not actually protect you from deep loneliness later on. People will hardly believe it, but it is true…'

'The attention has shifted elsewhere,' puts in the other officer, 'and the great past begins to feel like a dream … '

'Yes, one is not much affirmed any more,' says Monty, 'and I seem to be one of those who need constant affirmation … and since nobody much has been affirming me these last few years, I feel I must affirm myself, that's all.'

There is a longish, rather awkward, silence. 'But it makes you smaller,' says Richard, 'that's the trouble. It doesn't actually work!'

'I know that rationally, of course,' says Monty. 'But the good old war-fellowship is gone. Churchill has had different tasks in peacetime. I hardly ever see him. Good old Freddie de Guingand has gone off to South Africa. And so on … How often does one actually meet old comrades? And when one does, it is just not the same – the fire in the belly, the light in the eye, the sense of magic in comradeship, a fellowship growing hour by hour, the sense that somehow we walked in the heavens, even while we dealt out death, and terrible wounds … all that has gone.'

'All this is very sad,' says one of the officers, 'but extremely interesting if you are a reflective person.'

'I have had plenty of time to become a reflective person,' says Monty,' too much time, and too little contact of the kind that warms the heart and fills life with meaning … and this emptiness I fill with public appearances ... and travelling abroad. That's something, at least ... travelling ... for taking your mind off yourself, and the emptiness … it is very good while it lasts.'

'And while you are lionised by every foreign statesman you meet, and can assume yourself to be of equal stature ... and equally <u>current</u>, that's the main thing, isn't it?' asks Richard.

'You are a good soul, Richard ... and so very like your dear mother,' says Monty, 'Full of insight.'

'But I'm no good as a mentor and disciplinarian, as she was!' says Richard. 'You won't take advice or consolation from me, as you did from her!'

'True, true,' says Monty, 'but who could be the equal of her? If she were alive now, how very different my life would be! My vanity kept in check, a full sense of my own worth, with her love flowing towards me ... And to see her continuing to develop her painting, and teaching me so much that I don't know! Such fullness, such serene days!'

'It is something we will all have to face,' says the same officer, 'and perhaps something worse than battle.'

'Worse than battle!' exclaims Monty, 'I enjoyed every moment of a battle! I felt equal to everything that a mere battle-crisis could throw at me!'

'I'm sure you did,' says Richard, 'and so did Churchill, there's another resemblance.'

'But Churchill didn't particularly enjoy the politics of warfare,' says Monty, 'The war broke his health, nearly finished him. He was a big man, but the political challenge ... and the horrible military disappointments in the first three years of the war ... those broke him to pieces.'

'But your achievements helped to revive him,' says the first officer. 'We all owe that to you, Monty.'

'Yes, you do,' says Monty, 'But it all came a bit to late to save poor old Churchill's health.'

They all reflect on Churchill and the war for a while. Monty at last chuckles.

'Do you know what Churchill called me at one point? When Alanbrooke was trying to get me noticed and promoted? He said 'Montgomery? He's just a little man on the make!' A little man on the make!' Monty laughs uproariously, and they all laugh.

'Anyway, enough of this. As you know, I take to my bed early, as I have always done, and that time is fast approaching. However, if you won't mind, I will just turn on the radio for half-

an-hour, and we can all listen to the Goon Show, one of my favourites. Spike Milligan was out in North Africa, you know ... lampooned me, no doubt, but such a funny man. Anyway, do you mind if we listen?'
'A pleasure!' and 'Not at all!' are variously said.

So the radio is turned on, and the usual raucous music and shrieks and the collapsing of towers of saucepans and the like, are transmitted. At length the solemn voice of a narrator is heard.

'Deep in the wilds around Tunbridge Wells a strange and highly secret camp is to be found.'
'This must be it!' says a silky voice 'It is a completely sealed building and windowless. But there must be an entrance somewhere. We will all creep round it slowly to find the way in.'

Before they can begin to do so there is a faint clucking sound. There is also a regular tap-tapping.

'It sounds like a chicken to me,' says Eccles.

The tap-tap-tap-tap begins to flower into softly spoken words, like someone talking to himself.

'Listen harder, and we will make out the words,' says the smooth one.

'And we came up to the line around Benghazi, and Rommel was chasing us pretty fast,'

Monty slaps his thighs and laughs, and everyone leans forward in anticipation.

The voice resumes 'So I got on the phone to Wavell in Cairo, and I said, 'You fool, Wavell! Didn't I just tell you this would happen?' and he said, for Wavell was a decent chap when all is said and done ... he said, 'Certainly you did, certainly you did, O'Connor. But the point is, what do we do now?' So I said, 'There's nothing much we can do while that damned fool Dorman-Smith is throwing his weight about round here!'

'Good heavens,' cries Monty, 'Chink Dorman-Smith. A damned fool, indeed. The Goons have got him!'

'Shush,' everyone says.

They continue their creeping, and fragments are heard as they pass by.

'So I said to Alanbrooke, I said 'you fool, Alanbrooke ...'

And then another voice-fragment, 'And Alexander said to me 'What is your view on this?' And I answered, 'Alexander, you fool!'

And yet another, asking, 'Who in heaven's name is responsible for this fiasco at Arnhem?' And I replied, 'That damned fool Montgomery!'

Great roars of laughter from Monty and his guests. They rock up and down in their easy chairs, and Monty slaps his thighs again and thumps a small table.

'Genius!' cries Monty 'Absolute genius!'

'Shush!' cry the others..

There is a sound of a great creaking barn door being opened, then a loud announcement,

'Second World War Generals! Stand by your memoirs!'

This is followed by distressed clucking sounds, the scraping of chairs. And the creaks and groans of old weary men struggling to their feet.

There is then a shuffling of suede shoes on the floor of the barn, followed by a rush of same suede shoes, followed by shouts and curses and the noise of tables falling over, glasses of water smashing on the ground, and then a suede-shoed stampede towards the exit. Wails of the generals follow them. 'Give me back my memoirs!'

Finally a band strikes up 'It's a long way to Tipperary' in very quick time, out of tune with the tune, and with each other, in the usual way.

'Well, that's it!' says Monty 'And haven't they just livened up our evening!'

PART ONE - HOSPITAL

Chapter 1 – An Insect Bite

It is late August 1937

Monty, (now Brigadier Montgomery and aged 50), and his wife
Betty and their 10-year-old son David have been on holiday in
Bridgwater Bay in Somerset. Monty is walking alone through the
seaside town of Weston-super-Mare at a brisk rate. He is clearly a
happy man, and is in fine fettle. In fact he is so happy at the
moment, and in such a rare state of peace with himself and with
the world, that he is even prepared to be wise in his dealings with
those unfortunates, other people.

He is remembering a piece of advice sometimes given to him
by his dear wife – most certainly 'the idol of his life', as the song
says, and certainly to be taken with the utmost seriousness on
those occasions when she has seen fit to guide him and to warn
him against 'hubris', and other personality failings.

He has always taken these criticisms meekly as well as
seriously. The simple trouble is, remembering in time. The other
trouble is, setting them against that other idol of his life ... that is
to say, himself ... and finding in them enough weight to draw him
away from the practice of this latter worship ... and 'in time', that
was the main thing, 'in time'! The first difficulty was always
getting in the way as far as the second difficulty was concerned. A
momentary darkness passed across his face as he remembered
several embarrassing occasions of his own rudeness, and reflected
on the unfairness of Fate, and the way judgments are made about
oneself without knowledge of the inner complexities. On how
many of those occasions had he remembered Betty, and his
manners, the split second after having delivered himself of a
remark staggering in its insensitivity, and appalling in its
revelation of his own vanity and self-regard! He was repentant
within seconds, but it was nearly always too late, or he was too
confused, to repair the damage.

But today, today, he was remembering! He was warning

himself, as Betty had advised him to do, aloud, saying, 'Be careful, Bernard. This is exactly the moment to be careful!' There were delicate things to be negotiated, and he would need the best of himself to see them through without upsets. He would never have guessed that it was precisely in these times of tip-top physical condition, strong nerves and his own gusto for life and self-enjoyment, that the devil lurked and then sprang. But Betty had seen it many times, and Betty had said, 'Just watch out at those times, my dear old Monty, and then you will sail through, and be loved by everyone. Oh there's so much in you that is loveable, darling Monty, just don't spoil it. Just everyone would love you, almost as much as I do, if only you didn't blurt out those awful things sometimes. It gets you a reputation, you know it does.'

All too bitterly true, he knew. But he had enjoyed high hopes in these 10 years of his happy marriage of putting a few things right, and living down some of the bad reputation that he had acquired in the 10 or so years before his marriage. His own certainty about what was wrong with the British Army, particularly with its system of training, and its stifling class-system ... these certainties of his, which were in fact truths, and based on numerous first-hand experiences in the trenches of the First World War, were in practice thwarted in their operation by his own manner, his narrow, obsessed, military life, and his perceived bitterness, as well as his vanity and aggression. He spent many years as the Mess bore, to be avoided if possible, and laughed at behind his back. He knew he was laughed at and despised, for he had X-Ray antennae, and intuitions that could have been psychic. He saw and heard and sensed everything, knew his situation, but carried on, unable to change himself. Only married happiness had given him this wonderful second chance, the chance to be an unembittered teacher of men, and an inspiration.

He knew he could be an inspiration, even a genius, though 'genius' had hardly been a word in his narrow vocabulary until he met and married Betty, herself an artist, and with a circle of artistic friends. So the word 'genius' had gradually seeped into his consciousness, and it occurred to him that if the great Rembrandt had indeed been a 'genius', then why shouldn't dear old Monty be a 'genius' in his own way? He sensed that Betty believed it of him, and this thought alone filled him with delirious happiness.

As he walked along beside the beach, he found himself stopping several times, not through having observed anything out there, but through the force of his own preoccupation. He stopped abruptly, and several people looked at him, for his inner preoccupation was obvious, and striking ... and sometimes he was found to be talking to himself, just as he had persuaded himself to. His sharp foxy face had in it the most extraordinary eyes and glance, and this glance was just as penetrating when it was looking inward as when it was piercing the mildly shocked defences of some passing stranger.

For as Monty walked and passed people, he tended to spear each one with his glance, by force of habit at this particular time, rather than interest, for the main burden of his interest was clearly in his own mental world today, and for good reason. But even his 'spearing' of others was a powerful force, and people felt it, and wondered who this man was ... he was dressed nattily in holiday civilian clothes ... and what he might be up to.

He was clearly not just enjoying being 'beside the seaside', even though his health and vigour and brownness were also striking. He was a small lithe athletic man, spruce and alert. His casual clothes, though not pressed or smart, were startlingly clean and wholesome looking, and he seemed at home in them in a way that was almost as unusual as his penetrating glance. His health, and the relaxation that went with it, and the energy in reserve, like a coiled spring, and beneath that a sense of having his tap-root in a place of geniality that was both universal and in some strange way, out of this world ... all these things, but especially the last, gave a most extraordinary reassurance and happiness to the soldiers under his command. He was aware that he could inspire, as we have seen, but he was too simple a soul to be aware of the source of his inspiration. He attributed his power over men to his knowledge of military affairs, his supreme confidence in imparting it, his physical fitness, and his cliche-ridden little moral homilies ... these latter the residue of his education at St Paul's, and not at all part of the world of the mainly working-class men under his command. But they took it from him, where they would have inwardly sneered at others, because of the mystery and depth of his geniality, though of course most of these men would not have been aware of this. 'There's just something about Monty, I don't know what it is!' was the usual way of summing it up.

He had <u>been</u> on holiday, that much seemed certain to the passers-by today. But why these intense and unsmiling looks, and who was this solitary prowler, and why didn't he just 'join in' and smile, and why above all was he talking to himself? So said the looks and the shared smiles and jokes of many that he passed, and of which Monty was not at all oblivious, for all his inner concerns. Once a couple of young men affected to spring away from him in alarm, having just received the stab of his fierce glance. They went on down the promenade, giggling and gesticulating, and practising the sudden springs of frightened rabbits. Monty saw and registered it all, and took it quietly into his system of learning.

At last he arrived at the pier, and stopped again, knowing this would be the last pause for reflection and resolution before he set off into the town. He was developing in his mind a new aspect of one of his most basic teaching points. An inspiration had struck him, so that he actually blurted out 'Eureka' as he stood there, and so loudly that again people looked round and stared at him. He continued talking to himself, saying, 'But it's too early to say it. It will have to wait. It will have to wait. But meanwhile, exhilaration! That will do for now. Exhilaration! However, be careful Bernard, be careful!'

Then he set off at an even brisker pace than before, away from the beach and towards the main part of the town, sweeping the shops and the walkers with an even fiercer glance, and saying alternately 'Exhilaration' and 'Be careful Bernard' until he arrived at the hotel where he was due to meet his 10 year–old son David. He went into the lobby, nodded to the receptionist, and saw David seated on the far side.

'Hullo, my boy! We must get down to business pretty quickly.

Your mother has been found a bed in the hospital here, where she's likely to be for a few days, and meanwhile, as you know, I've got to find someone to look after you while you stay here in the hotel and visit your mother each day. Understood? Yes. Good. Now who would you like me to get for you?'

'Oh, I don't mind, anyone I can talk to a bit, and get on with, Monty.'

'Good. Well, I've the ideal person. I'll phone up your half-brother John, and I'll ask for Jocelyn. How would that suit you?'

'That would be best of all.'

'Right. Now where's that phone?'

He goes over to a small booth, dials, and rocks on his splayed legs while he waits for an answer.

'Hullo John, Monty here. Listen John, I know you're just back from India on leave and want to be with your wife, but I sorely need Jocelyn's help, and speedily. Will you bring her to the phone?'

' Hullo Monty! But can't you tell me first what it's all about? I mean I can get her of course, but I'd like to be in the picture a bit before you get at her, if you see what I mean ...'

'Yes, yes, yes of course. Though equally she could tell you afterwards, when it's all settled ... but as you wish. Hullo, are you there?'

Monty hangs on impatiently while John and Jocelyn exchange whispers.

'Yes, I'm here Monty. Carry on.'

'It's like this, John. Betty has had a little accident on our seaside holiday ... bitten by some insect on the leg. A nothing, but its flared up a bit, and she's in hospital for observation. Should be just a few days, at most a week, and I need Jocelyn to come and be with David in the hotel here and for visits to the hospital. It's perfectly simple ... just that ... Are you there, John? John?'

John is miming a message to Jocelyn who is at the other end of the room, and trying to conceal it from Monty by keeping on talking.

'Yes, still here Monty ... but there is just one point ... '

'Why don't I do it myself? Because I have these crucially

important training exercises on Salisbury Plain, and they start the day after tomorrow, and go on for several weeks. And I'm in charge John, that's the rub. Can't possibly miss them or even be a day late. Confounded nuisance this illness, but there it is ... So what does she say?'

There is a short silence, while Jocelyn gets the message and does a mime of protest a yard or two behind her husband.

'Confound it John, bring her to the phone, will you, and let us sort it out together. And confound it Jocelyn, stop prancing about and making horrible faces will you!'

'Jocelyn is suggesting her cousin Horace for the job, Monty. He's got nothing to do, and you know how well he gets on with boys. He'd be ideal, Monty, don't you think?'

'No I do not, John. Please bring Jocelyn to the phone, and I'll tell her why.'

'All right, Monty, here she is'.

'That you, Jocelyn? Now look here. Fwightful fellow, (Monty has a slight lisp on occasions) your cousin Horace, I'm afraid. Eats peas off his knife ... Not important, you say? In many circumstances, true, but this is different. Poor David has enough to put up with here, a bad end to a lovely holiday, his mother in hospital, me going away, his school term starting in a couple of weeks, and staying here in quite a posh hotel where everything is 'comme il faut', as they say. The last thing he needs is the social embarrassment of Horace's table manners in elevated company. Absolutely the last straw. Is that understood?'

'Yes I suppose so, Monty, but there is just one other thing, and that's my social embarrassment. I've never stayed in a hotel before.'

'What! Well isn't it about time you did, my girl! Isn't it time you did?'

There is a longish silence.

' So that's settled, Jocelyn, is it? ... Jocelyn, are you still there? I take it that that's settled, and I'll see you here tomorrow. The Bush Hotel, Weston–super-mare. As soon as you can.'

'Very well, Monty, I'll be there.'

Monty put the phone down, and walked briskly over to where

David was sitting, hunched up with a sense of the awkwardness of it all, and wishing above all not to be a nuisance.

'Well, that's fixed, anyway, David. Swift and to the point. That's the way. No problems, no dithering. I trust you're happy with that. And now we'll go and see your mother in hospital, and then we must see about some supper.'

And then, to himself quietly, 'Oh God, done it again!'

Chapter 2 - A Military Exercise on Salisbury Plain

September 1937
A magical dawn on Salisbury Plain. Soft masses of beech-clumps on grey-green chalk downs. The sun slips through quickly changing clouds, so that the shapes and lights of the hills and tree-clumps keep changing too, until the sun gradually establishes itself, and the clouds dissolve.

Tanks are seen lumbering down distant tracks on the hills. Army lorries rumble along the many small roads that converge on one road that leads to the plateau on which troops are assembling. They draw up in a long line on this road, stretching back some half a mile. Some are pulling artillery, some carry signalmen and their equipment, others field kitchens, others the pioneers with spades and wire. As each lorry is unloaded of men and their gear, it moves along to a huge parking bay another half-mile off.

The poor bloody infantry, as usual, are on the march. They are marched from the road onto the plain from various points along it. The first ones are marched to the far side of the plain, and the space gradually fills.

Eventually Monty arrives, sitting in a very large open car. He gives a quiet 'royal wave' now and again. He is not yet a public figure, but he is known to most of the men here, as he is their Divisional Commander, and already has some fame as a brilliant trainer. His car is driven from the road onto the plateau, and moves to the centre, where a small platform and a loudspeaker are being set up. The infantry still stream past him, and are still arriving from the road.

Gradually a large circle is forming at one end of the huge space, with Monty's car at its centre. A mild misty sun burns benignly over them all, the field kitchens are already busy, and the cooking smells drift over the whole assembly. The atmosphere becomes that of a festival. There is pleasure and expectation, smiles and the rubbing of hands, relaxation and a sense of the magical air and light of the day.

Monty at length gets out of his car and mounts the small platform, while NCO's and Officers rally their men. The cry

'Gather round' goes out on all sides in this particular part of the plateau-space.

'Come closer, come closer!' Monty barks out, as the hundreds of men at the front falter and stop at what they consider a polite distance. They are then shepherded by the NCO's right up to the car and the platform, and hundreds more press in around them, and hundreds behind them. There are something like 2,000 men in a large circle, becoming silent as Monty barks out again 'Can you hear me?' A patter of 'Yes Sir' cries come back from them, and a hush settles over them, as Monty's slight figure raises an arm. In this silence the hugeness of the space, the sense of the occasion, and the mystery of the silence itself become apparent to all. It is as though the event is already burying itself in the rich soil of significant memories.

Monty begins to speak.

'Welcome all of you. A hearty welcome. I have important things to say to you, but I shall not keep you long.

'I expect you are all enjoying this beautiful morning, and so am I. And I hope, when I have finished speaking to you, that you will continue to enjoy it, and to make yourselves as comfortable as possible while you all have your deserved and long-awaited breakfast. I can hear the pots banging and the crocks clattering as I speak, and the delicious smells are reaching me even now.

'It is indeed fortunate for you all that we have made such an auspicious start to our week-long exercise. For had it been raining today, and had we begun this manoeuvre sodden and ill-tempered, I fear that many of us would not have fared as well as we ought in the later stages of what is meant to be precisely an exercise in extreme endurance.

'Most of you know by now what an enthusiast for tip-top physical fitness I am. But in case some of you have never heard me speak of it before, and in case some of you have forgotten the finer points of what I believe and preach to you, I will go over it again. It is not a fanaticism on my part, I assure you. Nor do I believe in it merely because there's nothing else I believe in. It is not a doctrine springing from narrow-mindedness. There is plenty more that I think important, and these things I will tell you all again in due course.

'But for the moment, it is about fitness and endurance. The capacity to endure the things that will be inflicted on you in the next few days, such as forced marches, little sleep, little food, and moving our whole Division at night, in silence and without lights, as an exercise in surprise – all this, and hopefully some unpleasant weather later – this is of the essence. There is a promise of heavy rain, I will tell you that now. I will also tell you that my heart lit up when I heard of it! It is what we are here for.

'This is a Divisional Exercise, involving more than 10,000 of you. I have plans for all of you that will not be at all pleasant, unless you face them in the right spirit. Or rather, and to be more exact, they will not be pleasant even with the right spirit! Nevertheless, the right spirit is essential. We are here to prove to ourselves that we can endure and overcome the most extreme situations, organising ourselves and watching over our neighbour while moving forwards under precise orders. You will be expected to come through extreme hardships, and to bear them mildly.

'The beauty of the physical regime that you have already been subjected to under my command, is that it will enable you to surmount all the hurdles we shall create for you. It should also leave you, if the right spirit has been adopted, with a small surplus of will-power and potential energy. This, together with the physical and mental exhilaration that you will have experienced as your normal condition during normal times, this it is which can turn battles and win them. You will remember that special exhilaration even when you are dog-tired, and that memory will give you hope and will-power. That at least is my belief and my own practice. We are therefore talking about a mental strength of the highest order, that can turn battles at those times when everything seems to hang in the balance. This mental quality is at least as important as good weapons.

'But why am I talking of real battles, and implying war, when Europe, in spite of Hitler, is at peace – and when we are assured that Hitler can be and is now being successfully appeased? Yes, we are at peace, and I wish I could say we will remain so. But, alas, I cannot say that. Indeed, no sooner was the last war over than I began to have a dark foreboding of another one to come, and I have spent all these years preparing myself and trying to prepare some of our Army, for that eventuality.

'And who knows where we will fight? It may be in the frozen wastes of a Russian winter. It may be in the desert. It may be here in England. But wherever it is, and before I leave you today, I will make you a promise. Never, while you are under my command, will your lives be thrown away – and certainly, never never never as British lives were thrown away at that dreadful battle of Passchendale in 1917 that I myself witnessed. I will expect much of you. Endurance, courage, and a total commitment to our cause, as it will be a good one. But my aim is to conserve your lives, even while contriving splendid victories. This is my solemn promise to you, and with it I will leave you. Except for one last thing. There is yet another quality attached to my fitness cult, as some people call it. But this quality I will keep secret for now. It is in any case a belief, and only military action will show if my belief is correct or not. So I will divulge it on the eve of actual battle, not before. And then you will see why.

'And, as I have said, I expect that actual battle to come, and I expect to be your commander there. So, farewell … We meet at Philippi!'

Monty waves again, and a cheer gathers slowly in places, spreads, and becomes tremendous. Monty descends from the platform, enters his car, and it is driven away slowly to another huge circle of men about a quarter of a mile off, where he will speak again.

We see and hear parts of the endings of his speech in the different locations this same day.

'And this is my solemn promise to you ...'

The car is on its way again.

'This secret I will only divulge to you on the eve of battle ...'

The car is off again.

'My aim is to conserve your lives, even while contriving splendid victories ...'

The car is off again.

'But why am I talking of real battles, and implying war, when Europe is at peace?'

The car leaves for its final mission.

'And so farewell ... We meet at Philippi!'

We see passages from the week's Exercise. Fast route marches; men clambering over high obstacles in full equipment, jumping down some 15 feet, and rolling over; running up ramps, leaping across a gap onto rope netting, climbing up these and down the other side; men being woken in the night and made to pack up tents in darkness and silence, and then to move forwards in silence. Lorries are also loaded in silence, and move on the quietest engine and without lights, some carrying men, some pulling artillery.

Later we see pitiless hard rain, men donning capes, and pushing on through churned–up fields and slippery mud. We see tents erected in these conditions, and being dismantled again, in darkness and still in rain, and the troops moving forward again in silence.

We see men standing in the rain eating from billy-cans, and the field kitchens at work.

Later, men are crawling through thick undergrowth, with the rain still falling, up a hillside. Tanks, and lorries pulling artillery, pass through them. A little later the infantry rise to their feet, and at the double run past the artillery and the tanks, and establish themselves further forward. The infantry are now instructed to dig slip-trenches, with the help of the Pioneer Corps who have arrived with spades and duck-boards from the rear. A little later planes arrive and drop flour-bombs, as the infantry dash to their trenches, and pull the wooden boards over themselves.

Tanks and small field-guns then come up from the rear, and pass through and over the trenches. Then the infantry emerge, and move again at the double, passing through the tanks and the field-guns, again establishing themselves in forward positions. Orders come in quick succession for the infantry. They are told to rise, run forward, hit the ground, rise again, forward again, several times. Then to carry a wounded comrade on their back as far as various stretcher- bases in their rear.`

Later we see a specialist group of infantry being told to clear a way through a minefield ahead, a way wide enough for the tanks and infantry to pass through later on. This is done with fixed bayonets which pick at and disconnect the mines. Behind these come other men laying tape to mark out the safe driveways. Lastly, at night, this tricky exercise is repeated, and men with red lanterns on poles go forward, following map instructions, an Officer at their head. Searchlights are then used in tandem to pinpoint the apex of each safe driveway, so that the tanks can arrive from the rear to more or less correct positions. Once there, they adjust themselves more accurately according to the tapes, and then pass through, followed again by the infantry, who use the tanks for protection as much as possible.

It is morning again, and a fine one, the last day of the exercise, which is simply a breakfast, then a packing-up, and then a farewell greeting from Monty. He is standing up in his car, on the edge of the plateau, back at our starting-point, as the troops are marched back onto the approach-road, and where the lorries plough slowly forward. Monty salutes each lorry as it passes, and each detachment of infantry, shouting out congratulations. Sometimes he stops a detachment and shakes hands with a sergeant or the officer-in-charge, with a special warmth and a special light in his eye. The men in the lorries cheer as they pass

Monty and see his greeting.

The last lorry passes, and the last marching troop, and they are small and soundless along the road before Monty descends from his standing position, smiles at his driver and they set off slowly and grandly in the same direction.

Chapter 3 – Visiting Hospital

Monty is in the hospital with his son David and with Jocelyn. They are talking in the Ward Sister's room, with some concern.

'I'm afraid I can't say there has been any improvement,' the Ward Sister is saying. 'But then I sense that your wife, sir, has been under some strain before the accident, and her underlying tiredness is delaying her recovery. Would that be correct, sir?'

'We've just had a glorious holiday, Sister, but there is probably much in what you say. Betty has never properly got over that earthquake in India a couple of years ago. She was severely shaken, and had to leave for England with the other British residents. For several months she was without my loving care and protection. She probably experienced rather a lot of social invasion from her Bohemian friends. She loves them all, but doesn't say 'No' often enough.

'However, I'm sure she will receive love and attention and protection here, and I'm not seriously worried about her, good Sister. It's just going to take a little longer, that's all.'

Monty says this last with a significant glance at Jocelyn, and Jocelyn smiles and says 'I'm happy to stay, Monty, at least until David goes back to his school in a fortnight's time. After that, I must think again.'

'That's very sweet and kind of you, Jocelyn. I was going to beg you to stay just another week, but if you are prepared for a fortnight, that's wonderful. I'm sure it won't be necessary for that long, but thank you all the same ... Shall we go and see Betty now? Is she awake now, Sister?'

They walk into the passageway where David has been seated, and all four of them go into the Ward dormitory. Betty is composed on a thick wall of pillows, leaning back and smiling wanly. She has dark hair, a sturdy head, strong features and an expression that inspires complete trust. One senses a relaxed maturity and maternality, and a quick intelligence without 'nerves' and difficult temperament. Her artistic gift is serene, and makes no sharp break with the everyday and her everyday self. But she is truly gifted, and no dilettante. Some drawing and colouring materials are on a side-locker, and also some of her recent work done in the hospital.

Monty goes up to her and holds her proferred hand for a long time, and looking into her eyes, and with a deep breath. ' My dear, dear Betty, how long it has been. And soon, in two or three days, I must go back again for more Exercises. But as soon as they are over, I will come and see you again, and then I will go down to Portsmouth and put our new huge house in order, ready for your return. Won't that be lovely!'

Betty smiles back. 'Lovely, dear Monty. You see I try to do a little drawing each day. It is good for me in several ways ... But I am so tired, darling, so tired. I don't know when I have ever been so tired!'

'You needed the rest anyway, Betty, that's what we've decided. So just rest and enjoy it while you can. It would be madness for you to get up soon and go charging off to Portsmouth to see to the house. In fact, it's just as well you are ill, it's probably the only way I could have stopped you overdoing things. She's quite a devil to control!' Monty adds, turning to Jocelyn and to the Ward Sister, who is still with them. 'She is a good woman, but she does like her own way, and she will not be told! ... That's true, my love, is it not?' He turns to the Sister again 'A thoroughly good sort, but headstrong, and even a little bossy at times! That's the truth of it, Sister. Now let me look at your drawings, dear.'

Monty nips round to the other side of the bed and picks up the drawings from the locker. He is, or was, a complete ignoramus in these things, but genuinely wants to understand more, and shows a humility, not only with Betty but with her artistic friends that is quite touching in its sincerity and simplicity. He sits down and studies each drawing carefully, putting each one on the bed after he has finished with it.

'It's good to see you've been drawing the other patients,' he says, casting shrewd and penetrating glances down the dormitory and picking out various people. 'Oh yes, oh yes, you've got that one, oh yes' he says, keeping his voice low, but still sweeping the ward with his fierce glances. 'I do begin to see the difference, I think I do, between a mere surface likeness and something inward about the sitter. Yes, I think I do ... After all, I have to do something similar myself with my men! Do you know, it's very nearly the same sort of thing. It hadn't struck me till now, Betty. So when I'm ill in bed, Betty, and there are parades and exercises to inspect, I shall authorise you, Betty, to go down the lines and come back with a report!'

'I'm sure I won't put the fear of God into them as you do, Monty. And that's part of it as well, isn't it? It's not just what you find out about each one of them, is it? It's the thunderbolt they get from you, Monty. And I mean a good thunderbolt, Monty. That's your real secret and your gift, darling. And anyway, how did the Exercise go?'

'Oh, I don't want to talk about that. I'm glad it's over, and if I describe it I will only get more spadefuls of your flattery, and you know how I deplore all such things! I'm a simple man, as you know, modest, humble, quiet, kind, reserved and unassuming, one who just quietly gets on with the job, and never seeks the limelight!'

In spite of her tiredness Betty whoops with laughter at this, and Jocelyn and David join in, and Sister beams, and Monty writhes with secret laughter as he tries to keep the po-face appropriate to his last sentence.

Monty braces himself, and goes on, drawing himself up and gripping his lapels like a barrister in full flow. 'Men such as we are, our names are not trumpeted from the house-tops ... and nor would we have it so. We simply make speed to our humble abodes, and enjoy the quiet satisfaction of a job well done. That is our wish, and such will be our epitaph, ladies and gentlemen. I rest my case.'

Finally Monty too laughs, like an express train coming out of a tunnel, and bobs up and down banging his hands on his thighs.

'Oh yes, you're just a simple man,' Betty says, ' with few needs and simple tastes. All you need is adulation! Just that, and you sleep soundly in your bed. I've never known anyone who was pleased with so little!'

'You're quite right, my dear, as usual. All I need is adulation, and if all of us could be satisfied with just that, the world would indeed be a better place,' Monty says solemnly. 'A better place.' There are more hoots and screams, and several people in the ward are looking their way, some of them with smiles.

'But my dear darling Betty,' said Monty, going up to her again and holding and kissing her, 'You are laughing and we could go on like this for hours, but you're worn out just the same, and we mustn't tire you more, so we should leave you now, I think. And I can come in again for the next two or three days. And after that it gives me great peace and happiness that you, Jocelyn, will be here. Thank you again, and I'm sorry if I was abrupt on the phone with you, I truly am! I really don't know what came over me!'

Jocelyn puts her arm around Monty, then goes up to Betty and kisses her goodbye. David does the same. There are tears in Monty's eyes as he finally turns to leave. They walk out of the ward, along the passageway, Sister following. Sister stops, and the rest of the party turn left and out of sight.

Chapter 4 - With David

The house in Portsmouth is a very large mid-Victorian three-storeyed building, in solid order outside, but dingy and in need of decoration in all the rooms inside. Monty is walking around as four men go to and fro, from room to room, laying thick white dust-sheets over the furniture. Trestles are brought in. Monty follows the decorators to each room. The scraping of walls has already begun in one of them.

'It's a huge job, I can see that. I can see it will take weeks or even months. However, if we could just have a working and living house-area to begin with, in time for my wife coming out of hospital quite soon. That's what we'll do.'

Monty walks out of the room and towards his own large room, followed by the foreman.

'Now there's no need to do anything here. I shall be studying here, and eating and sleeping here for the time being. This room can be done last of all.'

He shakes hands with the foreman, and then goes by himself on a full tour of the house, to the upper storeys, looking meditatively out of the big windows in some of the rooms, and muttering to himself, 'Acres of space. Good heavens, I could run a training centre here, with my own hand-picked men. They could all stay overnight.'

He goes into a good-sized room with a very large window. 'Good. A north light. This can be Betty's studio. She'll like that. She's never had enough space before ... And a good solid oak door. I'll put a firm lock on that. Keep some of her pests out!'

He goes downstairs again, and towards his own room. Seeing a couple of workmen on the way, he says 'Bring me a very large solid table, will you. I think there's a scrubbed pine one in the kitchen area. Bring it to my working room please.'

Monty enters his room and two men come in with a wide pine table eight or nine feet long. He directs them to a suitable place, and then speaks with the foreman who has just come in. 'Look, I shall be working here, night and day. I don't mind how much crashing and banging you make – it's something I'm going to have to get used to in due course anyway. But I do mind interruptions. We've had a good talk, so can I rely on you all to get on with the job without bothering me every half-hour or so?'

'Most certainly sir!' said the foreman, and looking at his men, who nod quietly.

'Well, that's excellent then' said Monty, 'so now we can all get down to some hard work. Good, good' he said, rubbing his hands and looking intently and smilingly into each man's face.

Monty is then left in his own room. He closes the door, hauls a large trunk over to the table, and begins unpacking books and notes and maps and large sheets of blank paper onto it. His face becomes inward and lit up and intense. He pulls up a large wicker chair with cushions all round and wide arm-rests, tests it, flexes himself, and begins to read, with a sharp pencil in his hand. Inks in several different colours are near him, and half a dozen mapping pens stand in a glass.

We see him in late afternoon, in the autumn dusk, lying on his back on a simple army camp-bed with a rug over him.

Later still he is at the table again, and a maid brings in supper on a tray. Monty does not drink or smoke.

Later we see Monty bent over the table, the maid enter silently and carry away the tray. Monty does not move, but he says 'Thank you, Doris' as she reaches the door.

A fire is burning in the grate, and at one point Monty himself goes out to fetch more coal, and makes up the fire. We see him working at several times of the clock on the mantelpiece above the fire. We see it reach two in the morning before Monty seeks his camp bed again.

He is up at six, and while it is still dark he walks round the large garden, and as the light appears he goes off for a brisk walk in the streets of the neighbourhood. At half-past seven he is working at the table again and his batman brings in breakfast.

This pattern goes on for another two days and nights. After this Monty is seen again on an Exercise. He is making another speech on Salisbury Plain.

'I have talked about extreme endurance. But always remember, these extreme tests are only for a season, and not only here on

Exercise, but in actual warfare. At the earliest reasonable opportunity, I will bring you out of battle and send in other men. You will be safe behind the lines and you will be thoroughly rested before you are sent in again. Indeed, the battle may be over before that time comes. I know this principle was operated in the Great War, but not in the way I intend to operate it. I do not expect men to be gods, but only to be heroes, and that only, as I said, for a season. You are my most precious asset, and I do not intend to wear you out if I can help it.

'And if you are not capable of being a hero at some particular time, whether through having seen and endured too much on a previous occasion, or through being a complete novice who is not mentally ready for front-line battle, I will endeavour not to make use of you in that role. Of course that cannot be a promise, but it will be my endeavour. You can be a hero at some future time. And if you are an Officer who has seen and endured too much already, I will replace you and send you home for a while. People will of course say that I am a ruthless man, who struts around sacking people left right and centre ... but you will see that what I have spoken of in connection with Officers is not sacking, but compassion. This is not to say that actual sackings may not sometimes be necessary. I do have to have Officers and men who understand my methods and are keen to put them into operation, and who obey my orders at all times and without equivocation. All of this of course assumes an enormous power and authority on my part, which I do not at present possess. But one day I shall possess that authority, and those are some of them ways in which I intend to use it ... And so farewell ... We'll meet at Philippi!'

He is back at his table in Portsmouth again, working into the night. We see the night and day pattern repeated for two or three days, and we also see him on the telephone, asking for Betty's hospital, on several occasions, and we see gradually an expression of some pain and difficulty on his face. We learn that Betty herself is now in pain.

'But it was only an English insect-bite, Sister', he says on the phone, 'not a scorpion or a tarrantula. What exactly is the difficulty?' he says, trying hard to keep impatience out of his tone.

'Well, it is certainly more complex than we thought to begin with' said the Sister, 'but we are doing our best, and trying out new things. We must give it more time, sir.'

'Yes yes of course' he says. 'But meanwhile what am I supposed to do? I have a huge amount of work of all kinds to do, I am not good at sitting long hours at a bedside, doing nothing, but if I am required, please say the word, Sister, and I shall be there.'

'Your wife would most certainly like to see you again as soon as possible, if only for a short while. She is very strong mentally, as you know, sir, and a terrific fighter, but she is in some pain, and the raising of her spirits would be very good for her. So do come, sir, as soon as you can.'

'I'll be there,' says Monty, and rings off.

Monty is by his wife's bedside, looking troubled. Betty is visibly exhausted, but smiling at him, though twisted by pain. They hold hands. Monty is seated close to the bed, and Jocelyn is standing behind him, with David by her side.

There is no laughter this evening, and all are conscious of the difficulty of knowing what to say.

'I'll get a specialist to come in and see you,' says Monty quietly. 'I don't think there's anything else we can do at the moment. It's very puzzling. I just wish we knew why it's being do difficult.'

'You do hear of this from time to time ... something quite minor turning like this,' says Jocelyn . 'It just needs time'.

'I'll talk to Sister again,' says Monty. 'Meanwhile,' he says, turning to Betty again, 'I shall be staying a few nights at the hotel. Work is proceeding nicely on the house in Portsmouth, I've brought a few books along, and there are no more Exercises for a week. I'll come in and see you every day.'

'That'll be lovely, Bernard,' says Betty 'Things will get better soon.'

'I hate to see you in pain, dear Betty. Perhaps we can do something more for that.'

Monty kisses her again, gets up and talks quietly with Jocelyn. As they leave the ward, Monty says, 'You go home tomorrow, Jocelyn, and have a week with John. Should I need you back after that, bring John with you and stay in the hotel, or somewhere nicer if you can find it. All expenses paid for by me of course, and don't stint yourselves.'

He goes into the Sister's room for a few moments to talk and listen. Then they walk slowly out of the Hospital.

Out in the street Monty talks to David as they walk. 'It's school coming up now, my son, and perhaps just as well for you. You needn't come into the hospital each day from now on, unless you want to.'

'Oh I like to sit there with Mummy, and I'd rather see how she is than hear how she is,' says David. 'It's less frightening,' he adds.

'A good point, David. But as for myself, I'm quite the opposite. A bit of a coward face to face with pain and suffering. I don't like feeling helpless. I'd take the pain on myself, I think, willingly, but when you can't, you feel useless, as though there's nothing else you can offer. Somehow it seems conceited to think your own mere presence is a help'.

'But you don't say that about the soldiers under your command, Monty', says David. 'You always say you think you can inspire them, make them feel like lions!'

'O, you remember some of the things I go on about, my boy! How encouraging! But I hope I don't go on too long to you. But then again, I'm so vain and hungry for praise, I'll take it from a ten-year-old, and my own son. You don't mind that, do you, old boy?'

'No, Monty,' says David.

'But the difference is that my soldiers are fit and healthy. I can feel a connection with that. But as for the ... others ...' he trails off. 'Well thank God for the nurses!'

And then, very quietly to himself, 'Thank God for the nurses.'

All three cross the threshold of the hotel.

Next morning in the hotel. The three of them are sitting at

breakfast. Monty is talking with some animation.

'Such a dream I had last night. So realistic, such a complete narrative, so unlike most dreams.'

'What was it about? Or will it be boring, like most people when they tell dreams?' says David

'Well it might just be boring to you, but I don't think so,' says Monty. 'It was so vivid and alive, and it awoke the storyteller in me. Did you know that my father, a Bishop in the Church of England, was sent out to Tasmania to do missionary work? I might have told you, but I didn't tell you that we all as a quite large family went out with him. I was only about three at the time. What a magical world! It was best of all when father was at home, which wasn't very often. Then everything, even the hard things, seemed right, even joyful!'

'What were the hard things?' David asks.

'O the hard things were being got up by our mother at six o'clock in the morning and made to do chores. We couldn't afford servants, so we children did nearly all the house and garden work. We were out there in the garden in the early morning air ... O that lovely air, I could feel it and smell it in my dream ... I even stood there consciously in my dream and made a point of enjoying it. Anyway, we had to weed and clear the garden, and do digging and sowing and planting when necessary, and of course watering, carrying heavy watering cans. And we had to collect kindling wood for the autumn and winter fires, and also for the cooking. Kindling and logs and anything likely to burn. We learned to work hard, because our meals depended on it ... we also could not afford to buy in fuel. But I was remembering in my dream what a paradise it was when father was there. Work and play at the same time. Well, we had breakfast at about half-past seven, and then from half-past eight until one o'clock we had lessons, all of us in one big room together, with some of the children from the village to make up the numbers. Mother gave some of the lessons, and a teacher from the village also came in. All the families saved up to pay her. It was more fun than most schools. The smell of woodsmoke was everywhere, it was like a long camping holiday. And in the afternoons we just wandered and ran wild anywhere. There was so much space and freedom!'

'It doesn't sound very hard to me,' says David, 'I love camping and outdoor fires and all the work … and running wild.'

'Yes, but it was the beatings that were hard,' says Monty.

'Did your father beat you?' Jocelyn breaks in, 'I always heard he was so gentle.'

'O, he was,' says Monty, 'He did no beating. But mother beat us all, and me especially. She was so much younger than father, and I suppose felt helpless and exposed when he was away, and thought that continual beating was the only thing between order and complete chaos. But she beat us even when Father was at home. That was harder to understand, and Father didn't really think it necessary. He didn't approve, actually, and I think he remonstrated with her a little. But he accepted that she was boss in those things, so nothing changed.'

'So you've had a lovely dream of one beating after another!' says David.

'Well, even the beatings didn't hurt much when Father was at home,' says Monty. 'No, I didn't dream much about the beatings, except for some of the ones I got from my own fault, and when Father was away. When Father was at home I could go and talk to him after a beating, and he was all smiles and tenderness and apology ... and I would forget about the whole thing ... and the actual pain never bothered me.'

'Do you mean you got beaten sometimes when you hadn't done anything wrong?' David asks.

'O good Lord yes,' says Monty, ' My poor mother was like Mrs. Gargery in 'Great Expectations'. I'm sure you know it, David. Always on the rampage, always seeing sin and evil everywhere, and flailing her stick at all times as though it were an extra limb, always with her. But I got most of the beatings, because I thought it was only right and proper to do something wrong if I was to be beaten anyway. I had a strong will you see, and my mother had a strong will, so we battled it out between us, year after year!'

'And who won?' David asks 'Did anyone win in the end?'

'A very interesting question!' says Monty, 'Who won in the end? Well I think, in the end, mother won, but that would be too complicated to explain. I never stopped defying her while I lived at home, and refused to be afraid. But, since you ask it, I have to say that mother won in the end. She broke my spirit in other ways, and broke the connection between us. Nothing has ever been resolved. So you see, my dear boy, how lucky you are to have such a beautiful mother. Such a beautiful spirit. Have you ever seen anything like it? No, of course you haven't! ... But in my dream, to come back to that, there was a peaceful feeling of forgiveness, and that was partly what made it so memorable ... I don't mean that I personally forgave my mother, or that she came to me in contrition, but something lovely like that was in the dream. Aren't dreams impossible to explain? It was as though the very smell of the air and the garden and the wood smoke were forgiveness. I don't know if that makes sense, but that's how it was, and why it was magical, and why I am talking about it.'

They get up from the table at last.

I need to work this morning,' says Monty. 'I'll be going to the hospital in the afternoon, David. And I'll say goodbye to you, Jocelyn, and a thousand thanks yet again, and have a nice holiday with John.'

'I'm glad I came, Monty,' says Jocelyn, 'It's serious, and I'll come again if and when I'm needed, you needn't worry.'

Monty and David are walking back from the hospital.

'How about a game of cricket?' Monty says. 'We've got bat and ball and stumps from the holiday, and if we stroll down to the grassy area by the promenade, there'll probably be boys just out of school who will join us'.

As they reach the hotel David darts up the stairs and is soon back with the equipment. They walk rapidly back towards the beach. As they bang in the stumps with the end of the bat-handle a few boys begin to look hopefully in their direction. Monty turns to them.

'Come on then, if you want to play. We'll just have a knockabout till a few more turn up.'

David bowls to Monty, an innocuous ball, and Monty drives it into the covers, and the two boys give chase. Monty jogs two runs.

'Come on David. A bit faster ... and keep it straight.'

A better ball and Monty leans into it and pushes it for one run on the offside. David then bowls a shorter rising ball. Monty cuts it square on the offside and runs another two.

By this time a dozen other boys have arrived. The immediate impression of class in Monty's stroke-playing shows at a hundred yards and draws them like a magnet.

Monty calls out 'Now David here is a bit young for fast bowling. Is there anyone here who can bowl really fast?'

One 13-year-old holds a paw in the air.

'Good' says Monty. 'Now do your worst.'

'But won't you need pads, Sir?' says the boy.

'No, I'll be all right. But if any of you have got pads, we could do with them.'

Two boys shoot off at top speed to fetch pads from home.

Monty taps his bat on the ground and awaits the fast bowler, who is indeed fast for his age. But the ball comes at Monty's legs and he leans forward and glances it on the bounce. It goes racing for four runs on the leg side.

'That's four.' says Monty. 'Good ball, young man, but try not to wander down the leg side. Aim at the off-stump, or just outside.'

The boy runs in again, and bowls a fast good length on the off-stump. Monty plays elegantly forward and for once defends.

'A very good ball. Keep it like that. And don't worry about my unguarded legs. The faster they come, the better I like it.'

The boy runs up again and bowls another fast good length just outside the off-stump. Monty lifts his bat as though to let the ball go through, but at the last split second brings it down with a sudden twisted dab and the ball goes racing again for four behind the wicket.

'Very good ball young man, but I gave it the late cut, one of my specialities. I'm afraid it must be discouraging for you.'

But the boy is beaming with happiness, and is fired-up. The two boys with the pads arrive and Monty waves everyone into a circle around him, and fixes them all with his eyes, which are at once fierce and avuncular.

'Now let's get on with it' Monty says, 'We haven't got enough of you for two full sides, so you'll all have to field against your own batsmen. Too bad. But mind you do it with real verve, for I shall be watching you. Anyone not up to scratch will not be allowed to bat. Now, is there another fast bowler apart from this lad?'

A head of spiky ginger hair nods briskly.

'Good. So you two fast bowlers can be captains and pick your sides. I shall be wicket-keeper throughout, and umpire as well.'

The boys pick teams, a coin is tossed by Monty and a match begins.

Monty takes up his wicket-keeper position, and calls out just before the first ball is bowled,

'Don't think I can't see you, you boys behind me!' This is to third man and long leg, and backward square leg. 'You jolly well field like terriers, or I'll be on to you!'

The match proceeds, the fielders alert, and the pace brisk and efficient. As it draws to a close, Monty calls out,

'Now you need just four runs to win, last batsman in. Set your mind to it. And now, you ginger fiend,' he calls out to the ginger-haired fast bowler, 'Don't let him get there. Bowl faster and straighter than you have ever bowled before.'

The ginger boy comes racing up to the wicket and hurls down a fast ball just outside the off-stump. The batsman plays forward defensively, but the ball catches an edge low down and flies low and fast behind him. Monty dives hugely to his right, catches the ball and rolls over and over with his momentum, landing on his back and lifting his right arm up in the air at the same time, to show that he has the ball firmly in his hand. 'Game over!' he shouts.

Monty gets up, and all the boys converge on him.

'Another game tomorrow, same time, if you like.'

There is enthusiasm.

'And another the day after.'

Enthusiasm again.

'But after that I'm off, and so is my boy. Get here in good time. Same teams, best of three matches.'

Monty and David pack and go, with many of the boys walking

with them, curious to see where they are staying. They walk as far as the hotel, and say a courteous goodbye to the strange direct man, whom they feel must be well known in some capacity beyond their ken.

At the hotel that evening Monty and David are having supper, as Monty tells David of his early days.

'I was talking to you about the beatings I had, wasn't I? Well, there was one that was almost funny, I suppose. I had been caught smoking when I was about 15. My dear father was at home at the time. Smoking was, of course, a very grave offence. Why did I do it, when my father was there with us? Stupid of me. I let my rebellion against my mother override my reverential feelings for my father, and his love for me ...Well, so be it ... Anyway, what happened next was my being summoned to my father's room for a good talking to. He not only talked to me, and let me talk to him, and beg forgiveness, we actually went down on our knees together, and prayed together for God's forgiveness ... Now please understand that I am not mocking my father ... he had a clear and sincere religion, and so have I. My own is more simple, I don't have his theological intellect, though theological things are of course quite beyond you at your age, my boy, but never mind, let that pass. The point is, I was moved by our prayers together, and I believed, and believe, my father when he said God has a special task for everyone in this world. So, full of awe and chastened and sweetened by our talk and our prayers, imagine my surprise as I left his room to find a firm hand on my collar and a stick cracking me across the back of the legs. It was mother, hiding behind the door. 'Don't think you can get away with it like that!' she shrieked, 'You and your dear father, O yes, we know all about that, don't we!'. She hauled me off to another room, and gave me one of the fiercest beatings I've ever had.'

'But why didn't you protest?' says David 'And why didn't your father do something?'

'Well, it was not his way, though I know he spoke to her about it later, and told her she had been wrong. But for myself I thought it rather comical even at the time, and so I went through with it ... Nowadays it would make us think of Laurel and Hardy ... And anyway, I was hardened to beatings, and I loved the act of defiance.'

'What was that?' says David.

'Well, it was my determination never to utter a sound, no matter how much it hurt, far less to look sad, or to shed a tear. That was the game, that was the battle. And that at least I won.'

'What a game!' says David, not altogether approvingly. 'I suppose you couldn't stop yourself.'

'I felt I couldn't, which isn't quite the same thing. If father had been at home more of the time, I think his spirit in me would have won, and I'd have behaved differently. But what's the point of ifs and buts? When I was at St Paul's School I just wasted my time, I did no academic work whatever, and that was stupid of me ... the only subject I was good at was Scripture. I rather shone at that! I didn't have to work, I just knew it.'

'Didn't the Head give you warnings? You could have been expelled, couldn't you?', says David.

'No, I escaped warnings because I was so good at sports, every one of them. Rugger, cricket, athletics, football, everything. I was rather small, but extremely fierce and aggressive. I was nicknamed 'the monkey'. Here is what the school magazine said of me once, a propos rugby. 'The Monkey is vicious, of unflagging energy, and much feared by the neighbouring animals owing to its tendency to pull out the top hair of the head. This it calls 'tackling' ...'

Monty pauses, and shrieks with high laughter. David allows a smile to become a complicit laugh.

'To foreign fauna it shows no mercy,' Monty goes on, 'stamping on their hands and twisting their necks, and doing many other inconceivable atrocities with a view, no doubt, to proving his patriotism.'

'Well, it's harmless in spirit, isn't it?' says David, 'Anyway there was a referee at least, you must have been hauled up sometimes.'

'O yes, frequently, but I went on playing rugger like that. And even when I played the gentlemanly game of cricket and excelled there, (did you know, by the way, later on I made 87 not out against a a team led by W.G Grace! And I bowled him out as well. What about that!), but even when I excelled, and was admired, I never relented. I never became relaxed and friendly, I was the eternal rebel and misanthrope. I was much admired, but made no friends. That was a bad thing, a silly way to go on. I went to Sandhurst to do my military training a boorish, unmannered young man, ignorant, truculent, and self-satisfied in my ignorance. That's a terrible way to be, self-satisfied in ignorance, it's hard to think of anything worse ... Of course you're not a bit like me in these respects, thank God, but it's a very <u>English</u> thing, being self-satisfied in ignorance, and it goes on even in our public schools, and in temperaments quite unlike mine, so beware of it. Your dear mother has taught me so much ... to understand other things in life, to love music, for instance, and to respect those things in others that I don't and can't understand! Boorishness is precisely refusing to respect in others the things one doesn't have oneself. And the love of ignorance, a sort of refusal to grow up , very English, I'm afraid. However, if it were no worse that that, it wouldn't be so bad ...' he trails off in a quiet voice.

'If what were no worse than what?' says David. 'Now you are being mysterious. I've understood everything so far, even the bit about 'theological intellect'.'

'Oh, I've said quite enough for the time being. I've told you enough about myself and my ways. I talk about myself too much, and don't ask you enough about school and your doings.'

'Well, I write letters home about them. Do you mean you don't read them?'

'Of course we both read them, dear boy. We read them with interest. But you must talk to me more, and push me and my doings out of the way sometimes.'

'All right, I will.' says David.

'Good!' says Monty.

They both drift off into silence. Monty presses David's hand, they leave the dinner-table and make for the sitting room. Monty takes up 'The Times', while David works through a book of crosswords. As David later goes off to bed, Monty puts down 'The Times', and slips into a reverie.

PART 2 - RETROSPECT

Chapter 5 – Early Days in the Army

We see a huddle of Cadets at Sandhurst, with Monty at the centre, and the ring-leader.

'This new chap Berthon', Monty is saying, 'What a drip. Never joins in the fun and games. No horse-play in him at all. Reads Bernard Shaw, would you believe it? And poetry. Half French, I believe. What shall we do about him?'

'Challenge him to a boxing match?'one says.

'Put all his books in a heap and burn them!' suggests another.

'Put frogs in his bed!'

'Throw him up in a blanket till he hits the ground'.

'All of these,' says another.

'Not stern enough,' says Monty. 'Just listen to this!'

We see a group of them creeping along a dark corridor. Suddenly a door is flung open by Monty, the leader, to reveal a comfortable room with a fire lit, and a sensitive and intelligent-looking Cadet reclining in an armchair with his legs on the mantelpiece reading a book.

'What's that you're reading, Berthon?' sneers Monty.

'It's Shaw's 'Plays Unpleasant', Monty, if you must know. And what is it you want? Couldn't you knock before busting in?'

"Plays Unpleasant'! How very appropriate, Berthon!' Monty sneers again. 'We've come to perform another Play Unpleasant, if you must know ... forward, men!'

At this the Cadets all produce bayonets from behind their backs and advance into the room, making a circle round Berthon, and imprisoning him between themselves and the fire.

'Now get him, you two!' Monty snaps, and two more Cadets rush into the room, seize Berthon by the shoulders and heave him up from his chair, with his back to the fire.

'What the hell are you about?' yells Berthon, with a quiver of real fear in his voice.

'You'll soon find out!' says Monty, putting his bayonet into his left hand, and with his right hand picking up a twig from the hearth and placing it in the fire.

'Now pull his shirt out at the back', Monty snaps again.

The two men holding him do so, and Monty says 'Now, down with his trousers.'

Berthon struggles desperately forward, but the two men hold him, and the circle of bayonets comes closer, glinting in the firelight. They pull down his trousers, and Monty takes the twig from the fire and sets fire to the shirt-tails.

'Hold him firm till its properly alight', Monty shouts, 'Keep holding him'.

The flames creep up the shirt and finally burst into a large flame. A cry goes up from Berthon.

'That'll do' said Monty. 'Let's go!'

They all rush out of the room. Berthon tries to pull his shirt away from his backside but trips over the trousers which are around his ankles and falls face down on the floor. The shirt burns and his underpants are now also on fire. He is screaming with pain and fear. He rolls over onto his back to stifle the flames, but his clothes continue to burn. He screams as he sits up and struggles to get his shoes and trousers off, in order to move more freely. His screams have at last brought two or three cadets from adjoining rooms to the scene.

'O my God!' says one, and seeing the trouble seizes a heavy blanket from the bed, heaves Berthon over onto his front, and stifles the flames. All this time Berthon is screaming.

'Call the doctor!' yells the cadet. 'He's passing out, I think. Quick! Get a move on!'

Monty comes out of his reverie and is holding his head in his hands.

'O my God,' he groans, 'what was I thinking of?'

For relief, he lies out full stretch on the sofa, and puts 'The Times' over his face.

'In darkness let me dwell!' he groans aloud. He sinks gradually back into another reverie.

We see Monty the Cadet standing to attention in the

Commanding Officer's room at Sandhurst. The officer walks up and down the room, and around Monty himself once or twice, while Monty looks straight ahead in the correct 'military manner'.

'Can you think of one good reason why we should keep you here in the Army?'

'Well sir,' begins Monty.

'Shut up!' shouts the officer at the top of his voice. ' How dare you interrupt an officer! How dare you deign to speak! I'll do the talking, and you will keep your mouth shut, even when you are asked a question, is that clear?' he bellows.

There is silence.

'I said, is that clear?' yells the officer in a shrieking fortissimo.

'Yes sir!' says Monty.

'Well I can think of one good reason why we should keep you in the Army ... though why in the name of thunder we should be lumbered with rubbish like you I can't say. But the only reason for keeping you in is that you are no damned good at anything else. Isn't that so? What have you to say for yourself?' he says after a pause.

'Well, sir,' Monty begins again.

'Shut up!' yells the other, fortissimo again. 'How dare you presume to have something to say for yourself? Are you as shameless as you are stupid? I say without hesitation that this is by far the worst incident I have encountered in a long career. It is unspeakable, horrible, the work of a sick mind!'

The officer walks round and round Monty the cadet, shooting him angry glances.

'I understand that you yourself chose an Army career, against the wishes of your mother, who has herself told me she hoped you would go into the Church like your good father. So you haven't been pushed into this profession, it is your own choice. So I wonder what in the devil's name you were thinking of when you chose it. Do you think the Army is about random violence, from one day's end to another? Are you such a child? Well, yes, I think you are, and now you are going to have to grow up very quickly – and also to work very hard. For if you don't do both these things we will indeed throw you out. Can you deny that you have been bone idle in your few months here?'

There is silence.

'I said, can you deny you have been idle?' the officer shrieks fortissimo.

'No sir,' says Monty.

'No sir, indeed!' says the officer. 'No sir.' He says quietly, while mooching about, and circling round Monty once again. 'And can you deny that you have no plans, and indeed no aptitude, for any other profession?'

'No sir,' says Monty.

'No sir, indeed,' says the officer quietly. 'You are the typical one-track military mind, it is evident ... and the only excuse for being such a person, and for choosing such a profession, is to become damned good at it. Clearly you have some leadership qualities, but they are all going down the wrong channel. You can lead young men into evil ... But for your leadership qualities to flourish in the Army, you will need to be perceived as a good man, leading young men into what is necessary, even if it is not actually good. That is what war and the Army are about. Do you understand?'

Another pause.

'I said, do you understand?' he shrieks, fortissimo again.

'Yes sir!' says Monty.

'Very well, you have been reduced to your starting point in this College, and you will miss early promotion. But that is kindness on our part, out of regard for your good parents, and their concern for you. You will begin again, in the lowest grade, and your work and your conduct will be exemplary from this moment on. Dismiss!'

Monty salutes, about turns, and marches to the door, which is held open for him by an N.C.O.

Monty the Brigadier comes to on the hotel sofa, removes 'The Times' from his face and sits up. He holds his head in his hands for a few moments, then drifts off to bed.

While he is asleep, we see the rest of his life unfold, up to the present scene. He passes out of Sandhurst, shaking hands with the officer who had once scolded him. We see him as a Major in the trenches in the First World War, writing letters in his dugout to his mother, and starting 'Dearest Mother' or 'My Darling Mother'.

We see him on leave, bringing expensive presents for his mother. We witness her cold reception of them, and the hurt on his face. We see him wounded in action, as he springs forward with his sword to save a colleague from a bayonet attack. The German falls dead from rifle fire, and Monty is hit as well, and falls to the ground. A machine-gunner has his sights on him. As he prepares to fire, another body falls wounded on Monty, and another one in front of him. These bodies take the brunt of the machine-gun fire. Monty just lies there till the stretcher-bearers arrive, and carry him to a dressing station.

'Punctured lung,' the medic says. 'Some treatment, and then a spell in Blighty, you lucky man!'

'A punctured lung is not much fun,' says Monty.

'You'll live and flourish,' says the medic. 'You're the type.'

We see Monty in hospital in England, and then on leave again, and again taking expensive presents to his mother.

He notices the gold clock he had bought her is not in its place.

'What happened to the clock, mother? Is it in your bedroom?'

'O no, the clock', she says, 'I gave it away. I had no need of it. I was sure you wouldn't mind.'

We see him back in the trenches in November 1917. It is the battle of Passchendale, hundreds of thousands of British men being pushed forwards relentlessly into a sea of mud created by the heavy rains. German machine-gunners fell them, but more are sent forward.

Monty is in his dugout writing a letter to his father. 'This is the most appalling bloodbath I have seen in all my three years here. Men are being sacrificed in their tens of thousands for the sake of one General's vanity and self-regard. Good men, honest men, men who will follow and be loyal, and who naively believe in the good-will and the moral superiority of their superiors. I weep for these men. Most are not even professional soldiers, but were conscripts. How can a professional officer subject poor conscripts to such an ordeal, such slaughter? Surely the politicians will do something, surely the great Lloyd George is capable of knocking some heads together and creating some sanity, and surely the heads of some of the Generals must fall? This is not war, this is an abattoir, dumb animals led into the killing places without pity, and almost without pause. Such a method of war must never happen again. O dear father, when I chose the Army as a career, I never dreamed I would witness scenes like this, or be an accessory to them ... But what can the junior or middle-ranking officers do? We are under orders. The Generals direct the Staff Officers, and the Staff Officers push us into battle, again and again, regardless of casualties. And the Generals and the Staff Officers live mainly far off behind the lines, perfectly safe and inordinately comfortable. This is not war, father, this is the madhouse. Preach about it father, do what you can. Your loving son, Monty.

We see the Armistice signed, and the troops returning home. We see Monty arriving yet again with presents for his mother, and his mother saying to him 'O, not another lot of presents. I've sold or given away all the others. What do you mean by it, Monty?'

'What do I mean by it, mother? ... What do I mean by it? ... Well, I thought it was obvious ... what I mean by it ... isn't it obvious? ...' He trails off.

'I never thought you were such a mother's boy, Monty! What on earth's come over you? I prefer our old ways, don't you?'

'Well no, mother, no ... not any more ... I thought ...'

'A man cannot by taking thought add one cubit to his stature!' she pronounces triumphantly.

Monty crumples visibly, and gradually turns away. He gathers up the presents and walks out of the house with them and his luggage. He orders a taxi to the station and takes the train back to his regiment. As he enters the doorway of the Regimental Mess, two or three of the younger officers standing there take note of him.

'O God! That frightful Monty again. I thought he'd gone for

three weeks leave! What's going on?'

'Never mind,' says another, ' Your military education will be much speeded up thereby. You will be as wise as Solomon within a month, if you do but listen to the oracle!'

'More likely as drunk as Lot,' says another.

'Well, there's nothing to be done about it, short of covering one's face with 'The Times' while in the Smoking Room and pretending to be asleep. What a crashing bore!'

'We must stick together, that's the answer,' says another, 'the power of the pack. Never go alone into the Mess, it's not safe. We must go in twos or threes at least, and make a lot of noise at all times.'

'We do that anyway,' says another, 'It's not fool-proof. I suggest epileptic fits whenever the subject of the next war comes up.'

'Or the staggering inadequacy of our military training and out military strategy.'

'Or the frivolous nature of our officer class, and their upper-class bias.'

'Or what I saw and heard at Passchendale.'

'Yes, that just about covers it. One of us can always be taken ill, and we can then take off to the nearest pub, and continue our frivolous pursuits.'

They drift off into the Mess and order drinks.

Monty walks into the bar later and orders a fruit juice. He stands at a distance from the four fellow-officers who have been talking about him. It is a little awkward. They are caught between a desire not to be blatantly rude, and an equal desire not to have Monty spoil their tete-a-tete. Monty is quite oblivious to these tensions. He finds himself a seat in a far corner of the Mess, as far away from the smokers as possible.

The four officers at the bar eventually join Monty there, having perhaps sensed a hurt in him that evening, and feeling a little guilty for having run him down so thoroughly.

'Hullo Monty, mind if we sit here?' says one.

'Not at all,' says Monty, 'so long as you don't smoke.'

'O, I'd forgotten your moral objections to that', says another.

'Not really moral objections, you know. But I have only one

sound lung, and the smoke disagrees with me anyway.'

They sit down rather awkwardly. But Monty soon dispels that by launching straight away into a serious discourse.

'Did you ever have the experience of banging and banging away at a problem, giving your very best for year on year, and just coming up against a brick wall?'

They all think he is talking about his discourses on military reforms, and their awkwardness returns immediately. After a longish silence one of them says, 'We're sorry you feel like that, Monty. I'm afraid we haven't been a very receptive audience, have we?'

'You haven't been an audience at all, for I haven't yet told you the thing that concerns me.'

'O haven't you, Monty? Say on then!' he responds, somewhat relieved like the rest of them.

'It's to do with my mother,' says Monty.

'Your mother!' they all break out, and then shriek with relieved laughter.

A thin smile creeps across Monty's face.

'You may well laugh!' he says grudgingly, but with a laugh coming creeping up behind that.

'Thank you, we will!' they all say more or less together, and they do, and thump the table, and stamp feet on the floor.

'My mother is no laughing matter!' says Monty, breaking into a wide grin.

'O isn't she? Tell me why we are all laughing then! There must be something about her, I'd say!'

'Well, I can't help laughing either,' says Monty, 'and perhaps it's high time I did!'

'Yes, that's so, Monty. You've been bottling it all up, and depriving us of gallons of laughter!'

'But all I said was 'My Mother',' says Monty, 'What's funny about that?'

'I don't know!' one almost shouts, 'But it's a scream from start to finish. As I said, there must be something about her.'

They are all still spluttering, and Monty hits the sides of his chair and joins in, rocking backwards and forwards.

When it has more or less subsided, Monty speaks in a different tone.

'Well I've made a resolution. I will not speak of her any more!'

'O Monty! You've only spoken of her once, and now the fun is going to stop!'

They laugh again, and Monty grins at them.

'No seriously', he begins again.

'It's impossible!' one shrieks, and the laughing begins again. As it subsides again, he sneaks his request in again.

'Seriously', he pleads.

It explodes again, and at last all is quiet, and all are rubbing themselves, and easing various muscles, as though after a long cross-country run.

'Let me tell you a story,' Monty says.

'By all means, Monty,' they say together.

Monty collects himself, and fixes them one by one with his astonishing blue eyes, as he narrates.

'When I was a cadet at Sandhurst, before the war, I did a most dishonourable and stupid thing (I won't go into details, but I shudder as I think of it now). Had it not been for my mother visiting the Big Chief there, and impressing him with her concern for me, and with her indomitable character, I doubt if I would be sitting here with you now. The shock did me good, and one of the consequences was my determination to give credit to my mother, and to try to heal the rift between us. We had had a battle of wills since my earliest days in this world, and now I struggled to put that aside, and to become the devoted and the filial son in every conceivable way. And the upshot of it all is that it has not made a scrap of difference. She is unmoved, implacable ... and even cruel ... so there is my story, and the reason for my new resolution. And as you can see, it's not particularly funny ... but I didn't at all mind you laughing.'

'We wouldn't have laughed if we had known,' they say, 'No offence meant, Monty!'

'I'm getting a feeling that it was some sort of relief that made you laugh,' said Monty.

There is an uncomfortable silence.

'Perhaps you thought I was complaining about your attitude to my lecturing you all the time about war and strategy, and the next war and so on ... Pretty tiresome of me, I can begin to see that ... But I can't help myself, something inside me is on fire, you know ...'

'O my dear Monty, we forgive you ... and maybe we too will begin to see things differently ... But we are idle shallow things, Monty ... I mean, this is the life, isn't it, the Army in peacetime! Perpetual peace, and perpetual Army life! The war to end all wars has just happened, yet here we are in the bar, laughing our heads off, money in the bank, salaries flowing in, and 'all things found', as they say. Who wants to think about the next war?'

'Well, you know my views,' says Monty, 'but I hope I don't want the next war! That would be perverse! I mean I know I've become the Mess bore',

Loud protests at that...

'Come come!' says Monty, 'I'm not completely stupid! Pretty stupid most of the time, but not a complete ass ... Believe it or not, I have moments of insight about myself ... Totally forgotten by the time the shaving brush next addresses the stubble ... but there all the time really, and giving me little stabs of pain at unexpected moments.'

There is a pause.

'But anyway,' Monty resumes, 'I've decided to apply for the Staff College training at Camberley, where hopefully my concerns will find a readier ear ... No offence meant on my part either ... I can well understand, now that you've expressed it, your general attitude ... Were I to share your optimism about the future, I could possibly settle down into it myself, forget about the last war and the terrible mistakes and so on, and immerse myself in all the sports we have here. You know my keenness for cricket and rugby and all the rest ... and think of nothing else, not even promotion. But I don't share it, therefore my whole personal atmosphere is totally different, as you can see ... and thus I've become the mess bore ... Enough said.'

And Monty leans back, and takes a large draught of his fruit juice.

'It's all right now, Monty,' one says, and pauses. 'It's really all right ... And we wish you success at Camberley, and will watch your future career with interest. Come on all of you, let's drink to Monty!'

And they all do so, and there are genuine smiles and feeling. It is a good moment.

'Thank you very much,' says Monty, 'And I'd better be off now, before you start singing 'For he's a jolly good fellow' That would be too much ... And so, goodnight all of you.'

Monty rises, tries to conceal the tears coming to his eyes, and failing to do so, quickly turns away and makes for the door. There are looks all round, and murmurs, and then silence.

A few months later, Monty is seen entering Camberley College with his bag, with a batman helping him.

Later we see Monty and his colleagues being lectured to by Colonel Alan Brooke, the one person in authority Monty was able to look up to and stand in awe of. (Alan Brooke later called himself Alanbrooke, and was Chief of Imperial General Staff – or CIGS - for much of the Second World War.)

Later we see Monty and some colleagues talking in a Study Room. 'Not much about tanks and mobile warfare,' one of them is saying. 'Is the College really keeping up with the latest ideas?'

'It may be the latest idea,' says Monty, ' but it doesn't mean the British Army should carry it out.'

'What can you mean, not carry it out? Do you want static wars like the last one, and millions of casualties?'

'If we don't have good enough tanks' says Monty, 'we'll have to find some other way round the problem. With inferior tanks one becomes a sitting duck for the enemy.'

'Why should we have inferior tanks, Monty? Germany is being forcibly disarmed, Russia is decades behind all of us, and I can't think of another likely enemy ... '

'Nevertheless, if Germany does begin to re-arm at some time in the future, she will do it thoroughly. Meanwhile we also are disarming, and will probably be the last to re-arm when the crisis looms ... '

'It sounds as if you <u>wish</u> it, Monty' says another.

'I don't wish it, I assure you. I just know it. Don't ask me how I know it. I don't know how I know it, I just do know it, and I want us to prepare for it. A few years' backlog in re-arming could be fatal.'

1926. We see Monty finishing a lecture to students at Camberley (No sound ... we see through the glass door, his gestures and his eyes. We see smiles in the audience, and some laughter, and Monty laughing too).

We then see Monty leaving the lecture-room, and being driven by his batman to the nearest town. We see him mounting the steps of a tall smart terraced house, and see a plaque by the door that announces

MRS. O'HARA---- DANCING LESSONS

He rings a pull-bell, and a charming and lively middle-aged lady answers the door. They shake hands and Monty enters.

'I'm so glad to see you, Major Montgomery' she says, 'and I hope I can help you.'

'I've left it all rather late,' says Monty. 'That is, both the plan to get married, and the plan to learn dancing ... the one will surely help with the other, I imagine.'

'It's never too late Major, and we shall set about it briskly.'

They walk into the dance-room, where a wind-up gramophone is seated on a low table.

'We will try a slow waltz to begin with,' she says, winding it up, and putting the head on the revolving disc.

A pleasant schmaltzy music sounds out. We see the disc turning and turning while the dancers are invisible to us. We hear shuffles and the squeak of shoes, and the occasional 'I'm so sorry, madam,' and 'Think nothing of it, Major!' We hear a thump and a rolling noise as a small table is knocked over, and comes into view.

We see Monty leave, and enter the door again a week later, with the same disc turning and the same waltz tune being played, the same apologies and the same disclaimers. We see the same scene, and the same tune, some half-dozen times, as Monty enters and leaves by the same door.

Finally we see the two of them seated in elegant cane-chairs sipping China tea.

'Is there any hope for me at all, Mrs. O'Hara?' Monty is saying.

'Of course nothing is impossible, Major, given dedication and time. But I do have to say it will be a long haul ... I'm sorry to have to say this, of course ... '

'Not at all,' says Monty. 'Too bad. ... I'll just have to manage without this one skill, I'm afraid. Such a pity ... I love music ... and I thought I was quite musical ... '

'I'm sure you are very musical, sir ... but the movement of dancing is another thing entirely. That, and a certain fear, I think, which makes it difficult for you to relax. Never mind, Major ... it's been a delight to meet you.'

'And you too madam.'

They go to the door for the last time, and we see their parting handshakes on the steps, and Monty descending to his waiting batman in the car. The car draws away, and a few autumn yellow leaves fall from the lime-trees of the terrace onto the pavement.

Chapter 6 – Meeting Betty

We see Monty on a train arriving in Switzerland. He has skiiing gear, and is reading a skiing journal. We see him enter a hotel, and we see some of the guests in the large lounge in the evening, some seated, some moving freely about.

Two boys, aged about ten and thirteen, are seated at a small table playing chess. Monty comes into the lounge, looks round carefully, and eventually walks up to the chess table. He stands behind one of the boys for a minute, and then behind the other. He goes back to standing behind the first (and younger) boy. They become gradually aware of him. The first boy puts his hand on a piece and prepares to move it. There is a sharp intake of breath from behind him, from Monty. But the boy moves the piece nevertheless, and Monty goes and stands behind his opponent. There is a longish wait, till the boy puts his hand on a piece and prepares to move. Another sharp intake of breath from Monty, and the boy turns round.

'Look here, who are you? And what <u>right</u> have you?' he says rudely and without qualms.

'No right at all,' says Monty. 'Just interested – and can't help myself when a game or sport is going on ... And I'm an Army Officer having a well-deserved holiday. Who are you?'

'Our father was an Army Officer as well. Major Carver. He was killed in the war,' says the other boy. 'And there's our mother over there,' he says, pointing to a dark-haired woman in an armchair, who was looking around and occasionally making notes on what she saw. Monty looked briefly, and then looked at the chess game again.

'I'd be pleased to meet your mother, if you would be so kind. I remember your father as little. We could talk about him, should your mother wish to ...'

'We'll just finish this game, and then we'll introduce you,' the older boy said.

Monty then pulls up a light chair, sits midway between them and watches the game, with no further comments or noises, till it ends.

The boys get up and go over to their mother, with Monty a little way behind.

'Mother, can we introduce an Army Officer who says he knew father,' says the older boy.

'I am Montgomery, Major Montgomery,' says Monty. 'I am sorry to hear about your loss.' He extends his hand, and Mrs Carver takes it. She is of a comfortable build, with a strong face, that soon shows itself to be full of kindness as well. Sweetness and strength is Monty's first impression, and a very good one. He likes her immediately, and has no fear or shyness, mainly because he senses her complete honesty and openness, and lack of malice or pride.

'How do you do, sir,' she says, 'These are my two sons. They are good boys, but they miss their father in more ways than one – I do hope they weren't rude to you?'

'I fear I was rude myself,' says Monty,' and was justly rebuked for it.'

'O dear,' she said, 'what did you say, Richard?'

'Only what right had he to interfere in our game,' says Richard quite testily.

'Well there was no need for such language,' she says, 'none at all. I'm sure the Major was kindness itself. Never mind, Major, I hope you will forgive them.'

Monty then sees a few scraps of drawings she has on her knee, and asks to look at them.

'O, they're nothing much, just something to be going on with. We're supposed to be learning to ski ... or rather, the boys are, while I continue a bit of my painting.'

'It sounds as if you are quite serious about your painting,' says Monty. 'That's good. I like serious people. I'm serious, and very ambitious, myself. But I don't understand anything about painting,' he says,'so I can't comment at all, or encourage you in any real way ... I take it you are not a military family on your parents' side, then?'

'Quite the opposite. My maiden name is Hobart, and they were military, and I have a brother, Captain Patrick Hobart, who is an ambitious military thinker ... '

'Good heavens!' says Monty, 'He is at Staff College with me. Camberley, you know. Dear old Hobo!'

'He knows Hobo!' says Richard, 'What a lark! Isn't Hobo a lark?' he says.

Don't talk about your uncle so disrespectfully,' says their mother, 'He has brilliant ideas, and might even be famous one day.'

'I am sure Major Montgomery has as much chance of being famous as Hobo,' says Richard, with the clear implication that it was extremely unlikely for either of them.

'Don't judge superficially,' says Mrs Carver, 'You have to look behind the familiar surface sometimes. Too much familiarity … as the saying goes, 'No man is a great man to his valet' '.

'Exactly!' says Monty, 'And sometimes not to his family either. Or to his friends.'

'Well, what's the use of being great and famous, if your friends and family don't make you feel it?' asks John. 'Where's the pleasure in it?' he repeats.

'A shrewd point,' Monty replies, 'but one doesn't think about those aspects of the thing if one is ambitious. It is ideas that are the passion. Look at your mother, now, boys. A dedicated artist, working on and on, entranced by her subjects and a passion for seeing. I'm sorry, I know and appreciate nothing in this area, but it is common sense at least to know that much, and to respect it. Do you have many artistic friends, Mrs Carver?'

'You can call me Betty from now on,' she said, 'and yes, we do have quite a few artistic friends, some of them a bit Bohemian, I have to say. But nothing extreme in that direction. Genteel Bohemians mostly. There's a lot of middle and upper class Bohemians that likes to play at being romantically Bohemian, down-at-heel, and down-and-out. It's probably harmless, mostly. Some of our friends are like that, and others not at all like that. And others are military people. And one or two quite the opposite, pacifists, in fact. We live in Chiswick, a pleasant part of London. Plenty of artists there, and a good feeling, in spite of the terrible gaps left by the war … '

'What about your skiing, then?' says Monty.

'The boys, I'm afraid, haven't learnt a good deal in their week here, and we're going home tomorrow. But we are coming again next year, and perhaps they'll do better then.'

Monty thrills with the knowledge, even while he experiences disappointment at their early departure. He feels surrounded by warmth, and so easily accepted into their circle that he can scarcely believe it.

'O, off so soon!' he says, 'I already feel I shall miss you all. But please do let me know the dates that you are re-visiting, and I'll endeavor to be here too.'

'Yes we will,' says Betty Carver, 'I've enjoyed meeting you. Perhaps you could visit us at Chiswick in the meanwhile.'

'I'm afraid I'd be somewhat shy and in awe of your artistic friends,' says Monty, 'I've been called a one-track military mind, and I fear it's true.'

'Never mind about that,' says Betty Carver. 'Just come, and we'll see what we can do to ease you into our circle.'

'They all talk about incomprehensible things!' says John.

'That's just what I feared,' says Monty. 'I might be asked for my opinion.'

'Dear Major Montgomery, do try not to worry about that! Anyway, you can sit with your ten fingers pressed together and look wise in your silence. That has a way of putting some people off their stroke!'

'I can easily imagine it,' says Monty, 'and it worries me just as much! Damned if I do, and damned if I don't. An impossible situation ... still, I'll think about it ... And if I am to call you Betty, then you are to call me Monty. And that means the boys as well ... So, goodnight Betty, and Richard and John, and I'll come and see you off tomorrow.'

'Goodnight ... Monty,' says Betty, and with the boys he shakes hands and leaves.

Autumn 1927. At the Swiss ski-resort again.

Monty is with Betty's two boys, out in the open, teaching them to ski. He is dressed in a thick, extremely baggy pullover, that comes right down over his knees. He looks dapper and comfortable, as usual.

'Follow me', he says, and sets off on a cross-country ski, crouching down, with the baggy jumper at his ankles. The boys follow, and all three gradually disappear into the far distance.

It is evening in the hotel, after dinner. Monty is sitting with Betty in the lounge.

'What these boys need is a few days away from you, and under my tutelage,' says Monty.

'I'm sure they do,' says Betty, comfortably and with smiles. 'But can you put up with that?'

'You know very well I will be in my element, and that you can then get on with your own work in peace ... what could be better? And they need a bit more discipline and order, Betty, I have to say it ... they do rather lean on you.'

'O, it's being away at boarding school, and having no father, I do feel I have to indulge them at times ...'

'It's not good for them, though, Betty ... and I promise I won't be harsh or unfair. They will enjoy themselves. So I've booked a lodge and there they will lead a simple existence and do huge cross-country journeys, and be tested to the limit of their strength, bit by bit ... It will be a good experience for them, I promise you!'

'Dear Monty, of course it will. I'm so glad for them ... and the way they have taken to you! How do you do it?'

'I don't do anything that I am aware of, just follow my own instincts and enjoy myself. But I want to see some results from my work ... I mean, I want to see your work when we get back, and check that you have not been idling!'

Next day, we see Monty and the boys arriving at a lodge. The boys are bringing in logs from a shed and lighting a fire. All three of them then prepare a meal, with Monty very much in charge. Then they sit down to chess in front of the fire. Monty plays against John, while Richard sits with Monty, and Monty whispers explanations of some of his moves. It is peaceful and happy.

'Up at first light!' Monty says, as the game draws to an end. They go off to their bunks, and as first light shows, Monty is ringing a school hand-bell he has picked up somewhere. The boys sit up in bed, look at each other, groan, and get up quickly.

They are inside the lodge doing loosening-up exercises before breakfast, with Monty demonstrating, shaking the ankles loose, and then the wrists, and then head and neck, and then the whole body, and letting out noise.

At length we see them set off, up and down, and around, into a far distance, and disappear over a far hill.

When they get back in the late afternoon Monty has them take off heavy clothes and immediately do more loosening-up exercises, inside the lodge. This time there is even more noise made, as the boys struggle against their exhaustion.

'Now, log-fire and hot baths, you boys,' Monty says, 'while I start to prepare the supper.'

There is a copper boiler under which Monty lights a small fire, while the boys rouse up the log-fire, and fetch more logs from the shed.

'Don't sit down yet,' says Monty, as a breathless John makes for a chair, 'Fatal to sit down, however tired you are. Just do the jobs ... get through the jobs ... you will enjoy your relaxation a hundred times more!'

Goodnight boys,' says Monty later on 'I'll just sit here and read for an hour. I'll try not to wake you.'

The boys go to their bunks, and are seen to drop off to sleep immediately. Monty joins them later and is soon peacefully asleep.

In the early hours Monty wakes to see the two boys crouching on the floor.

'What on earth are you doing, you two?'

'O Monty,' says John, embarassed 'We are just trying to use the chamber-pots, without waking you ... I'm sorry we've woken you up.'

'That's neither here nor there!' says Monty, 'But the point is, that's no way to use a chamber-pot!'

Monty gets up from his bunk and grabs his chamber-pot from underneath it.

'Just follow me, and do as I do!'

We see him walk to the door of the bedroom, and facing outwards splay his legs like a pair of compasses.

'Like this!' says Monty, 'Like this! Standing up, like gentlemen. Come on, follow me ... we're not praying, you know. We're peeing, so do it properly!'

The boys follow and stand beside him in the wide doorway, and do likewise.

'That's more like it!' says Monty. 'I can't think what they teach you at that school of yours!'

Then they all seek the lids of their pots, put them on the pots, and slide the chamber-pots under the bunks.

'Up at first light!' says Monty.

The boys in their bottom bunks look at each other, and allow a faint grin, and a rueful shake of the head, before turning over to sleep again.

Back at the hotel it is evening in the lounge, and all four are enjoying their last hours of the holiday. Monty is thumbing through Betty's drawings, and sitting very close to her without quite being in physical contact. Betty is smiling and looking very well.

'It's good for me to do some figures in action for a change,' says Betty. 'A lot of quick sketches, very good exercise, if not very tidy or finished! I've had a very relaxed time ... thank you Monty. It's done us all good.'

'It's easy to appreciate these,' says Monty, 'But I need to see some more paintings, they're harder.'

'I've begun a couple,' says Betty, 'They're in my bedroom ... I don't want to bring them into the lounge ... anyway, the paint's still wet, and I'm going to have to find a way of getting them home tomorrow, a way of packing them safely while wet. You can see them later, Monty, and help me to pack them.'

'A snow painting must be rather monotonous,' says Monty.

'Not at all!' says Betty. 'Not when you've learnt to see! A different colour or tone every time the plane or angle shifts ... and sky-blue shadows on these blue days, Monty ... so delicious. It's like eating a delicious cake!'

'I look forward to seeing them,' says Monty, with the deepest of relaxed smiles.

Next morning they are all standing waiting for the cable-car to take them down. Betty points out to Monty the colours in the snow, taking his arm from time to time to direct his gaze. There is a blissful look in Monty's face as he submits to these directions.

'You are quite right,' says Monty, 'I can see blue shadows, and areas of pale violet higher up the slopes, and even flecks of pink here and there ... and many subtle greys of all shades. Do I enjoy it, though? Too early to say ... but it's certainly a change from my monochrome existence. But wouldn't a really good photo be enough?'

'That's so hard to answer,' says Betty. 'Sometimes it's hard to say 'No' convincingly. But we painters are not trying to be clever ... not trying to imitate in detail what a very good camera can do. I can't explain it, Monty! It's very hard.'

'Never mind,' says Monty, 'I'm sure I'll learn in time.'

There is a silence. The cable car arrives, a small body of people get in and descend. Then the train brings them across Europe to the English Channel, and a train to London.

Monty is seen with Betty and the boys entering Charterhouse Public School for the beginning of the Summer Term. The boys take their luggage from the taxi and struggle with it out of sight. Monty and Betty go to the office, greet the Headmaster, and then walk about the grounds, eventually settling down in the Fives Court in a shady area.

'You're looking a bit nervous, Betty,' says Monty. 'Are you thinking I shouldn't be here with you?'

'People are talking,' says Betty. 'And did you know that Hobo's military career is now hanging by a thread?'

'What can you mean?' asks Monty.

'Hobo had an affair with an officer's wife,' says Betty, 'His career is almost certainly in ruins ... all that ambition and ability!'

'Yes, I see. Very bad ... But how does that connect with us?

We're not exactly 'having an affair', are we?'

'People look, and people talk,' says Betty, 'I'd hate it for the same thing to happen to you ... I see such talent in you.'

'Very kind of you to say so, Betty. However, I can't see there's anything to fret about ... er ... nothing 'improper' has occurred, has it?'

'They don't know that. And my own family have experienced the effects of the most dreadful snobbery, you know. All about us being 'trade', you know ... and unfitted for a high marriage, and so on. It can be awful.'

A silence.

'I really think we should separate for a few months at least, to put a stop to the wagging tongues, while you consolidate your position at Camberley College, and shake this off ...'

'But Betty ... ' says Monty, puzzled, and not finding his words, 'This is cruel!'

'Not exactly cruel, Monty, but necessary. Even the boys might gossip at school here, and it will get worse and worse. You just can't risk your career just to be kind to me and the boys ... It's disproportionate ... You've done us a lot of good, but now I think you should go ... and in the nick of time. We'll always remember your kindness.'

'But Betty!' says Monty again, 'There's more to it than that! It's not just kindness ... Betty dear, I <u>love</u> you ... can't you see that? It's love, Betty ... I've never known anything like it before! I've never loved a woman in my life ... and now it's upon me. And it's about care and kindness and concern. I can even forget my ambition sometimes ... though there's no need to, of course!'

By this time Betty's head is bowed, and the tears are running down her face. Monty, overwhelmed, seizes her hand, and at the same moment the two boys walk into the Fives Court.

'Hullo you two!' shouts John, boisterously and rudely, and 'O, I'm sorry!' as he gets nearer and sees them more clearly.

'Your mother is a little tired and upset,' says Monty, 'Just leave us alone for a while and she'll be all right again.'

The boys steal off quickly and quietly.

'Thank you, Monty,' says Betty. 'It's strange, but I think I love you too, Monty, I really do! ... I never thought I could love again.'

A silence. Monty's face is transfigured. He has to fight off tears.

'Betty, I can't believe it! It's the most wonderful moment of my life! In which case, dammit, we can get married, can't we, and stop all the wagging tongues that way ... We can get <u>married</u>, Betty. Think of that!'

Chiswick, November 1927

A car draws up. Betty gets out and speaks to Monty, who is in the driving seat, 'I won't be long. I'll just call on the Herberts for a few words ... '

In the house she sits on the edge of the sofa, while A P Herbert and his wife attend on her with drinks and snacks.

'No, I'm just leaving you this book, then I'll have to go.'

'What's the hurry, dear Betty,' says Mrs Herbert.

'O, there's someone in the car, I can't leave him too long.'

'O it's a <u>him</u> is it Betty?' says A.P.

'Yes. We'll be married soon, and then I'll bring him on a proper visit.'

'Betty!' they both cry, 'My dear! Why didn't you say? Bring him in!'

'O dear,' says Betty, 'He's much too shy ... not an intellectual like you and me, Just a simple soldier. He'll feel very awkward.'

'Bring him in!' they insist, 'Surely we can between us make him feel welcome!'

'Well, if you must,' says Betty. 'But we won't stay long.'

She goes out awkwardly and fetches Monty. He is gracious and quiet in the introductions, as are his hosts, but they sit silently for a while.

'Betty says you were too shy to come in,' says A.P.,' Are we so frightening, now you are here?'

It's more of a statement then a question.

'I fear I know very little of the matters that interest people such as yourselves ... though I've begun to be interested in Betty's painting. And I know you all like to talk, and I can contribute nothing. However I <u>am</u> something of a talker ... a <u>considerable</u>

talker ... but I do like to know what I'm talking about, which is solely the military thing. All my own fault, of course, I took no interest at school, or afterwards, apart from sports.'

There is a pause, and Mrs Herbert continues 'Sometimes I think it's a pity that the artistic world does so much talking. Most of it is gossip, anyway. And it is off-putting to those who feel outside it.'

'But don't worry about me, anyway. I am happy to sit here and listen while you converse in your usual way ... consider me invisible ... and unshockable ... and uncritical, as I'm sure I am in these matters.'

'That's very gracious of you, Colonel Montgomery,' says A.P, 'However, we do have some military common ground, if you'll forgive me for bringing that in so early on. I fought in the Great War, and have even written a book about it called 'The Secret Battle'. Perhaps you would like to take it away with you when you go.'

'O certainly! All military experience interests me. There are quite a few books coming out now, aren't there, mainly those written by conscripts and volunteers and non-regular servicemen. A rash of them, one might say. Robert Graves' 'Goodbye to All That' has recently come out, and I'm in the thick of it already.'

'A very good book, I think,' says Mrs Herbert. 'But A.P.'s is just as good, though much less well known. A.P. didn't wait ten years before writing, his was written immediately.'

'I thought I'd better get it out of my system straight away,' says A.P, 'so that I could take up normal living and feeling as soon as possible ... though I do understand when others say they couldn't begin to speak or write or even think about it for years ... In fact I knew a military padre who literally couldn't speak about anything whatever ... and still can't. He is still under treatment. All that, and shell-shock, and the rest ... doesn't it rather make you think that man is not after all made for war, Colonel? That it is too much for us?'

'It was certainly too much for a lot of people, the way the last war was fought,' says Monty. 'It was almost too much for me. And certainly, if wars are to be fought in future largely by civilians in uniform, there will have to be serious changes in training and in methods of fighting.'

'O, in the <u>future</u>, Colonel!' says Mrs Herbert, 'Surely we're not going to have another major war! Surely not! Nobody is thinking about that now, are they?'

'Well, I'm afraid ... ' Monty begins, but at that point another figure enters the room.

'This is Dick Sheppard, our local curate, Colonel. It looks as though he wants to sound off,' says Mrs Herbert.

'I was hiding away in the other room,' says the Rev Sheppard, 'but when I heard the way the conversation was developing I had to barge in ... I was wanting to say that if this country does begin to prepare for a major war, I will stir myself to oppose it. As things stand at the moment, I think millions in this country would even sign a pledge to refuse to participate in such a war. I can't see that feeling changing, not in a long while, can you, Colonel?'

'It will change if the threat is great enough' says Monty.

'Perhaps,' says Dick Sheppard, 'But meanwhile we and some others are disarming quite considerably. Surely that must be a good thing, even in your book, Colonel?'

'It depends,' says Monty.' It seems the right thing at the moment. But if the time for armament comes, and we are tardy in that respect, then the consequences will be that we will probably lose the war ... or be unable to fight it at all.'

'That may well be the best consequence after all,' says Dick Sheppard, 'Isn't it time we just stopped fighting altogether? Isn't it just primitive, outmoded? And isn't our Christian message one of peace?'

'I fear that there is a spirit in Germany that is angry and resentful and unappeased,' says Monty. 'I fear it will rise again. And I fear it will be vengeful, vicious ... much worse than the last time.'

'But Germany seems peaceful just now, apart from a few fringe lunatics like Hitler,' says Mrs Herbert. 'Why should that change?'

'But if it <u>does</u> change,' says Monty, 'and if, as I say, we are tardy in re-arming, we will suffer not only inferiority in number of weapons, but in quality, which is much more serious ... I know this will cut no ice with you, Reverend Sheppard, but as a military man I have to stress its importance. It is not fair to send men into battle with vastly inferior weapons. It will be like the last war again. Unspeakably cruel, but for different reasons.'

'Your case is a strong one,' says Dick Sheppard, 'and I have no answer to it, in your terms. But speaking as a Christian member of a Christian culture, can we not find a better way?'

'I too speak as a Christian,' says Monty, 'though I more or less lost my faith during the recent war. My dear father, the Bishop, is a good Christian, full of love of the most genuine kind, and yet he does not take the pacifist view, Reverend Sheppard. I learnt my Christianity from my father, and through his love for me ... It is the one strong reality in me in addition to my being a military man. One does not have to hate in order to wage war. That's the crux of it, I think.'

'But the carnage, the destruction, and the mental wounds of war,' says Dick Sheppard, 'The broken hearts and spirits, the broken societies! Aren't these as important as winning a war? And indeed, wouldn't it be better to lose a war sometimes ... in the right spirit?'

'If you are going to lose a war, or refuse a war, in the right spirit, you are going to have to have the whole of the Church in our country, or a significant part of it, leading the rest of society in a spirit of martyrdom. You will need a martyr Church, followed in the same spirit by a martyr population ... many of whom no longer attend any kind of church. It is theoretically possible, it is even beautiful, but it will not happen. Pacifists will have to take their stands as individuals against war, and be very much on their own. Isn't that so, Reverend Sheppard?'

'That, of course, is the least we can do. But I very much hope we can do more. A large part of the population willing to be martyred rather than fight! I find the prospect exciting and challenging, and will do my utmost to support, even to lead such a movement, if the occasion arise!'

'It's good you can talk about this without rancour, you two,' says AP 'I know several military men, and what's more, several pacifists, who are not able to do so. Congratulations!'

'Thank you,' says Monty, 'but why rancour? When one has looked right through things to the end ... when one has been thorough, and even cold ... then one will see why some other people will think and feel differently, and one will accept it, even if reluctantly. All men are different ... that is one of the things I'm beginning to teach in my military training. One man can do some things, but not others. Not just a matter of skill or intelligence, but of feeling, of cast of personality. If a commander can't spot these crucial differences and make allowance for individuals, and use the differences, then he's not worth very much. However, I mustn't go on ... it's getting more like Camberley every minute! You must excuse me.'

'O certainly,' says Dick Sheppard, 'I think you're a good military sort, Colonel. I'm not sure there are many like you. though perhaps when you've trained a few more ...' he trails off.

'It's time we were going,' says Betty, 'It's been enjoyable ... if that's the word. But we should go. More another time. We'll come again.'

'O yes, do!' says Mrs Herbert, 'where's AP?'

'Here I am,' says AP, coming back into the room. 'I'll be most interested in your opinion on my little effort,' he says, handing Monty a copy of his book. 'And many congratulations to both of you! Betty tells us you will be married soon!'

'I know I am very lucky,' says Monty, 'and certainly I will read your book. Thank you for your kind welcome.'

Monty and Betty leave the house. They sit in the car and join hands.

'Not so bad, then, Monty!' says Betty.

'No. They're good people. I felt at ease immediately. Betty, you're a wonder. You know such splendid people. I will be a changed man in no time, just you wait and see.'

'It's good to see you hold your own, Monty ... You have charm when you want to use it, Monty! Why don't you use it more often?'

'Can't stand the idiots above me in the Army. Idiots, most of them, idiots all of them except Alanbrooke at Camberley! Don't need charm, need kicking ... damned good kicking ... ', he says, easing the car away.

1928. Monty is a teacher at Camberley Staff College.

A sunny day in June. Monty and his two stepsons are walking up a gravelled drive. Part of the drive bears leftwards at one point towards the front door of the administrative buildings ... elegant grey brick half-covered in ivy. The other fork carries on rightwards past the buildings, and out of sight. The path is bordered all the way with well-kept grass, and warning notices about keeping off it

As Monty and the boys come nearer to the offices, Monty steps onto the grass, and veers leftwards, towards an old chalky wall adjoining these buildings, and covered in tough creepers and other mature vegetation.

'Come on you two, let's take the short cut!' says Monty.

'But Monty,' says John 'It says 'Keep off the grass'!'

'O floojam woojam!' says Monty, 'It does no harm'.

'No harm!' the younger boy snorts 'But someone in the office might see us! What then, Monty?'

'O flotsam jotsam, jolly old wotsam!' says Monty. 'Come on, you two!'

'But Monty,' says John, the elder, again' 'You're so strict about your orders being obeyed! What about other people's orders?'

'Hubble trouble boil and bubble!' says Monty. 'Are you coming or not?'

'No we're jolly well not!' they both say.

'All right. I'll go myself. I've got to scramble over that wall, but I'll beat you to the house anyway. Strictly no running though, it's a walking race. You'll have to walk pretty fast to beat me. Right. Go!'

The boys set off at a smart rate, while Monty strolls over to the wall, seizes a thick creeper, and is up and over in a few seconds. He is greeted in the thick shrubbery the other side by an angry voice.

'Hey you there!'

A gardener comes through the thickets and emerges with a hot and angry face.

' Oh I'm sorry Colonel Montgomery! I didn't see it was you sir!'

'A fine day Mr. Weatherby!' says Monty.

'It certainly is sir. It certainly is. Ah.'

'Well I must be on my way' says Monty, 'No time to lose, on such a day ... I wish you well Mr. Weatherby ... and ... must be on my way!'

Monty ducks his way through the small trees and comes out onto the grass. A quick look to his right shows him the two boys about halfway to the Officers' Mess and going very strongly. He sets out in great strides, with his arms working energetically, and then breaks into a run. A cry goes up from the boys as they see this.

'Monty, you said no running!' they scream, and soon break into a run themselves, but it is too late. Monty is a good twenty yards to the advantage, and is now sprinting. He reaches the Mess well in front of them, and does not wait for their remonstrations but goes straight round it and towards their house. The boys follow yelling and screaming, 'Cheat! Unfair! Bad bad Monty!'

Back among the shrubbery Mr. Weatherby and his young assistant are watching.

'Well I reckon the Colonel got caught short!' says Mr. Weatherby ' 'ed of done it right here, I reckon! ... Nice old boy ... Bit of a rum 'un, by all accounts.'

'Eccentric, you mean?' said the young one.

'Eccentric baint the half of it, boy! A law unto isself, more like!'

At the house the boys arrive panting and shouting. Monty is standing on the threshold, arms folded, smiling and happy.

'But you <u>cheated</u> !' they shout again.

'Nonsense!' said Monty 'Everything went strictly according to plan. Any complaints?'

'A hundred complaints!' they say.

'All complaints in triplicate to the Commanding Officer here. Do the thing properly, if you must do it at all.'

They arrive at him and punch him on all sides, he ducking and weaving like a bantamweight boxer, and taking the punishment with ease.

The next morning we see Monty addressing a class. Some of the students there will later become his chosen commanders in the field, both for their innate qualities and for their appreciation of his teaching. Monty is checking them in.

'Mr. Harding.'

' Here sir'.

'Mr. Leese'

' Here sir '

'Mr. Gatehouse'

' Here sir.'

'Mr. Dorman-Smith'

' Here sir'

'Well gentlemen,' says Monty, 'I look forward to having you in my class, and to giving you an outline of some of the ideas which are now being generally discussed in Army circles. In considerably more detail I will reveal to you my own ideas, which I am convinced you will find even more valuable. Some of these ideas of mine are not yet accepted. To give you but one example, it is already an anachronism that we have only an Army Training Centre here. The next war will require the closest co-ordination between ground forces and the Air Arm, and to an extent with the sea forces as well. We really need a Joint Services Training Centre here, so that the rather childish barriers, and indeed animosities, that exist between the different branches, have been sufficiently broken down and neutralized well before the real war begins. I need hardly remind you, gentlemen, that battles have been lost in the past through lack of co-ordination between different Generals in the same land-force. Vanity and vaingloriousness and self-aggrandisement have been at the heart of these failures of co-ordination just as much as actual strategic considerations. It needs little imagination, gentlemen, to conceive of the follies and disasters that may follow if you add to these personal failings the institutional vanities and jealousies of the separate Arms of our Armed Forces. How, in the thick and the fog of war, are they to be sorted out?

'Let us anticipate these difficulties now, and let us vow that, in the absence of any institutional reform before the next war is upon us, we will all be fully aware of the problem, and will be early in spotting difficulties arising therefrom, and will be unafraid and vocal about them, bringing them to the attention of the authorities concerned. And let us learn coolness and calmness in these acts of persuasion, gentlemen, and try to avoid all shouting-matches and stormings-out and slammed doors, and so on and so forth. And let us also avoid as far as possible being guilty of the vanity and jealousy stemming from our own position as soldiers of the Army, which is merely one Arm in our Forces. It may sound banal saying this, but believe me, gentlemen, these institutional crusts will grow on us, and particular loyalties will expand into our being until we are hardly aware of them. Be on your guard, gentlemen.'

Monty makes a pause in his address and relaxes his gaze, which has all the time been both intense and fluid, ranging from one man to another, and altering slightly as it does so, registering psychically the different reality it finds in each man's eyes. Incommunicable skills are being exercised, by a man aware of his power and grasp of things, but not fully aware of his ability to speak to most conditions of men.

Monty resumes, 'And thank you, gentlemen, for not coughing or spluttering during this introduction of mine. It disturbs my concentration, and is in any case quite unnecessary. I imagine you have all been present at a Concert of Music at which sundry persons cough at all times ... both in the interval between the movements, and during the music itself. It is psychological ineptitude, gentlemen. It shows lack of respect for the musicians, and for the other members of the audience. A moment's reflection by these perpetual coughers will reveal the complete irrationality of their behaviour. Let them ask themselves, did they cough all the way in the car, or on the bus, or on foot in going to the concert? Of course they didn't! Let them remember <u>one</u> single cough in the car or on the bus ... and let them further ask themselves, did they cough in the foyer of the Concert Hall? What do we hear there but a babble of voices, no coughing discernible. Of course they didn't cough there, not once! And let them further ask themselves, should they have met with some friends in a cafe before the concert, did they spend their time with their friends coughing? Of course they didn't! Had they done so, their friends would surely have prevailed upon them to go home immediately and take to their beds! Also, considering the vast number of people who cough incessantly at concerts, what would our little gatherings at cafes beforehand be like if, say, at least half of these people were perpetual coughers! Imagine it, gentlemen! All social intercourse would come to an end. No, let these coughers ask themselves what is the cause of their coughing. Is it lack of true interest in music? If so, let them abstain from public concerts. Is it a more generalized boredom, and so an awkwardness relieved by coughing when concentration and a show of interest is required of them? Possibly ... Or is it a terrible fear of being moved by the music, a fear of feeling? Some of us do fear being moved by anything, gentlemen. It might ruffle our perfectly styled hair, gentlemen, or cause us, if we are ladies, to heat up our make-up, and find it running down our faces.

'Well, these are all interesting questions, gentlemen, and worth some consideration. I could use a more telling if slightly outrageous example, when considering how real interest and indeed passion will always conquer coughing. Consider gentlemen, do you find yourself coughing when you are entwined in the arms of your loved one and engaged in a totally absorbing occupation? Of course you don't! So by analogy, let me promise you, gentlemen, that when you are in the thick of one of my lectures you will be equally absorbed and equally gripped, if I may use the expression, so that all possibility of coughing and spluttering will be quite beyond you. Yes, I can promise you that kind of an experience, gentlemen. However, I am a realist, and believe in safeguards, so before I begin the substance of my lecture to you, I will allow a full three minutes for coughing ... and talking. After that, no more coughing at all. I hope that is clear, gentlemen.'

Chapter 7 – Holidays

<u>1929 - On Holiday in the Lake District</u>

A large car edges uphill to a T-junction just south of Broughton, in the Western Lake District area. Monty is driving and his wife and their baby son David are in the front seat together. In the back seats are Betty's two sons, and her brother Patrick Hobart, another military man who until recently, as we have seen earlier, was on the way to military renown through his original ideas.

As the car reaches the junction, at which it is to turn right and go downhill on the way to the bridge over the river Duddon, we see a mischievous smile playing lightly over Monty's features. At the same time we can see that he is happy, as are all the party except perhaps Patrick, or Hobo. They soon reach the river-bridge, and here they turn right, to proceed inland parallel to the river. There is a very steep hill facing them to begin with.

'Hold onto your saddles!' cries Monty, as they approach the hill. He rushes at it full speed in third gear, then has to change to second and then into first as they tackle bends and increasing steepness. At last they are out of it and more or less on a flat course. There are cheers from everyone, except Hobo.

At length Hobo makes his contribution. 'We've been travelling over an hour, Monty. Couldn't we have some more air? All the windows are tightly closed.'

'Quite right, Hobo,' says Monty.

'What do you mean, Monty? Do you mean it's correct when I say 'All the windows are tightly closed'? Or do you mean it's quite right that they should be closed?'

'Both statements are true, Hobo. Both statements,' says Monty with sly equanimity.

'Right!' says Hobo. 'I'll begin again. Considering that there are six of us in here, and that we've been travelling over an hour, and that the day is quite hot, it being July, in case it has escaped your notice, might it not be reasonable to request that at least one window be slightly opened, if only for a while? Now what could be more moderate or polite than that?'

"Polite,' certainly, Hobo. "Moderate' only on the most

superficial view of the matter. In actual fact, you could not have made a more extreme or dangerous request. 'One window slightly open', you said. Worst option of all, Hobo, the very worst.'

'I don't see that, Monty ... nor does anyone else, I'm quite sure.'

Hobo half turns to the boys for support, and to Betty. There are titters between the boys, and Betty is unconcerned at this stage, and even enjoying this little encounter.

'I can explain my position later on, but meanwhile let me ask what is wrong with the status quo?'

'But it's hot and it's a bit stuffy, Monty. It's just common sense. We need more air.'

'You may feel you would like more air, Hobo,' says Monty, 'But as to needing more air, that's quite another matter. We do not need more air, Hobo. There is enough air in this car for all of us for at least a night and a day, of that I can assure you. We could travel on, sleep in the car with all the windows closed and emerge none the worse for it. I don't say it would be a pleasant experience, Hobo, what with you bellyaching all the time, and arguing the toss about every conceivable thing, but a danger to life and health, certainly not.'

'Have you gone quite mad, Monty?' says Hobo, 'Where is your common sense? Where is your humanity? We're all suffering Monty!'

Hobo again half-turns to the boys, but again only finds titters. They are smiling broadly, and nudging and tickling each other.

'I haven't heard any suffering yet, Hobo,' says Monty, with maddening equability, 'only your bellyaching. At the first sign of real suffering I will stop the car, and we will deal with the situation as it needs to be dealt with. Meanwhile, though the air in here may not be of the freshest, it is perfectly adequate for our needs, and is the least dangerous of all the options open to us.'

'Least dangerous of the options, Monty! You talk as though we were at war, as though this were some kind of crisis!'

'Who exactly has been making a crisis out of it?' says Monty.

'Very well then,' says Hobo, 'I will begin again. First, it is not a crisis. I will grant you it is not a crisis. I will grant you also that the air in here is adequate for our needs. I will even grant you, for the sake of argument, Monty, that it will continue to be adequate for the rest of the day, and perhaps the night as well ... and whatever of that sort you wish to maintain. My simple point is this. Would it not be more <u>pleasant</u>, - would it not be more pleasant, Monty, if we were to have a modicum of fresh air passing through the car and passing through our systems? Is <u>pleasantness</u> a sin Monty? Is our mere pleasure something to be sneezed at?'

'While we are on the subject of sneezing ...' says Monty.

'We are <u>not</u> on the subject of sneezing, Monty,' Hobo is almost shouting, 'We are not on the subject at all. Why go down such side-alleys?'

'While on the subject of side-alleys...' says Monty equably again.

'We are <u>not</u> on the subject of side-alleys!' shouts Hobo. 'We are not. We just are not.'

'Just as you wish, Hobo,' says Monty, pacifically neutral and quiet.

'Well answer my point then!' Hobo snorts.

'Very remiss of me, Hobo, but what exactly was your point? You made a statement of personal preference, then you asked a somewhat rhetorical question, but nowhere did I find it coming to a precise point or proposition.'

'Right!' says Hobo, ' My proposition is this – that we should open one window just slightly, because it would be more <u>pleasant</u> for us all to have a little <u>fresh</u> air to add to the admittedly adequate supply that we already have.'

'Perfectly clear now, Hobo, perfectly clear. Unfortunately, as I've already indicated, what you propose is the least attractive proposition you could have made. It is quite a dangerous proposition, something not to be trifled with.'

'Here we go again!' moans Hobo, 'O saints in heaven, send this sufferer patience! O please do!'

'A little less of your melodrama, Hobo. There's no need for that. I'm being perfectly plain. 'One window slightly opened' constitutes a draught, Hobo, and a draught can be a terrible thing.'

'O this is indeed news!' snorts Hobo again.'Here is our great commander of the future, here's our physical fitness fanatic, who proposes to train his men in all weathers, night and day and all the next night again, without sleep and without much food ... this seeker out of mud and damp, of hail and driving rain, of burning sun, and of fog and mist, all in one great gulp and swallow ... and what is worrying him? A little draught! Can I be hearing you right Monty?'

'Yes you certainly can,' says Monty, 'A great aunt of mine in my Tasmania days comes to mind. Into the drawing-room, all fresh and glowing from tennis. Still in her long tennis shorts of course. Sits down. One leg exposed to draught from window. Evening air ... cooling ... thought nothing of it ... caught chill in the night ... high temperature ,,, off to hospital ... three days ... finished.'

'Three days in hospital because of a chill from a draught,' muses Hobo. 'Certainly a bit extreme. Freakish. She was probably a bit run-down. Not at all typical.'

'She was not run-down. And she was not three days in hospital and then out! She was three days in hospital and then dead! That's what I'm saying, Hobo. The draught killed her.'

'Well, that's certainly serious. An extreme case, no doubt. Something a bit freakish there. Probably a bit run down.'

'She was not one little bit run down, my aunt Gwyn! Did you know my aunt Gwyn, Hobo?'

'No, of course I didn't know your aunt Gwyn. All I am saying is that you like to pretend, you know ...'

Monty interrupts, 'All you are saying is that you just like to talk for the sake of it, and that you like to have opinions in the teeth of all the evidence!'

'What evidence? What in the name of thunder is all this talk of evidence? Evidence of what, for God's sake?'

'Have you read thoroughly the books on Wellington's campaign in the Peninsular War?' asks Monty, 'Have you read them thoroughly, Hobo?'

'You know I read all military things thoroughly. You know I'm as particular as you are on these matters, Monty, so why do you ask?'

'Do you know how many of Wellington's men died mysteriously, from sudden chills, almost certainly from draughts, on that campaign?'

'I confess I am not at all aware of any factual material on that subject, Monty ... and I'm not sure you're not pulling my leg ... '

'Most certainly not! You say you read thoroughly, Hobo. Do you always read the footnotes?'

'I usually read the footnotes, yes. I don't always read <u>all</u> the footnotes ... I read them if my interest draws me to them, if I think they are significant.'

'You can't always know if they are going to be significant until you actually read them! It's never safe to ignore a footnote, Hobo. Never quite safe. In this particular case, in the standard 3-volume study, the footnote refers you to Appendix 5. I wonder if you picked that up?'

'I couldn't be absolutely sure of that. But only pedants read Appendices, Monty!'

'O dear me, O dear me! A sad gap in your knowledge here, Hobo. For had you taken up that footnote, and referred to that Appendix, we would probably not be having this rather tiresome argument now, dear Hobo.'

'You expect me to take seriously the idea that campaign-hardened soldiers, those who put up with hunger for days on end sometimes, who suffer impure water, dust, lice, and every kind of germ, who are baked into an incredible toughness by these experiences, are going to succumb to a chill because of a <u>draught</u>! Why, they will sleep in the open night after night, even in extremely cold conditions. Do you take me for a complete fool?'

'No, my dear Hobo, but your information is not as full as it could be. By all means ask your soldiers to sleep out in the open, in the cold, if there is no comfortable alternative. But, if so, let them be properly exposed, let the body be all over more or less the same temperature. And if you are going to cover yourself with a blanket, cover yourself, and do not let the cold air in through a side-alley, as it were That's why I was glad you raised the subject of side-alleys, as I said at the time. A side-alley, however minute, will induce <u>sneezing</u>, (another subject you raised, if you remember), and once sneezing has begun, there is sometimes no stopping it, and chills and pneumonia can follow. That's what happens. A small cold <u>spot</u> on the body can put the whole system out of joint. Even if it does not induce sneezing, it affects the brain, and then everything begins to go wrong. So I hope you see now that I was perfectly serious in refusing your request for a small opening of one window. That, in my judgment, is a side-alley, or draught, and is extremely dangerous.'

'Well, you begin to persuade even me, Monty. But by hell, I'm going to check out your damned Appendix when I get home, and if you've been having me on, there's going to be a rumpus!'

'By all means check the facts, Hobo. I could, of course, have mis-remembered. I don't remember everything I read.'

'Don't you, Monty? I rather thought you did. I really don't know what to think at the moment. But perhaps, on your own principle, the thing to do now is to open <u>all</u> the windows wide and have a real gale blowing. That wouldn't offend your principle, would it now? A proper and salubrious gale, total exposure to freshness and the wild. How about it, Monty?'

Quite a long pause.

'I'll give it serious thought,' says Monty.

The conversation at last subsides. At the same time the road broadens a little, and the stone walls vanish from the roadsides as the landscape begins to be less precipitous. They are descending through an area of bracken and rocks and scattered yew-trees, with no pasture. Here the sheep run free, and wander across the highway, often sitting down on it, sometimes right in the middle, where they chew languorously and long, like American GIs at rest or at play. The long loops of this descent bring them at last to a wide, flat area at river level, where a few holiday-makers are strung out along the water's edge.

As they are approaching this area, with the car slowing down for all to take it in and appreciate it, Patrick breaks the silence almost explosively.

'It's no good, Monty! Stop the car, stop the car!'

Monty turns to look at him questioningly.

'This is unfinished business, Monty, stop the car. You and I have to leave these people in peace, and have this thing out properly, on our own. Stop the car, Monty, can't you hear me?'

'As you wish, Hobo,' says Monty, slowing down and pulling the car over onto a grassy flat area beside the river. They both get out, and Monty says, 'At your service, Hobo!'

'Over here then,' says Patrick, striding with very large, angry strides to a point about thirty yards away.

Here they take up positions, with Patrick more or less facing towards the car and its occupants, who are seething quietly with amusement, and Monty more or less in quarter profile as he faces Patrick and looks upwards at his much taller friend. It is the same look of friendly curiosity and gentlemanly courtesy with which Monty was to look, nearly fifteen years later, after the battle of El Alamein, at the battered General von Thoma surrendering to him personally, tall and covered in smoke and grime, but saluting as to a fellow-soldier and comrade, and as though with the last few ounces of his strength.

A dumb-show begins, for the windows of the car are thick, and still closed, no one having the courage to open them. Hobo is gesticulating and throwing his body up and down as he releases his vehemence and frustration. It looks like toe-touching exercises, done to a hidden and unheard voice of command. Monty meanwhile is as still as the flat rock that stands between them. After a minute Hobo stalks off and comes back with a long straight branch of birch, takes up his position again, and now begins to thwack the rock with his weapon after every loud tirade. This goes on for some while, during which their positions shift a little, so that Monty has his back entirely to the car. At this point a boy's hand reaches out and stealthily winds the window down about six inches.

'Shut that window please!' shouts Monty without looking round.

The boy's hand shakingly winds it up again, and there is writhing and slapping of hands on knees, while Betty bounces her one-year old up and down, singing a cheerful bouncing song.

'What did he say?' says one boy to the other.

' He said 'Shut that window,' says the window-shutter.

'I know that!' says the other, ' What did Hobo say?'

' I'm not quite sure ... But I think he said, 'And ninthly' '

There is a pause.

' 'And ninthly,' says his brother. 'O I see. Ninthly!'

'Yes. 'And ninthly' . Yes yes yes. Ninthly.'

Shrieks of merriment in the car, even the baby taking it up, adding his own shrieks of joy, as though in perfect understanding. As they are still shrieking the front doors open and the two men get back in.

After a while Betty asks 'And what was the upshot of all that?'

'Collapse of stout party!' says Hobo triumphantly. 'Surrender on all fronts! Aunt in Tasmania died of old age, (right Monty? 'Right'). Appendix a total fiction, (right, Monty? 'Right'). No evidence that draughts ever hurt anyone (yes Monty? 'That's not so clear.').

'I meant, what is the upshot concerning the windows?' asks Betty, a little impatiently.

A pause as Monty puts the car into gear and begins to drive away.

'My car,' Monty says. 'Windows stay shut.'.

Stifled screams of laughter from the back, and Betty smiling, but ruefully now.

'In any case,' says Monty, 'you've all had a bit of an airing this last twenty minutes, haven't you?'

The car pulls away, as the boys in the back shriek, 'We haven't!' in a unison of indignation. 'You told us to close the window. We've had the windows shut, all the time!'

Monty ignores this. The car speeds up and crosses a small bridge over the river Duddon and proceeds on the other side of it, going inland still. Soon they come to a left turn that climbs a very steep and winding hill. Just before this point Monty brings the car to a stop.

'Right,' he says, ' Everybody out!'

And then, 'Right. Betty and the baby in front with me. The rest of you walk. Hill's too steep for the car and all the luggage.'

Hobo and the boys start to walk towards the hill.

'I said 'And all the luggage',' snaps Monty. 'Come on you boys, get yourself as big a knapsack as you can carry. Here Hobo, here's a really heavy one for you. Right. Now gentlemen your tasks are three. First, to carry this luggage up the hill, and beyond, to a place where I can pull away easily. Second, to prepare to push the car should it fail at any point on its ascent. Third, to maintain cheerfulness and high spirits throughout. Right. Off we go!'

Monty and Betty get into the car and Monty again hurls the car at the start of the hill and shortly disappears round the first bend. The walkers hear the car engaging the lower gears and spluttering and groaning up the hill, as they, glad of the fresh air and the shady woods covering the hillside, lean into their climb. They stride out admirably and soon go round the first bend, while the car is only some fifty yards ahead, growling its way round the third. Cool breezes on two happy faces, and on one impassive one. Onward and upward.

The car is by now well out of their sight, parked where the hill flattens, and where the full sun is shining, and both front doors are open. Betty and Monty are sitting hand in hand, enjoying the bliss of sudden high moorland air, bringing its scent and cooling the sunshine.

'Is Hobo all right, do you think, Monty? Haven't you taken things a bit far? I mean he feels his recent military humiliation very keenly. Enough is enough, Monty. Don't bring military matters into it.'

'I agree, Betty. No more Army stuff ... I only mean fun you know. Hobo's so serious. He does rather ask for it.'

'Let him be, Monty! How would you like it?'

'I'll try to ease off dear,' says Monty as he goes to meet the party now emerging from the last of the trees and bushes and into the sunshine. Monty takes the younger boy's pack and they reach the car.

'Right. Betty and the baby in the front with me, you three in the back.'

When all are settled he says 'Right. All windows open. Moorland ahead. Lovely air. So, windows down, everyone.'

The windows go down, but Hobo's only halfway.

'Right down Hobo!' says Monty without turning his head.

Betty nudges her husband sharply in the thigh.

'Sorry for that Hobo. I've changed my mind. Keep it where you like it.'

Betty opens her door, and struggles out with the baby.

'This is ridiculous. I won't sit here while all this is going on. Come on Patrick, you get in the front with Monty.'

Hobo labours out again, and into the front seat. The car pulls away, and reaches the bare ochre stretches of Birker Moor. The wind and the clouds are looser and less earthbound. A gaiety returns to the party and Hobo suddenly bursts out, 'Ah, this is wonderful! Such a place, such a day, such a summer! O frabjous day!'

The boys begin to recite from Lear, 'Far and few, far and few, are the lands where the jumblies live!' and Hobo carries on with the quotation.

He is looking ahead laughing and smiling, and up into the free sailing clouds, and down into the boggy wastes, until suddenly tears are running down his face, and Monty's hand steals out and rests on his knee for a few moments.

The car climbs a long shallow slope, and then goes over its top, and is out of sight cruising down the other side.

About 1930, in Chiswick on holiday

Monty and family are on holiday at Betty's family home in Chiswick. Their son David is two years old, and is being looked after by a Nanny. The two stepsons, John and Richard, are also at home on a school holiday. Betty is painting a pot of irises in her studio, while Monty walks from place to place to make sure everything is going 'according to plan'. He consults a notice-board in the entrance-hall, and looks at his watch.

'Nearly 10.' he says, 'You two boys, where are you? Your cricket-practice begins at 10 precisely. Why aren't you ready?'

John and Dick come tumbling down the stairs in their stockinged feet, and holding bat, ball and pads.

'What, still no boots on!' says Monty, 'Do you never consult standing orders for the day? Why do I have to check and check that they are being carried out? Do you think I've got nothing better to do?' Monty is only half serious in his officiousness. It is his great game at home, but it is not entirely a game.

'How can your mother get on with her painting if the whole place is in chaos! She needs to know that the household is running smoothly before she can really settle to work ... that everything else is being seen to ... can't you two boys understand that?'

'We <u>have</u> consulted Standing Orders, Monty, and we are only a minute behind time. It doesn't take a minute to get our boots on, and now you are wasting that minute by going on at us!'

All this is said while they crash upstairs again to find their boots, and crash down again, ready to go.

'Betty will paint till 12 noon,' says Monty, 'and I want you boys back on the dot of noon to help with laying the big table for 1pm. We have the Herberts, and a couple of painter friends coming ... it should be good fun.'

'O jaw-jaw-jaw!' says Richard, the younger one. 'Thank heavens there'll be good food!'

'Just do your best to be polite to our guests, all of whom are very interesting people from whom you both might learn something, if you weren't such a couple of dedicated philistines,' says Monty, with a hint of self-irony.

There are hoots of laughter from the boys at this as they go out.

'Right!' shouts 16-year-old John, as they go down the street. 'Philistines versus Greenery-Yallery Tendency. You're the Philistines, Dick, and Greenery-Yallery will give you a damned good thrashing.'

Monty closes the door, smiles gently, and makes his way to Betty's studio, and stands quietly behind her as she paints.

'I'm liking this one very much,' says Monty, 'This could be one of your best so far'.

'Thank you, dear Monty. Yes, I think the essential <u>is</u> coming through.'

She is seated well away from the easel, her eyes are screwed up, and she is working boldly and incisively with quite a large brush, trying to co-ordinate the strong action lines of the painting into a coherent design, with strong colours.

'I must not get bogged down in detail,' she is saying, half to herself. 'Look for the shapes ... and for the shapes between the shapes,' she goes on quietly.

'What are the shapes between the shapes?' Monty asks.

'Look here!' Betty points at a large stem of an Iris, and then at another one. I've not only to paint these stems accurately, and with life in them, but the space between the two stems must also have an artistic, shaped quality ... do you see?'

'Not quite,' says Monty, 'Why? Do they have an artistic shaped quality in real life? I can't quite see that they do ...' he says, but without assertion, and looking at the real irises in the vase.

'Well, they do and they don't, that's the trouble,' says Betty. 'That sounds peculiar. But things are peculiar. If you look for them, they are there ... all except for a twitch or two of alteration. Once I have stopped looking for them, they are suddenly not there ... until, that is, I have had years and years of looking and painting, and then the shapes between the shapes will hopefully be there all the time, even when I'm not painting ... the world itself becomes more significant, more beautiful.'

'It's still a bit beyond me, dear Betty, but I will get there, with your help, in the end. That word 'significant', it's the word of the hour, isn't it?'

'Yes,' says Betty, 'something of a fashion.'

Monty sits down. 'Do you mind if I stay and watch for a while, Betty? I won't talk, and you mustn't talk unless you want to. I'd like to keep a close eye on the subject itself and what you are doing with it.'

They both sit quietly, and Monty switches his intense eyes from painting to subject, and back, from time to time. At last he gets up, touches Betty on the head with a hand, and steals from the room. He goes to the sitting-room, and takes up 'The Times'.

As noon approaches, Betty is cleaning her brushes. Monty is at the door looking down the street, and the boys in the distance are waving and shouting.

'Excellent, excellent,' says Monty, rubbing his hands as the boys come in, 'Everything on time, and everybody happy!'

All now bustle around to get the table ready. Betty picks up

David in her arms, and sits talking with the Nanny in the sitting-room. There is a happy atmosphere throughout the house.

The doorbell rings, and Gwen and A.P. Herbert are there. Monty answers the door.

'Hullo, Monty, hullo, hullo,' says AP, and they enter the house, beaming with pleasure. 'Everything going to plan, Monty?' says AP again.

'Splendidly,' says Monty, 'splendidly. Good work has been done this morning, and everything is in order.'

They walk into the sitting room to join Betty, who gets up with David on her shoulder, and greets them warmly.

'I understand we've got Duncan Grant coming to lunch,' says Gwen. 'He's quite something, Monty, in the world of painting. One of Bloomsbury's top men, isn't he, Betty?'

'O certainly,' says Betty, 'and we're lucky to get him. Our other guest is a younger painter ... just calls himself Reilly. I don't know much of his work, but Duncan thinks highly of him and wants to bring him along.'

We see them an hour or so later, finishing lunch, drinking coffee, ... and even smoking. (Monty tolerates this for Betty's guests, though for no-one else).

'So how are you getting on in the world of Bloomsbury, Colonel Montgomery,' asks Duncan Grant, a rugged-looking man, not the aesthete of conventional legend. 'Don't you find us all a bit effete?' he adds, knowing full well that he himself will never be accused of that.

'O I don't know,' says Monty, 'I don't know. It's not entirely as I expected.'

Reilly is a small quick dark man with a foxy, amused face, rather like Monty's. He loves looking from face to face as the conversation proceeds, peering intently and amusedly into the eyes of each speaker. He is now looking at Monty.

'And I am beginning to get the hang of it, even from a military point of view, I can say,' says Monty.

'Military!' repeats Reilly, with an Irish twang, ' How's that?'

'Well, I understand most of you live in squares,' says Monty, picking up a large square table-mat and placing it in front of him.

'Some truth in that,' says Reilly, 'but how does that help you?'

'And love in triangles,' says Monty, picking up the white serviettes and shaping them back to their original triangular shape, and then placing four of them round the four sides of the square.

There is a laugh.

'I can see that that helps you a little with us,' says Reilly, 'it gives you a kind of entry-point.'

'It is what pleases my simple military mind,' says Monty, 'A good clear shape, something tangible ... It is also, by the way, this square and these triangles, a military device of the 17th century fortification ... at Vauban, I believe. So I only have to think of Vauban, and there I have you all!' he says, with a high-pitched burst of laughter.

'Not quite all of us,' says Betty, 'I hope. Not myself, at least.'

'Nor me,' says Reilly, 'Not me either!'

'O dear,' says Monty, 'that means I'm already losing my grip. Help me somebody! I'm drowning!'

'Well, it's true enough,' says Duncan Grant, 'we are a sort of commonwealth of free love, so-called ... in a way ... which is more like a prison in practice.'

'And of bitchiness,'says Gwen. 'Such self-important people, such snobbery, you've no idea, Monty! Betty protects you from the worst of it. You see only the best of us.'

'I'm sure I do,' says Monty. 'And it is a great pleasure to me to see you. I am enjoying myself far more than I could ever have believed. And I never thought such happiness possible as we're experiencing, Betty and I. I never dreamed such a thing was possible, did I, Betty?' says Monty.

'We mustn't talk about that here,' says Betty, 'We mustn't flaunt ourselves quite so much, I think ...'

'Why not?' says Duncan Grant, 'It's quite rare, the thing you have between you. I can say this, though it's the first time I've seen you together. It shines out from you both. I only wish I could say the same of most of the others in our Bloomsbury lot! Or of myself ... we're such egos, you see, Monty. A certain unavoidable ruthless egoism in being an artist ... making sure, first of all, that you have the conditions and the time to pursue your work. That comes first, middle and last, to be absolutely candid, Monty. A military man is necessarily very different from this, isn't he? His life on the line whenever called on ... what a horror for the artist that is, the military man can hardly conceive of!'

There is a loud laugh from the company, especially from Monty.

'It's not quite as you say, Mr Grant,' says Monty presently. 'Not quite like that ... not in my case at least ... I have been known, just once or twice, to insist on my own way in things ... It has not been unknown for me to assert my ego at times ... that naughty entity just does peep out at intervals ...' Here he explodes into his express-train-coming-out-of-a-tunnel laugh, and beats the table with his fists.

'Steady on, Monty!' says Betty, 'This is not the Officer's Mess ... we do not smash wine-glasses here and throw the pieces on the floor, you know!'

'Seriously,' says Monty, 'seriously. There is a soldier type, I'm sure of it. For that type, all the emotion that a painter or composer of music feels for his work goes into his sense of himself as a fearless guardian of others. He lives for being looked up to as fearless and absolutely reliable in his function. When he is admired for his courage and resolution even unto death, it is as though the collective emotion of a whole people is gathered up into him, and joins with his own sense of himself and his task. He becomes a reservoir of enormous feeling, and of value and self-worth. For those things that he gets back from the people, he will willingly fight and die ... die young, and happy, I mean ... which of course is the horror of the dedicated artist, if I'm understanding you, Mr Grant!'

'Certainly.' says Duncan Grant. 'Speaking for myself at least, unless I can have life and time, I cannot fulfil my own function. And how are we to reconcile these things, Monty? I can hardly go to a Conscientious Objectors' Tribunal and say simply 'I am a painter, and therefore I must live, while soldiers must die!', can I? Though of course that was partly what was at the back of some of our minds in the last war. We had to find, some of us, better reasons in order to cover that up!'

'A perfectly reasonable defence, your first one,' says Monty, 'why on earth should civilians of any kind fight in war, let alone artists? It is the logic of the technological development of war, and of a mass society, of course. But that doesn't make it right. In the old days, apart from the Press Gang for the Navy in the Napoleonic wars, only people of the soldier-type fought in wars, though thousands of civilians got killed nevertheless. I think I am on your side, Mr Grant, in an ideal sense. The trouble is, the realities of modern societies. In present circumstances, even a democratic society in time of war acts like a Press Gang when it introduces conscription. It is an imposition, I agree with you.'

'Well, well, well,' say Duncan Grant and Reilly together. 'Why aren't there more military men of your type, Monty? Are you being sincere, or just diplomatic ... for the difficult evening with the artists?' asks Reilly with an impish look.

'I'm being perfectly sincere, am I not, Betty? Betty has heard me talk like this ... '

'Not quite like this,' says Betty.

'Not quite, it's true,' says Monty. 'But you are all making me think, and I am developing my thought bit by bit. It takes time, you know, to sort out one's thoughts.'

There is a silence, into which no-one wants to intrude. There is a deep breath all round, and the silence begins to be fruitful in itself. Monty at last speaks, more quietly, with the silence being part of his meaning.

'In the last war, as we know, millions of young lives, on both sides, were just thrown away, without cause, and without shame ... and without sufficient explanation as to why civilians should be conscripted and join the militarists' game. White feathers were touted, and all that nonsense. No-one ever bothered to tell people that we were in a very different situation, and that it was an imposition on ordinary men to conscript them and to force them to kill and die. That oaf Haig, that cold, bloodshot military thunderbox ... well, he didn't care how many died. He just went on as though military values were everyone's values.'

There is another deep silence, till Monty goes on, 'And why didn't the politicians do something? At the battle of the Somme in

1916 ... Lloyd George went to the front himself, he knew perfectly well the slaughter that was going on ... Why didn't he sue for a general peace, in the name of simple humanity? Humanity on all sides, I mean, Kaiser and all. Of course, the Kaiser wouldn't have responded. But many of the German people might still have responded. It was worth a try. Why didn't Lloyd George try? Because no-one could touch Haig ... because of his links to the Royal Family. I'm sorry! I'm telling you what we all know! And we all know, as well, that the Royal Families of Europe, with all their inter-family connections, could have prevented the war, if they'd cared to, in the first place, but for that damned Kaiser, who lied and lied up to the last moment. But where is this all going? What was your question, again, Mr Grant?'

There is a laugh, and a pause.

'Just about how we reconcile the general public, and artists in particular, to having to wage war themselves, rather than by proxy. The general public do not particularly want to fight and die, unless they are whipped into a state by vicious propaganda? And I certainly don't want to fight and die, Monty. I want to live, and produce the work of the vision I see. Something that many people will also enjoy seeing ... if 'enjoy' is an adequate word in this context ... it does sound rather frivolous.'

There is another longish, but refreshing silence. At length Betty speaks.

'Monty often says to me that he wants to tell his conscript soldiers (if we have conscription again in the next war) that he wants them to fight and live, if possible, not fight and die. With just the hope that at least some of them will be more reconciled to dying if they are told one is genuinely trying not to throw their lives away, that even the Army cares for life, not just for death and glory. And of course it has to be sincere on the Army's part, you can't just blarney it through to them. Condemned men spot blarney and ... er ...'

'Bull,' says Monty.

'Ah yes,' says Betty, 'straight away, straight away. No bull at any time. I like that, don't you?'

'It would make a lot of difference to be honest like that,' says AP, joining the conversation at last. 'Of course, in any case the army doesn't, from a purely military point of view, want a lot of soldiers to die, but to kill and live. But if it were deemed necessary, it would throw away scores of thousands of lives. It did not care how many ... or only strategically, never morally. I wish the Services had talked to their men like that in the last war ... such emotional confusion everywhere ... where there wasn't just a kind of whipped-up hysteria ... and unreality ... a military, a Services-imposed unreality. 'One law for the Lion and the Ox is oppression', said Blake. Quite right too. We are all different, aren't we, Monty?'

'I believe even every soldier-type is probably different! For the rest, it goes without saying. However, we've spoken quite enough about war and soldiering, haven't we? Let's talk about something else ... Let's talk about ... Significant Form! 'he proclaims triumphantly. 'You see, I'm quite up to date, and have even read some of your Roger Fry and Clive Bell, though I don't think I understand it.'

'It's only a way of speaking,' says Gwen Herbert, 'by artists and appreciators of what we <u>do</u> ... of trying to get some understanding of what we actually perform more or less instinctively ... What I am saying is that it's not very important itself, our theories about what we <u>do</u> ... don't you think so, Betty? It's interesting to try to understand these things from another angle, but it doesn't much matter if the theory doesn't quite add up, does it?'

'That's good enough for me,' says Betty, 'But I'm not sure it'll be good enough for Monty. He wants to understand, and he wants things to make perfect sense, don't you, Monty? No loose ends of any kind! Isn't that so?'

'I'm afraid I can't quite grasp how one can be <u>said</u> to understand <u>anything</u>, unless all loose ends are cleared up, and the thing makes perfect sense. Is that my little military mind getting in the way again? Possibly such an approach is not appropriate for painting, in which case I will have to give it up, and try something else!'

'No no no!' says Reilly, 'Don't give it up. Just to allow

ourselves a little bit of haze in the mind, a little magic mist, a gap that can only be crossed in the end by a sort of magic ... a night journey of some kind. After all, show me God, and I will show you exactly what this all means!'

'How strange you should say that!' says Monty, 'For I could see God clearly, as a boy, in my father's face, whenever he was at home ... which was not often, unfortunately. When he was away, I couldn't see God at all, or feel God in myself. So I said to my father once or twice, 'is God always there?'. He, of course, said 'Yes.' So I thought to myself, it's my own fault. He's there, but I can't see Him. And of course my own (military) type of logic could not summon Him. I've had to learn other ways to see God, so perhaps you are talking about something similar in this world of painting, and one can learn to see what it is! But is it as big a thing as God ... I wonder?'

'O Monty, you are so relentless!' says Gwen. 'You ask such huge things of us! It makes me feel quite small ... a mere book-reader and dilettante artist, faced by a questing Colonel. It's not fair!'

'But it's you people, if I may say so, who make such a big thing of the Arts. If they are not such a big thing after all, then why make such a fuss of them? And if they are a big thing, then you won't feel small, as you say, Gwen, when challenged to give an account of their importance. I mean, I didn't invent this thing, Significant Form, and nor did Field Marshall Haig, to my knowledge! What in the devil's name is it? If you don't mind me pursuing it a bit longer ... '

'I think it could be called seizing the essential, Monty,' says Betty, 'as I was trying to show you this morning with my painting of the irises. More than that, of course ... finding that this simplification, this shedding of inessential detail, is something very satisfying and mysterious. In fact, so satisfying that one wants to call it significant. That's the best I can offer,' Betty added.

'But purely decorative work,' Duncan Grant intervenes, 'what we would call decorative twaddle, is just as simplified, as shorn of detail, but remains twaddle all the same! How would one show, in a formal and concrete way, the difference between decorative twaddle and the real thing? Especially as we sometimes, or even often, produce twaddle ourselves, and don't always know, certainly don't <u>immediately</u> know, that it is twaddle. Some of my own work has been rubbish, some of Roger Fry's is rubbish, and even some of Cezanne's work, dare I say it? is rubbish ... knowing the real thing is quite a problem. <u>Showing</u> it to others, to the novice, or aspirant, even more so. And I can't do better than that, Monty!'

There is another silence.

'Yes, one just comes to <u>know</u> the difference, in the end, there seems no way of prescribing it,' says Betty. 'And one is sometimes, or even often, wrong. And only time sorts these things out ... quite a long time in some cases ... I mean, generations. It <u>is</u> mysterious, the process.'

Another silence, into which Monty at last enters apologetically.

'Excuse me again,' he says, 'You are using the word 'significant'. You are suggesting your art <u>signifies</u> something. To my mind, that must point to something beyond itself? As a pure object, a painting is so much wood or canvas, and a finite quantity of paint, and so on. So in the end, the painting is held in your mind, or soul, and in the minds and souls of others, as though only there does it properly exist. Isn't that rather a big idea? Aren't you really creeping into another world? And isn't the fact that it is often difficult to grasp the beauty of it ... or rather, to know that one art-object is true and beautiful, while another, though looking like it, is 'twaddle' ... doesn't this mean that our very highest faculties, our spiritual and religious senses, are actually at play here? In which case ...'

'Hold on, Monty,' says Reilly. 'Many of us have given up God and the Soul, and have Art in their place. Now you want Art to lead back to the things we have thankfully given up! You will have a hard and thankless task there, Monty!'

'Never mind if I'm to have a hard and thankless task,' says Monty, 'I have hard and thankless tasks in the Army, much of the time. Nevertheless, I think and <u>know</u> that I am right in military matters, and right <u>all of the time</u>, so I continue in my tasks, and continue to proclaim that I am right! And if I were an art-critic, and were seeing things clearly and rightly, I would want to proclaim my rightness there too, and go on doing so until people came round to my view. The only question is, is Art a big enough thing to be worth the struggle? It seems, by your account, that it sometimes <u>is</u>! Yet when I welcome its entry into another world, and ultimately into God, hands are thrown up in horror, and suddenly it's a rather small, or smaller, thing, after all! I mean, make up your confounded minds, you artists! I mean, come on, make a decision, and stick to it!'

There is an amused silence, a sigh of laughter, until Duncan Grant says, 'Monty, I think we should all put some money in a pot to enable you to buy yourself out of the Army ... in a short while you would become one of our most interesting Art critics. A gadfly, a nuisance, a provocateur!'

There is laughter all round, and Monty leans back in his chair grinning, and places his hands palm down on the table.

'I shall certainly sleep on that,' he says, and, after a longish pause, 'I'll let you know in the morning, Mr Grant.... Perhaps you could effect some introductions!' And he laughs his express train laugh, and there is general merriment.

Through all this the boys have been silent, the elder listening intently, but the younger boy by now wilting visibly.

'Come on, you boys, stir yourselves,' says Monty. 'Clear away the rest of the things, and start the washing-up. I'm sorry you've had to put up with me for so long ... Anyway, we've gone some way past our standing orders deadlines, all of us.'

The boys get up and busy themselves.

'Standing orders, Monty?' says Reilly, ' Are you serious?'

'O, he's perfectly serious!' says Betty, 'It's the only way he can cope with domestic life. Anyway it's very useful in some ways, especially for myself ... boundaries, clarity ... equals freedom!'

The boys, having taken dishes to the kitchen, come back with the Standing Orders in their grasp.

'Standing Orders say,' says John, '3pm Betty will rest! It's now 3.45pm, what has become of your system, Monty?'

'O never mind, boys! I have broken it myself, which means it's all right, and everything is still in order! Betty will rest now, you boys will work in the garden for an hour, and our guests will please themselves, stay and talk, or wander round with me, or take themselves home. I am sure they all have tasks to attend to ...'

'It's time for us to go,' says AP, with Gwen nodding agreement.

'I'd like to see some of Betty's work,' says Reilly.

'Splendid,' says Monty. 'I'll show you around.'

'I'll come with you,' says Duncan Grant.

Chapter 8 – Postings to Egypt and India

Early 1930s – Monty and family are posted to Egypt

Monty's life here is a combination of enjoyable dinner-parties (a complete change, for him) and a military concern with desert exercises, and especially exercises at night.

We see the first dinner party, with Monty cheerful and bustling about, and talking a great deal, but also listening patiently and seriously.

We see him saying goodbye to his guests, and then he and Betty sitting quietly together.

'I didn't think you could continue being sociable like this, out here, with just military people to invite, and nothing to talk about except 'shop',' says Betty.

'I loved all your dinner parties at Camberley and Chiswick and wherever we were in England,' says Monty, 'I never knew I could come to like such a lot of different types of people ... it's all your work, Betty. You've begun making me human ... I can even listen to other military opinions with you beside me, Betty, instead of needing to boil them in oil!'

'Good!' says Betty, 'It's more enjoyable, isn't it?'

'It certainly is,' says Monty. 'And we're not going to stop at military people. There are plenty of other British sorts out here, scholars, archaeologists, people interested in the old religion, even artists and musicians ... possibly even poets.'

'There's even Lawrence Durrell,' says Betty.

'O I don't think I can take Durrell!' says Monty, 'what should I call him? Confounded <u>aesthete</u>, is that right? Sorry, I've met him once, and once is enough. Conceited, bad-tempered puppy. So full of himself, so ...'

'Yes, yes, Monty, never mind, we don't have to have him. I don't think I like him myself. There are plenty without him, as you are saying.'

Yes,' says Monty, 'we'll begin the education of some of these military men, won't we ... Make them come up against different sorts of minds. Very good for them. Some of these military men, Betty, would you believe it ... <u>unbelievably</u> narrow! No art, no music, no science, no theatre, no philosophy, not even <u>nature</u>, except for polo, and hunting, shooting and fishing ... talking about which, it would be wonderful to have dear old Alan Brooke out here, if he can wangle a short holiday, or some 'mission' or other. He's a great bird-watcher, you know. He'd love it out here. He's the only military man above me I've really been able to respect. He really understands strategy and tactics, the whole thing. A serious, dedicated man, and a <u>good</u> man ... and I suppose what we're looking for, a human being!'

'A little bit at a time, Monty,' says Betty. 'Don't get too excited. Yes, we can have mixed dinner-parties, and we can even propose a subject for discussion after dinner, as we relax ... We could even talk about the ethics of war, as we've done before, in Chiswick. What's wrong with being <u>serious</u> from time to time?'

'Absolutely!' says Monty. 'You know I'm hopeless at small talk, at least until we've had some real talk to hang it on. It's much more relaxing ... People's small talk, repeated on one occasion after another, for fear of offending anyone ,,, it's mind-numbing. Every person brings up the same old bit of himself, and you bring up the same old bit of yourself, and you both, as it were, say 'snap!', and the game is more or less over! We can surely do better than that, even if we have bad-tempered arguments from time to time!'

'We shall elect a Chairman for each occasion,' says Betty, 'to ensure fair play. No one will get away with pure abuse, or with not listening to a point of view properly. The Chair will put them through it.'

Egypt, 1930s

We see Monty and fellow-officers exploring the desert in a special staff car.

'What we need here is a really prolonged exercise,' Monty is saying, 'Not some 9–5 kind of thing. Something to last a couple of days in the first instance ... then, perhaps, a week-long exercise ... with various night-moves interspersed. Also, we must seek the co-operation of the Air Force and the Navy.'

'That could be a problem, Sir,' says a junior officer.

'I'm only too well aware of that,' says Monty, 'So the sooner we tackle it the better. I'll also need to practice the Artillery. One of my ideas is that Artillery should be concentrated in a small area, and should concentrate all its fire on a relatively small area. We've got plenty of room here to practice that. I need a car, and a few colleagues to go really deep into the desert, to plan on a big scale. Do you think you can help me in that?'

'Yes I can, Sir, I've been out here some time, and I think I can pull the right levers,' says one of the officers.

'Good!' says Monty, 'You get on with the logistics side of things, and I'll go and pick my colleagues. I believe Brigadier Harding is out here,' he mutters, 'He'll be invaluable ... understands my ideas ... ' he wanders off, both in his speech and into the desert.

'Strange,' Monty says, 'Hard sand and then soft sand, so soft that you sink in it ... is there much of the desert like this?'

'There are real quicksands in some places,' says another officer, 'some of them mapped, some not. Still a lot of work to be done here, Sir.'

'Then we'll do as much of that as we can,' says Monty. 'It seems to me that a tank could hardly move in a soft-sand area like this. Very important to know. We'll find out if there's some civilian out here who's passionate about the desert, and who knows more than we do. If necessary, we'll have to fund him to do more research ... I'll find the money somehow.'

'Yes, Sir, such people exist out here,' says the same officer, 'I can find them for you quite soon.'

'Good fellow,' says Monty, 'Good fellow'.

We see the night-life of Cairo in a series of 'snapshots'. First the Shepheard's Hotel with its clientele of military and other big fry; then Zamily's Island in the Nile, with the Egyptian upper classes, and royalty glittering and voluptuous, all reflected in the water, and the clear stars in the sky; then a belly-dancer both there, and another at a smaller seedier venue, with the British occupying troops in civilian clothes enjoying themselves; then the dark narrow half-lighted streets of the poorer quarters, with their brothels, and the British troops going in pairs, and nodding to the various seated locals as they pass by and go inside.

Outside there are groups of street-musicians here and there, playing in the precincts of outdoor cafes shadowed by trees. The clientele are mainly Egyptian men, but a half-dozen British squaddies arrive at one, and rudely order and shove the locals out of their chairs and tables, and take their places. One bangs the table for service, and shouts in a loud voice at the same time. Another turns to the musicians and shouts, 'And you can stop that bleeding noise, for a start! Sounds like the bloody belly-ache to me!'

And the musicians are silenced, and hardly dare to show their resentment. First one, and then several, muezzins sound the call to prayer.

1935 – Posted to Quetta in India.

A large colonial bungalow, with verandahs all the way round. It is evening with pale violet skies and exquisite shadows cast by the trees across the garden. It has been an intensely hot day, and the earth and the gardens as well as the servants and guests are almost overwhelmed with relief at the relative coolness. Everyone is still pared down in dress. There are no draughty corners or cool areas in the shade. It is warm but blissful. There is a general feeling that this is how it should always be on earth ... a warm lit-up evening with lovely but restrained colours, and everyone at leisure after a not too toilsome day, and free to roam from group to group in house and garden, and to talk or be silent as they wished.

This is Betty Montgomery's military quarters, and the family house she has made of it is typical of herself and her talent for friendship. People feel they can be themselves, and her formal dinner-parties are reckoned to be the most enjoyable the military people and civil servants who come here have experienced. The lack of stiff formality allows the expression of different views, even on contentious subjects such as the struggle for Indian independence, and on Mahatma Gandhi himself ... whom of course many British military men have expressed violent feelings towards. Monty himself darts through the serene atmosphere like a dragonfly, flitting from drawing room to verandahs to garden groups and then to the kitchen, amiable and witty and relaxed.

Colonel Patrick Hobart, or Hobo, is here on a prolonged leave. Monty has ceased to tease him in the old way and feels genuinely sorry that a career that promised exceptional things has been blighted by a sexual peccadillo that in many other walks of life would have done no harm. But the Army is by necessity something of a close community and suffers the perils of its own virtues, and this is understood. Monty feels protective towards Hobo these days, and even ashamed of his previous 'ragging' of him.

As darkness swiftly comes over the delicious evening light, most of the party gradually make its way indoors and sit on sofas and easy chairs. There is no standing for politeness sake. Also there are no compulsory dinner jackets. Most of the male party is in white loose shirts, as the Indians dress, and the womenfolk in coloured cottons or in silks, smart but not flashy. Betty has quietly discouraged 'show' and rivalry ... and of course those who must have those things simply don't come.

Monty loves the brass gong and stands next to the chief servant in the hallway and wields the soft-headed sounding instrument himself, with a deep smile as the ripples go out and out. He sounds it thrice, like a magician. His treating it as an important and poetic ritual generates in each one there his or her own thoughts and imaginings. If there is, for some present, things about India that are frightening and alien and not to be compassed in their own categories of thought, the sounding of the gong both acknowledges that mystery and fear, and at the same time smoothes it out to an extent. The first shock of sound, and then the lessening, and at last the dying but expanding ripples ... all these together produce a feeling that is universal, and this lessens the seeming strangeness of India, helps people to 'settle in'.

For some, of course, there is no mystery, whether good or evil, only an alien climate and people, assumed to be inferior, and fair game for the gallant and resourceful Britishers who have, as it were, 'bothered' to come all this way to sample them and hopefully to improve them. But those at the Montgomerys' party will at least lend themselves to a willing suspension of disbelief as far as mystery is concerned. It is enjoyable to do so, and fits the ambiance created by Betty ... her benevolence and charm allied to her artistic sensibility. Her paintings around the house reinforce the impression.

As the guests come from all directions towards the dining-room and see Monty with his deep smile by the gong, they can almost imagine themselves the devotees of a forgotten cult. Some find themselves unwittingly walking with a soft ritualistic tread towards their place at the table ... and indeed when they are seated Monty says a grace from the heart. The atmosphere remains serene and full of quiet promise.

There is a relaxed silence for the most part, and a few murmurs, as the Indian servants come round with the dishes and with wines.

'Welcome, all of you ... and, your health!' says Monty, holding up a glass of wine. They all do likewise, and the general conversation begins. That is to say, it begins with each one talking to his or her neighbours. Monty keenly listens to scraps of different conversations, as he watches and gestures to the servants as they offer food. At last he begins his meal, still with his ears, and other antennae, well forward.

At length he holds up a hand, and then bangs on a bronze dish with a spoon. There is a silence.

'The present consensus among us seems to be that this new Status of India Act is not going to do the trick, as far as allaying Indian national unrest is concerned. We need to go much further in that direction, or become considerably more repressive. One or the other, but not this useless half measure. I must say, I agree. And it looks as though we will enter the next war with a hostile India at our back. Very serious, we could lose our Persian oil-fields.'

'Possibly,' says a Major half-way down the table, 'but the

Indian regiments are amongst our most loyal. We shouldn't forget that. They fought for us once, why not again?'

'Simply because Gandhi and his movement have begun to change that,' says his wife, seated next to him. 'his influence is enormous.'

'But not quite as universal as he sometimes likes to claim,' says another man. 'He is a skilful propagandist, and he gives the impression that all India knows who he is and supports him. In my experience, quite a number have never heard of him, let alone support him.'

'India is vast,' says another, after a silence.

'In short,' says another, after another silence, 'he is a politician.'

'And he does deals with our politicians, and these are enshrined in statutes, and then all the politicians think the problem is just about solved.'

There is a light ripple of laughter round the assembly, while all resume their meal, and all these military people consider quietly the illusions of politicians, and their own much better qualifications for solving political problems. Into this self-congratulatory atmosphere Monty then blurts, 'All politicians should be put up against a wall and shot!'

There is a burst of noise, partly expostulatory, partly laughter, and out of this emerge a few specific voices.

'Now Monty, that's naughty of you!'

'Yes, that's going much too far! You imagine you are reading our thoughts, I suppose.

'Not fair on us, Monty, not fair on us.'

'Outrageous as usual, Monty ... over-simple. Not my ticket at all.'

'How could you, Monty? How could you spoil things so?'

'So it's back to military basics is it, Monty? The old school, eh? Damn all these political niceties and shilly-shallying, well, well, well!'

The hubbub subsides, and the individual interjections cease. After a pause of a certain length, exactly measured, and the key to all comedians and their effects, Monty says,

'Discuss!'

A moment of silence, and then an explosion of merriment, going around the table several times like a wave.

'So it's our topic for the evening then!' says one of the wives. 'But still, a bit below our normal level, I'd say. I mean, are we still so crude as to even consider things from that point of view? Aren't we beyond these crude oppositions?'

'Not at all,' says Monty, 'we can never be beyond considering what is the correct relationship between the military and the government. Perfectly serious issue ... needs discussion ... on the one hand, politicians often make a mess of foreign affairs ... trying to balance too many considerations, to keep everyone happy, including some very nasty types. On the other hand, military men usually make things worse when they take the law into their own hands. Think it's simple ... isn't simple at all. Retire hurt, like the Australian batsmen after facing Voce and Larwood, our body-line fast bowlers! No good retiring hurt, is it? Expecting sympathy ... done our level best, hasn't worked, now we want little pat on head and 'Well tried, you folk, well tried, old man!' Retire in peace, medals given later, honours list, honourable retirement, all done and dusted ... and goodnight, ladies, goodnight.'

Monty subsides at last, and a benign murmur settles on the company. Yet no-one seems disposed tonight to take up the issue for discussion. At length someone pushes the public part of the conversation in another direction.

' I see your brother John is doing very well in the Navy, Hobo,' says an officer, one who knows little of Hobo's history, and thinks he is making a contribution to the general good and atmosphere.

'Very well indeed,' says Hobo quietly, and with his head almost in his soup.

Before anyone more knowledgeable can intervene, the man is off again, 'And I see the Navy has designed a most wonderful uniform for off-duty hours. Such elegance and panache. Must make them feel like demi-gods when they're on leave! What say you, Hobo?'

'No doubt,' says Hobo quietly, 'but I don't say anything about it, I really don't know anything about it at all.'

'Well, to be sure, it won't be on the top of your mind ... ', the wretched bull in a china shop was saying again, when Monty briskly intervenes.

'Nothing is to be gained militarily, in my opinion, by walking down Picadilly in elasticated boots!'

There is a pause, and then delighted laughter.

'I've no wish to sound dogmatic, of course,' Monty goes on, ' but I am not persuaded of it ... morale is everything in war, of course, and there is no saying what a civilian elasticated boot might not do for general morale in the Navy. Nonetheless, I am not persuaded of its importance in this case ... in this particular case ...', he repeats with a humble seriousness.

All are laughing, and some are thumping the table in delight. Unseen in the tumult, Monty shoots a quick glance and a wink at Hobo, who returns it with gratitude.

As the laughter subsides, another noise is heard. It is a rumbling, as of thunder. People are surprised.

'Not exactly the season for storms, is it?' says one.

'Such a beautiful serene evening and sunset!' says another.

'India must be getting unpredictable like England,' says another.

There is another deep rumble, and a scraping sound, like heavy furniture being moved across a room.

'Good heavens, it means it!' says another.

'And then the floor itself begins to move, and the jugs and bottles on the table to wobble and then fall.

'It's an earthquake,' says Monty lightly. 'We must get ourselves outside.'

They all rise from the table and make their way to the gardens, away from the trees, and well away from the walls of the house. Some hold hands and look into each other's eyes.

'What a terrible thing!' somebody says.

'It may not be so terrible,' says Hobo, 'possibly just a tremor.'

A telephone rings from inside the house.

'That'll be news, and possibly instructions,' says Monty. 'I'll go and answer it.'

'O Monty!' says Hobo, 'I'll go.'

'No, you stay here and see to everything,' says Monty, already on the run. 'Nothing will touch me.'

Monty is in the house, while all wait anxiously. He emerges within the minute.

'It is serious,' Monty says, 'In fact, it is terrible. The whole town of Quetta is engulfed at the moment ... luckily for us, our offices and HQs are outside the town area. Nevertheless, the orders are for all wives and families, and all except essential personnel, to be sent home, with immediate effect. No packing, Betty, everything will be provided at the airport and on the ship. I'm sorry, but there it is ... and that means you too, Hobo ... perhaps you will take charge of some of the party and see to everything.'

'Gladly,' says Hobo. 'And I've got a hired car here. I can take you to the airport now.'

'And I'll bring the rest,' says Monty.

In fact, three cars set out for the airport, everyone piling in, for the goodbyes to be said properly when the aircraft are prepared to leave. Monty, at the airport, takes down a long list of personal valuables to be gathered from the houses of those civilians departing, and sent on later. Practical arrangements of various kinds, messages to kith and kin, transport to pick up the travellers once they reach England ... all this predominates over emotion for the time being.

Monty, Hobo and Betty stand together.

'It'll be great to see David again,' says Monty to Betty. 'Tell him on no account to worry, I shall be all right. And you can tell John and Richard as well. I'll keep in touch regularly. Perhaps we'll all be evacuated in due course. Where next? I wonder ... '

A Dakota plane taxies along the runway. Meanwhile food and comforts and toiletries are arriving on trolleys. Soon an official sections off a group, including Betty and Hobo, and a few others from the dinner-party, with some strangers. Betty and Monty embrace silently. Then Monty turns to Hobo and they shake hands tightly and almost fiercely.

'Many thanks, dear old Monty,' says Hobo, looking into his eyes.

'Keep your chin up!' says Monty.

The sectioned group are ushered away, carrying their newly acquired personal properties, towards the gang-plank of the plane. Within a few minutes, the plane is again taxiing towards the runway, and soon after is in the infinite air.

The silence left behind is blank and a little strange. Monty pays it no attention.

'Anyone wanting to come with me,' he says, 'I need to get nearer to the centre of things.' He is speaking to the military remnants of his dinner-party. 'Get some more recent news.'

Two officers agree to come with him, and they set off in Monty's car.

We see the earthquake devastation in Quetta itself, and the rescue parties moving around in the rubble. Every now and then a stretcher party brings a body from the wreckage, whether alive or dead to be ascertained later. In one terrible case, a woman has lost both legs, and is being sealed and bandaged as well as can be done on the spot. She is then hurried by the bearers to a waiting ambulance, which speeds off to the army field-hospital.

PART THREE – MEETING DEATH

Chapter 9 - Death

Suddenly we are back in the Weston-Super-Mare Hotel, in September 1937. Monty wakes from a long sleep in the lounge there, and we are to understand that the whole sequence from childhood onwards can be taken as his dreams.

'Where am I?' says Monty, on waking, 'O thank God! Not in that bloody earthquake!'

But then he says, 'Something terrible is happening.'

He looks at the clock. It is 10pm. He shakes himself, combs his hair a little, and leaves the hotel, walking at a cracking pace We see him soon arriving at the hospital.

'I know this is an unorthodox hour for visiting,' says Monty to the Matron, 'but I felt I had to come.'

'I'll take you to the Ward Sister,' says the Matron, and they walk along a dark corridor.

'Sister, Brigadier Montgomery has arrived,' she says as she enters the Sister's office on her own. 'Can he come in?'

He is brought in.

'The sooner the better, as a matter of fact,' says the Sister. 'I'm afraid that things have moved swiftly, your wife has been in very serious pain, and we are coming to the conclusion that the only thing we can do is to amputate the affected leg. It is serious blood-poisoning. There seems nothing else to be done, according to the Consultants here ... it should save her pain, anyway.'

'And her life?' asks Monty.

'Her life, yes,' agrees the Sister.

'Is this the last chance?'

'I'm afraid so.'

'Then you must do it,' says Monty, 'And I will tell my son, and the rest of the family and close friends.'

'Good,' says the Sister.

'May I see her now?' asks Monty.

'She has been given sedatives, but is probably awake.'

They go into the ward and stand by Betty's bed. Monty peers into her eyes, and sees she is far away, but awake. He takes her hand.

'Darling Betty,' he says, 'So much has happened since this morning. You poor lamb, why must you suffer so?'

Betty smiles as from a vast distance, and presses his hand.

'I'm feeling much better now,' she says, 'Not so much pain ... But I must have a serious operation ... You won't mind, will you?'

'I know,' says Monty, 'I know.. No, you must have it ... and we'll all see you well at last ... Don't worry, Betty, everything will go well. Dear Betty, what can I do?'

'Nothing except be patient, and hopeful, and loving,' says Betty.

'All these things are easy ... but I would like to perform a miracle, Betty, a miracle!'

'Save for battlefield,' says Betty weakly.

'She is very tired, and weak,' says the Sister, 'we must let her sleep now.'

'Yes,' says Monty, tears coming into his eyes. 'Yes ... Yes' They walk away, as Betty drifts into sleep.

'Thank you so much, Sister ... I must go and try to sleep myself. Trouble is, I've been dozing on the hotel sofa for hours ... think I will go for a long walk.'

'Good idea,' says the Sister, 'Walk yourself tired ... we'll see you tomorrow.'

Monty walks back along the corridor, thanking the Matron as he goes out.

We see him walking through the lighted streets, and finding his way to the promenade and beach, and walking along that until a tiny figure and out of sight.

We see him walking the streets again, dark now, and returning to the hotel. It is 3am by the hotel clock. We see him in bed and turning off the light.

We see him next day, with David, walking to the Hospital.

'Your mother has been in great pain,' Monty is saying.

'You mean, worse than before?' asks David.

'I'm afraid so,' says Monty after a pause.

They walk together for a minute or two, until Monty says, 'They have decided to do some rather drastic surgery, David ... you must try not to be too shocked.'

'What is it?' says David.

'Well, as you know, your mother was bitten in the leg, and the leg just refuses to heal. The poison is in danger of spreading to the rest of the body ... '

'You mean,' says David, 'they must cut part of the leg off? That's terrible!'

'Yes,' says Monty, 'part of the leg ... we're just going to have to get used to it, the same as Betty ... we must help her all we can, and not show any fear or distress – not now, nor after it is done.'

'It's hard,' says David slowly. 'It gets worse all the time.'

'Yes,' says Monty, 'we'll all need to be brave ... I can't say any more just now. It's hard for me as well.'

'You can't stand illness and wounds, you told me,' says David.

'That's true,' says Monty, 'I feel helpless ... but we must trust the surgeons and nurses ... they have all sorts of skills we don't have ... not just the technical skills ... other sorts ' he trailed off.

At the hospital bedside David is sad and troubled. Monty, while silent, is supportive.

'We will operate this evening,' says the Matron. 'Come again tomorrow evening.'

Monty and David walk off.

'Do you want to go back to school now, and come back to visit when all this has been done, and your mother is well again?' asks Monty, 'It might be the best thing,' he adds.

There is a longish pause.

'I think I'd like to stay here,' says David, hiding his fear that his mother will very soon be dead.

'As you wish,' says Monty, also hiding his fear. 'Perhaps we can play some more cricket,' he goes on, 'If we can't find those lads again, we'll find some nets and I'll bowl to you there.'

Later on we see Monty bowling to David in the nets. There is little joy, or forgetting. As they pack up and leave, Monty says 'I can try to help you with some of your school work ... You'd better not get too far behind.'

In the hotel lounge they sit together, and Monty is helping David with some simple mathematics, and then with English.

'Just remember to write exactly what you mean to say,' says

Monty, 'Just be clear and precise. No frills ... All the best writers write like that. People think it's easy, too easy, just to say what they mean. So they add all sorts of clever bits. The trouble is, in doing so, they actually forget to say exactly what they mean. Nothing adds to the plain truth, after all, something is subtracted, and we end up confused ... Do you understand what I am saying?'

'Just common sense,' says David, 'Yes, of course I do.'

'Good lad,' says Monty.

Monty leans back and reads 'The Times' while David concentrates on a piece of writing.

The next day Monty and David play cricket again in the nets, and sit down together again to study, in the hotel. Monty is teaching David map-reading, with a compass. Later they go out to the cricket field, and Monty teaches David how to walk on a compass-bearing.

There is rather a melancholic evening meal in the hotel, and then they set out for the hospital.

The Matron meets them, and takes them to the Ward-Sister.

'All safely done and over,' says the Sister. 'But Betty is sleeping heavily, and I don't think we should wake her. There is no point you sitting here for hours. Come back tomorrow afternoon.'

We see Monty and David returning the next day.

It's not particularly good news, I'm afraid,' says the Sister. 'Betty is still struggling with all sorts of pain ... and then there's the shock of the operation ... I think you should just come and say hullo, and then go back to your hotel.'

Monty sits by the bedside and holds Betty's hand. She smiles from a great distance. Monty sighs, and leaves again, in a silent walk with David.

The next day they are back again. Sister is serious.

'No improvement,' she says, 'A lot of pain ... we fear that the poison is spreading, and there's not much we can do.'

Monty takes it in, and grips David's hand. 'Stay here a few moments,' he says, 'I want to talk to Matron privately.'

'What should we do?' he is asking the Matron in her office.

'I think you should send David back to school now,' she says, 'it's only a matter of days now … either a recovery then, or no recovery at all. Her pain and suffering are too much for David to have to witness. Send him to school with as much reassurance as you can honestly muster.'

A pause.

'He sees right through such things, I fear. But I'll do my best. Can I just say goodbye to Betty for a few minutes?'

He sits again at her bedside, holding her hand, with David close to him.

Then another silent walk to the hotel, and next morning Monty is driving David with his luggage to the station. Monty joins the train, and they are seen arriving at David's Prep School.

Monty is with the Headmaster in his office, explaining the situation. 'I must hurry back to the hospital. Look after the poor boy. I will telephone with news, good or bad. Goodbye.'

Monty emerges from the office, hugs David, and then leaves.

We see him back at the hospital the next day, and then the next. On the third day, the news is that Betty has died. Monty takes the news from the Matron, lifts the sheet that is over Betty's face on a moveable bed, looks for a few moments and then leaves.

Later we see a small funeral, at Chiswick, with David and Monty, John, Richard and Hobo standing close together. The vicar is Canon Dick Sheppard, the pacifist, with whom Monty had had a discussion years ago. He has remained a family friend.

After the funeral, Monty and Dick Sheppard stay in the church awhile, as the rest of the party go to the family house. Dick Sheppard has his arm round Monty's shoulder.

'Shall we kneel and say a prayer together?' asks Dick.

'Yes, that would be good.' says Monty. They both kneel.

'God keep and protect Betty,' prays the vicar, 'and keep Monty and David and the others in good heart, in spite of their grief,' he goes on, 'May they be joined together in the living world of the Communion of Saints both here and hereafter. God bless us, as we suffer and struggle, and lift up our hearts to Thee, O God. Amen!'

'Amen', says Monty.

They get up and walk slowly out of the church.

Chapter 10 – Coping Strategies

Next day we see Monty arriving at David's Prep School again. He goes to the Headmaster's house, and talks to the Head and his wife, a Mr and Mrs Reynolds.

'I would appreciate it if you would look after David for me in the holidays, on those occasions when I am forced to be away.'

'Yes, of course,' says Mr Reynolds, 'that would be our privilege and our pleasure.'

Mrs Reynolds nods. She is warm and maternal.

' Thank you so much,' says Monty, 'such a weight off my mind. Our new family home at Portsmouth is now so bleak and empty. I must be there for some weeks, and David can join me in the Christmas holidays, to get used to the confounded place, and for he and myself to learn to get on together in the new circumstances. But after that, I'd much appreciate your loving care. I'll visit you all here as often as I can manage ... but please don't allow any of my family to share these arrangements with you ... I don't want to explain this, please just accept my judgment and decision.'

The Head and his wife look at each other, and then face Monty with an acceptance of his request.

'Thank you very much,' says Monty, 'I have every confidence in you two good people. I shall do my best to sort out my own life and feelings ... and get back to my work.'

He leaves the house and makes for his car. He sets off, and arrives at the large house in Portsmouth some hours later. His housekeeper makes him an evening meal and then leaves. He is on his own, seated in an armchair, by a coal-fire, staring into space.

The phone rings.

'Hullo. Montgomery speaking.'

'Hullo Monty. This is Jocelyn. I wasn't at the funeral, but I wanted to be there, and I'm concerned that you shouldn't be on your own. Do you have to be at Portsmouth just now?'

'Yes and no,' says Monty coldly.

'Look ... come and stay with us, Monty! We'll look after you for a while. You've got compassionate leave, why spend it in a large, gloomy, empty house?'

'I'm as well as I ever can be, down here,' says Monty, ' No-one can help me in this, so it's no use pretending they can.'

'It's not help, Monty, it's just human presences. Some alleviation.'

'Thank you, but no,' says Monty. 'I shall manage.'

'I'm sure you will, in your own way,' says Jocelyn, 'But I'm not happy with you just 'managing'. Look here, if you don't want to come here, why don't you let me come down there and be with you for a few days? How about that, Monty?'

'It's kind of you,' says Monty, a little more warmly. 'Yes, it really is. But you must let me manage ... and after all, I can throw myself into my work.'

'I'm hearing you, Monty, but just remember, if you change your mind to let me know ... In any case, I shall phone you again in a week ... at least you won't mind that, will you?'

'Not at all,' says Monty, 'I don't mind phone calls. Goodbye, Jocelyn.'

'Goodbye,' says Jocelyn.   .

We see Monty 'throwing himself into his work' by resuming his reclining position in the armchair and staring into the fire. We see the clock at 8.0pm, then at 9pm, and 10pm and 11pm and midnight, and Monty is still staring, either into space, or into the ashes of the fire. At midnight he stirs himself, takes off his slippers, jersey and shirt, and gets into his camp bed still in the rest of his clothes. He lies on his side and stares into space, then switches off his bedside light, and stares into the dark. We see the clock pass 1am and 2am, and Monty is still wide awake and staring. He finally drifts off to sleep about 3am, and wakes around 9am, with his housekeeper bringing tea and toast.

'O Mrs Humphreys, thank you ... I'm sorry for the disorder here. I should have been up hours ago.'

'You do just as you like, Sir. I shall fit in with whatever hours you want to keep. Such a shame for you, Sir, my heart bleeds for you. And such a shame Mrs Montgomery never lived in the house here ... it's very bleak for you, Sir'.

'Bleak indeed,' says Monty, 'Still, I must do what I can. Today I will get on with some work.'

The volumes of military history are on the table, with maps spread out still, and Monty stands over them when his housekeeper has left the room. His gaze is at first on a particular map, of Spain and the Peninsular War. But we see his gaze going from focussed to unfocussed. He is looking through the map, not at it. He appears to be trying to look through everything in the world, in order for his gaze to arrive at something beyond the world. He is looking into space again, out of the window.

The phone rings. It is Canon Dick Sheppard.

'Hullo, Monty, how are you faring?'

'Frankly, not all that well, Dick ... But that's to be expected, isn't it? ... But I've been thinking, what have I done wrong to deserve this blow of fate? I can't help going over and over my life looking for an answer ... '

'O, you mustn't think like that, you really mustn't,' the Canon says, interrupting him. 'I'm absolutely sure it doesn't work like that ... though Christians in the Valley of the Shadow of Death will generally tend to fall into that way of feeling. Monty, you need good company, good loving friends, if that's the way your thoughts are tending. Come and stay with us, Monty ... or I'll try and get away for a few days and stay with you.'

'No, no, no,' says Monty, 'no need for that. Thank you for your wise words ... they will help me manage my thoughts ... and then I shall learn to cope ... In any case, I'm pretty well throwing myself into my work at present ... that'll see me through.'

'Just as you prefer, Monty. But I'll phone again before too long. Cheerio, Monty!'

'Cheerio,' says Monty.

He picks up a military history from the table and walks with it to a comfortable armchair. The fire has just been lit. A calendar shows the date, 20th October.

The clock shows 10.00 a.m. At 11.00 a.m., Monty is clutching the book, unopened, and again staring into space. At noon, Mrs. Humphreys looks in and Monty is asleep in the chair and the book has fallen to the floor.

'I'll just make up the fire, Sir', she says, affecting not to notice that he is asleep, and waking him up in the process.

'Oh dear, Mrs. Humphreys, you mustn't do that … I do think I'm capable of that', he says, and takes the coal scuttle from her hands.

'I'll be back around 6 o'clock to make you a little supper, sir.'

'Don't bother tonight, Mrs. Humphreys, have a night off. I'll do it myself.'

'If you're sure, sir' says Mrs. Humphreys. 'Tomorrow morning, then, Sir.'

Monty then walks up and down the room, ashamed of having fallen asleep. He goes to the kitchen, makes himself a little bread and cheese, and eats it standing. He then walks out of the house, and takes a bus into Portsmouth City Centre. He walks round all the main streets, peering into shops and cafes, at last buys a newspaper, enters a dark little cafe, orders a pot of tea and sits in the darkest corner. He reads his paper, then pretends to read his paper. He is again staring through it rather than at it. He even pretends to enjoy his tea. He leaves, walks the streets all over again, and more streets, before walking all the way home. The fire is almost out, he revives it and sits in his armchair, his head in his hands, looking a pitiful old man.

It is 10.00 p.m. before Monty goes to the kitchen, and fries an egg and some bacon. And it is 2.00 a.m. before he goes to bed, again staring into the still-glowing fire, and again in his day-clothes.

We see Mrs. Humphreys arrive in the morning. She finds him still asleep again, and brings in tea and toast.

Monty excuses himself.

'Sorry, Mrs. Humphreys, I've been burning the midnight oil again. Still, no law against it, as yet,' he goes on.

'No indeed sir,' she says, 'work when you can sir.'

Monty takes himself off, runs a bath, and shaves for the first time in two or three days.

'I'll go out walking for the morning, Mrs. Humphreys, and do my work later,' he says. 'No need to hang around. If you could just prepare me something I can re-heat later.'

'Certainly sir.'

Monty goes out to his car and drives off, and into the countryside. He parks in the yard of a small pub, makes himself known to the landlord, and goes off walking in good boots and jacket. It is beautiful late October weather, the last balminess before November mist and mizzles and rains and the later leaf-stripping winds.

When he returns a couple of hours later, he goes into the country pub and up to the bar. It is round about noon and they have just opened for the short midday stint.

'Tell me, landlord, what would be an acceptable alcoholic drink for one who doesn't normally drink alcohol at all ... and on a day like this?'

'On a day like this, beautiful late October weather ... and for a man such as yourself, sir ... well, you could hardly do better than a pint of good rough cider, from just over the border, sir ... I'll pour it for you and bring it to you, if you'd care to choose your seat, sir.'

'Thank you, landlord. And a hunk of bread and cheese as well, thank you ... it makes a change to be hungry,' he says, half to himself as he wanders off and chooses a dark corner-seat that looks out on the sunny world through a small scullery-like window.

The landlord comes with the rough cider in a clay tankard, and the bread and several cheeses on a large wooden plate.

Monty sips and eats and then drinks more deeply and begins to look benign in his corner. What looks like a farm worker comes in. He nods at Monty and Monty at him, goes up to the bar and orders a pint of rough cider. When it arrives, he lifts it up, winks at Monty and says

'Your health, sir.'

'Your health indeed,' says Monty, lifting up his tankard and trying to look like a seasoned drinker.

'Some drink, some outlook,' says the labourer. 'The rough for the rough, the smooth for the smooth, eh?'

Monty just nods.

'Would you call yourself a bit rough, sir?' the labourer enquires at last.

'Certainly a bit rough, just at the moment, yes indeed,' says Monty.

A longish silence.

'This stuff roughs you up even more,' says the labourer, 'until you begin to enjoy being roughed up. I roughs myself up just about every day of the week with this stuff. It do me good.'

Monty smiles and nods, and takes another sip. The room is beginning to swim before his eyes.

'It certainly seems to loosen the joints a bit,' says Monty at last. 'Ar,' says the labourer. 'In its rough way, that's what it does. Think of some old gnarled-up mower or seed-drill. They need rough treatment 'afore they'll go again. I holds 'em with one hand and gives the buggers a good kicking with my boot. That makes the joints work again, it certainly does. They needs a bit of the rough stuff ... and so do we at times.'

There is a long philosophical pause, until the labourer begins again. 'The winter is the worst sir. I'm up and about by seven most mornings ... in the pitch dark by late November ... I can't say I enjoy it, I don't say I hate it ... But my old joints: how do you say it sir ... they begin to <u>resent</u> it, and I begin to snarl up, like ... Well, it ain't no good trying to kickstart myself with me own boots, so I come in here and have this pint, sir – midday sir. Well, in the wintertime it sees me right, it really does ... I goes back to work a little bit groggy sir ... and the sight of the winter, all those bitter grey days we get in this country, it don't quite get into me sir, it don't as it were bite me to the bone.'

Another philosophical pause.

At last Monty says 'So it's your mind that needs the cider-medicine, not just your joints?'

'Ar,' says the labourer, 'I hadn't thought to separate them, but you're right sir. Left to itself, the mind is not quite strong enough to get through these winter months, that's right ... Of course, if I've a companion it's different ... you don't notice the bitter grey days, nor how many bloody months they go on ... But most of the time I have to work on my own ... I get bloody sick of myself and what goes on in my mind, sir, I can tell you ... I'm not Einstein, sir, as you can well see, so I'm not a-working out how the light of the stars reaches us and the like ... You can't escape from things into your mind, unless you've really <u>got</u> a mind, that's the trouble sir. Why some of us should be cursed with such little minds I can't say, sir. And then to have day after day working on your own ... it don't seem right, sir. Do you ever experience what I mean, sir?'

'Well I certainly do at present, I must say ... But when I can escape into my work the problem is much less. When work absorbs me almost totally, there's of course less pain and trouble ...'

'That's if the work absorbs <u>enough</u> of you, I suppose ... I work with sheep mainly ... I know them all, and there's often new ones I have to get to know, but it's not what you could call <u>totally absorbing</u> sir ... I fear I get more and more like a bloody sheep myself, one day after another ... What's your line of country, if you don't mind me asking sir? I'm curious, and I feel there's something distinguished about you, sir.'

'Of a military nature,' says Monty. 'Something in that line.'

'Now don't be coy, sir, can't you be more precise? I'm being too nosey, is that it?'

'Well, since you ask, I'm a brigadier in the Army, and my main job is the training of troops for battle. I enjoy my work, but I've hit a bit of a snag just now – which I don't really want to talk about.'

'I shan't stick my nose in there sir, but I sensed you was troubled ... as well as distinguished, sir. Brigadier! That's quite high up, isn't it sir?'

'Not as high as I would like .... but we must wait and see.'

'Perhaps you will be a General ... or .even ... what comes after that?'

'Field Marshal,' says Monty.

'A Field Marshal,' says the labourer. 'Er, might I know your name sir? If that's not going too far?'

'Montgomery'.

'Brigadier Montgomery,' says the labourer. 'I shan't forget you, sir, but I must be on my way.'

He drains his glass. Monty does the same.

'Nor I you,' says Monty. 'Can I give you a lift anywhere?'

'Well, if you've the time, sir, I've a mile or two to walk ... a lift would be a boon, sir, even on this lovely day.'

They walk out into the autumn sunshine, paying and then waving goodbye to the landlord, who has been silently listening the whole time. The labourer gets into the car, in the most polite and deferential way.

We see the car set off and wander about a little on the road. Monty is smiling and seemingly happy. The car climbs a hill onto the top of a chalk down, where it stops and the labourer gets out.

'Thank you, kind sir. I shall enjoy this fine day all the more for not having had to climb that hill. Perhaps I should join the Army, what do you say, sir?'

'If you were in my unit, I would give you a responsible job and rely on you ... I would say you have great potential, so don't think too unkindly of yourself,' says Monty.

'Very kind of you to say so, sir ... You've given me hope, sir. Maybe I'm not just Hodge after all ... and there's others like me down here, sir.'

'I believe you,' says Monty. 'And now I must be on my way.'

The labourer's hand comes suddenly through the open window and Monty shakes it with his left hand.

'Goodbye,' says Monty.

'Goodbye,' says the labourer, as the car turns round and goes down the hill a little unsteadily.

It is the day after Monty's little country expedition. He is much more alert than he has been recently, and is actually reading at the big table. The phone rings.

'Montgomery here.'

'O hello, Monty, this is Jocelyn.'

'Oh,' says Monty 'Jocelyn. Hello.' A neutral tone of voice.

'Monty, we were wondering why you haven't given David into our care ... You must be wanting some help there.'

'I've made other arrangements,' says Monty coldly.

'Have you?' says Jocelyn. 'May we ask who with?'

'Certainly,' says Monty 'with the Headmaster of the school and his wife. Very good people, Mr. and Mrs. Reynolds.'

'But Monty, why didn't you ask us first? David can be with his half-brother John, who's been his companion for so long ... At least as long as John is here with me in England.'

'I came to hear of things you did during your care of David that did not please me,' says Monty.

There is a long silence, while Jocelyn struggles with her emotions.

'But Monty, you thanked me profusely for my work with David! You thanked me, you were grateful for the support ... ' She is on the verge of tears.

But Monty goes on coldly 'I did not at that time know of the incident I'm referring to. It was only later, in conversation with David.'

'Incident ...' says Jocelyn weakly. 'What incident?'

'I understand that you gave David cider to drink one evening at the hotel, and that he became tipsy and loquacious.'

'Oh that!' said Jocelyn. 'Surely you are not going to hold that against me. It was completely harmless, Monty ... Monty, what are you doing? Why are you being like this?' Jocelyn's voice is shaking with tears.

'Not harmless at all!' says Monty. 'I take a most serious view of the matter.'

'But cider!' says Jocelyn, half crying. 'A small glass of cider ... Monty, for heavens' sake! What harm is there?'

'A boy of only ten,' says Monty. 'And cider, a drink stronger than all ordinary beer. Not at all harmless. A foolish act on your part, Jocelyn ... which has influenced me strongly in the direction I have taken. I'm sorry, but there it is.'

'But there it is!' repeats Jocelyn bitterly. 'A rift in the family at a tragic time ... we are family, Monty, family! Does that mean nothing to you? What on earth are you doing?'

'I'm sorry, but there it is,' says Monty again, offering no softening, even around the edges.

Jocelyn puts the phone back on the hook, and sobs bitterly. John comes into the room. 'What is it, Jocelyn dear?'

'It's Monty!' she cries, 'He's put David under the care of almost complete strangers, and won't let us have anything to do with him! It's so cruel, so unfair!'

'After all you've done!' says John.

'It's not even that,' cries Jocelyn, 'It's that we're family, and Monty doesn't seem to want his family ... He's turned cold and distant. It's unbearable ... and all because of a little incident with a glass of cider!'

'I'll go and see him shortly,' says John. 'I'll bring him round.'

'But why should you have to go and see him?' Jocelyn cries again, 'What is the matter with him? He's like ice!'

'He's got some queer dark corners in him, especially where family is concerned. I expect Betty's death has unhinged him a little. He may be slipping back into old ways ... But of <u>course</u> he should stand with us at this time! How does he imagine I am feeling about my mother, and how <u>could</u> he injure any of us, in the circumstances? But I will go and see him all the same.'

'The deed is done, whatever you say to him,' says Jocelyn. 'David is in the care of the Head of the School and his wife, and I don't see how that can be undone.'

'Perhaps not,' says John, 'but at least an apology from him, and some resumption of warm relations.'

'I'm not sure if I'll be able to bear a resumption, after what's been said and done.'

'O families!' says John, 'These things happen all the time!'

'Not in my family,' says Jocelyn. 'I'm just not used to it. It's cruel, and most unusual.'

"Cruel and unusual punishment", John quotes, 'Monty is an unusual person. He seems to need to hurt people sometimes. And he tries always to provide a cover for it ... a rationale ... it's never just his own spite and cruelty. He rationalizes it, as though that fools anyone! Does he fool himself? That's the mystery ...'

'I'm really not interested in that,' says Jocelyn, 'I'd like to kick him!'

'Several people, to my knowledge, have felt like that over the years,' says John. 'But mostly he's a good man. Sometimes he retreats into a lonely place, where he feels alone, and totally righteous, and totally cold. He has to be coaxed out of it ... he'll come out of it in time.'

'But I've been cruelly slighted, and how will I care whether he comes out of his lonely bunker or not? I will still hurt and hurt.'

'Yes, dear, there's no denying that,' says John. 'But I must go and see him all the same.'

'Yes, you go ... for your purposes,' says Jocelyn 'I don't want to prevent you ... '

'Maybe you will feel differently, in time,' says John.

'No!' says Jocelyn, flaring up, 'I will not feel differently! But you go, do as you say, and never mind me ... I mean it ... never mind about me!'

'I will go, and do what I can,' says John.

Next day. John rings the bell at Monty's house in Portsmouth, in the early afternoon. Monty answers the door and they go into the working-room.

'Monty, Jocelyn is terribly upset,' says John.

'She should have thought of how she would feel before she committed her act,' says Monty.

'But she didn't consider it a terrible act, Monty. It is a difference of valuation, Monty, not a deliberate slighting of your standards.'

'I can't see how that could be,' says Monty, 'She knew well enough my views on such things.'

'She thought she knew,' says John, 'But clearly she didn't know well enough ... that's not her fault, Monty. It's a mistake of judgment, of knowledge, not an irresponsible action! Jocelyn is a good, responsible woman ... and she's your friend, Monty, a good friend. And she is family, Monty ... we are all family, and need to stand together.'

'Damn all families!' says Monty, 'Damn all families! They are nothing but pain and trouble.'

John pauses and walks to the large bow-window before replying. 'So many happy family years with us, and now you say that!' he says at last. 'How are we supposed to feel?'

'Yes, they were happy years,' says Monty, 'And now they are over. And I have to re-make my life somehow ... I have to take a

128

different course.'

'Why a different course?' says John, 'Why not the same old course, with the same old people, the people who love and care for you, and also you once loved ... doesn't that matter any more?'

'I don't yet know what matters now,' says Monty after a long silence. 'I am having to find out.'

John is beginning to see a hopelessness in the situation. He is baffled, and has no longer much faith in his skills.

'Is this what my mother would have wished?' he says, as a kind of last throw of the dice.

Monty is silent. He walks about the room, up and down.

'I suppose anything that reminds you of Mother is now anathema to you?' ventures John. 'That's the only way I can make sense of it ... Is that how things are?'

Monty is still silent, and still walking up and down the room. 'I am not prepared to discuss Betty with you, or with anyone.' Monty says at last.

'But she's my <u>mother</u>!' John shouts, 'And we are part of one another, you and me! You can't just <u>break</u> everything, because she's died!'

Monty is still walking up and down. 'I have to preserve myself somehow,' says Monty, 'I have to survive.'

'So you go off to a desert island, and make friends with the natives there, whom you don't know, and pretend that everything new will be better than the old ... I suppose this is called 'Going Forward Bravely'! And everything to do with the family is to be called 'Falling Back Weakly on the Past'? Monty, this is pathetic, this is just stupid. What is the matter with you? What <u>have</u> we done to upset you? Nothing, just nothing ... you just like being awkward and stubborn ... you're enjoying it, hurting Jocelyn, and others ... You think it will make you suffer less, I suppose ... in the short term. But in the long run, you damage yourself as well as us, and make things harder for yourself. Can't you see that?'

Monty says nothing. John gives him a hopeless look, picks up his coat, and leaves the house.

We see the date 20 November on Monty's calendar in his Portsmouth house. We see him at last getting down to work at his large table with the books and maps. Outside it is foggy. A low fire burns in the room, and every now and then Monty gets up from his chair, walks about the room, warms his hands at the fire, and returns to his work. We see the morning hours tick by, and in the afternoon Monty puts on a coat and walks briskly for a mile or two in his area. He returns to work, taking a snack to his table, and brewing up tea on a small primus-stove. The hours go by, and he makes a larger fire as evening comes, and moves to the armchair with a hefty volume, and with just a pencil to mark passages.

The hours go by, and he goes to bed at 11pm, this time washing and changing into pyjamas. As he drifts off to sleep he is still staring into the darkness, and moving his lips in a quiet prayer. As the clock moves to 3am, we see him wake, and stare into the darkness again. At length he gets up, and pulls a loose pair of trousers over his pyjamas, finds a loose jersey as well, puts on a coat and boots, and walks out of his house.

We see him finding Portsmouth Docks in the foggy night, the visibility only about ten yards. It is totally silent as he walks alongside tall warehouses. Night-lamps are placed at each end of this warehouse complex, and about every thirty yards along the way. The lights from the lamps go only a small distance into the fog, and as Monty walks, he goes into a tunnel of darkness, to emerge briefly into the next lamp-lit area. We see into these tunnels, and see a very small, lighted aperture at the further end, making it seem much more than thirty yards away. The fog is dense and unmoving.

Monty would like to find oblivion in the tunnels of darkness, but when we see his face it is fully alert and aware, with the eyes full of pain. His eyes are like lamps themselves, seeing through darkness, and, as it were, seeing through comforts and consolations as well.

He comes to the end of the warehouse complex with its night-lamp, asleep or dozing compared with Monty's eyes. He stops here for a short while, and then sets off, turning left, and along the other side. There is darkness and fog and pathetic lamps, as before. As he peers ahead, Monty spots a figure standing by a lamp. He stops, and thinks of turning round, but the figure has already seen him, and calls out a loud 'Hoy!'

Monty walks on calmly towards the figure that is now moving in his direction. 'Probably the night-watchman,' Monty says to himself. 'Not a problem.'

The figure moves into the next lamp light, and Monty can just about make out a policeman's helmet.

'Ah, a policeman ... never mind.'

They walk towards each other, and meet in the darkness of one of the 'tunnels'.

'Who are you, Sir, and what are you doing here?' says the policeman, middle-aged, placid and burly.

'I can't sleep, officer,' says Monty, 'and I find walking here somehow more restful than walking the streets of the town. Am I illegal?'

'Well, more or less,' says the policeman. 'The night-watchman should have spotted you, but I expect he's deep in the land of dreams! You can't sleep, you say ... sleeping pills, Sir?'

'No use to me, officer! I have to be fully alert in the daytime. They're quite useless for my purposes.'

'Indeed,' says the policeman, 'and what might be your purposes, Sir, if I may be so bold?'

A pause.

'Of a military nature,' says Monty, 'that kind of thing.'

'O indeed,' says the policeman, becoming acutely suspicious, as though he has an unbalanced man on his hands, and looking acutely into Monty's intense eyes. 'Perhaps you could elaborate a little more on this 'military nature'. And indeed, Sir, perhaps you could accompany me to the station in order to do so.'

Another pause. Monty composes himself, and tries to switch off his eyes. 'I see it from your point of view, officer, but really, that is quite unnecessary. You are welcome to accompany me home, and then you can have full proof of my identity, and get to know the nature of my interests.'

'That is most irregular, Sir, if I may say so.'

'And so are pyjamas,' says Monty, unbuttoning his coat, lifting his jersey and showing a gather of pyjamas. 'Would a serious criminal come out in his pyjamas, officer? And without wallet or money or tools of any sort,' he says, turning out all his pockets.

'No sir,' says the officer reluctantly, 'A serious criminal probably would not ... but on the other hand ... ' and he pauses.

Monty picks up his thought. 'But on the other hand, a serious loony might well do so?'

'Something of that sort ... ' murmurs the policeman, a bit defensive now.

'I'll willingly come to the station, officer, but as I've said, I've absolutely no papers on me, nothing to indicate who I am. Why don't you at least go to where I live first, so that I can pick up a few bits and pieces?'

'Perhaps there'll be no need for that, after all, sir. Perhaps I can see you home, sir, and leave it at that.'

'I was beginning to think I should get home officer ... I'm not going to make things any easier for myself, I've concluded, by walking around warehouses on a foggy night. It doesn't seem to help very much.'

'Help, sir?' says the officer, as they set off together.

'What I must have had in mind, officer, was that this desolate place and the foggy conditions might be some relief from the desolation inside ... You see, my wife has recently died, and I am affected by the loss more than I can say.'

I'm sorry to hear it, sir ... I can't imagine what I would feel in the same circumstances ... Desolation, I suppose, as you say ... I see a lot of desolation in my job, sir, and desolate nights and places like this ... '

A longish silence.

'I've always thought of myself as strong, you see,' says Monty, 'But I'd come to rely on a wonderful woman ... a woman who transformed my life, turned me into a proper human being. And now I'm not sure if I can manage that any more. All the old bitterness begins to come out. I feelnot only lonely, but afraid for the future, afraid of my own emptiness. Death is humbling, officer ... it shows one up.'

'It has to be got over, sir, so I'm told. Got through. You will come right in the end.'

By this time they have emerged from the last of the warehouse lights and are walking towards the gates of the whole complex.

'I've left my bike over there, by the gates,' says the policeman. 'We'll just walk that way, sir.'

'Certainly,' says Monty.

As they arrive at the gates the policeman retrieves his bicycle, and then says, 'I don't think I'll need to come with you after all, sir ... I'm dropping all my plans of arrest ... but if I might just know your name and calling, sir ... just for my own interest, that's all, not for the records'.

'Brigadier Montgomery,' says Monty. 'I live at ... ,', and he gives his address.

'I know it, sir. Large house. Still being done up inside. And you all alone in that big house, sir ... No wonder you sleepwalk!'

'I'm getting used to it,' says Monty, 'Doing a lot of military reading. Getting ready for the next war in Europe.'

'It's looking more and more like it, sir ... I was in the last one ... perhaps you were as well. Enough was enough, I say.'

'But unfortunately Hitler doesn't,' says Monty.

'It's been good to meet you and talk to you, sir,' says the policeman. 'PC Haines, in case we meet again ... Good luck, sir, in both your struggles!'

PC Haines puts out a spare hand and shakes Monty's hand. He gets onto his bike, puts the lights on, and sets off, red back light soon swallowed up in the fog.

PART 4 - War

Chapter 11 – Alanbrooke and Churchill

Early June 1940, just after the Dunkirk evacuation.

Alanbrooke returns to England on May 28th, and is in
conversation with Churchill, now Prime Minister, concerning
the remainder of British troops in France, to the west of Paris.

Churchill is saying, 'We must at all costs keep our troops in
France, to link up with the French Army, and mount a counter-
attack, what say you, Alanbrooke?'

'A cheerless prospect all round, Prime Minister. Not something
I think we should embark on. I'd like to get them all home alive,
and prepared to fight another day.'

'That's not a very adventurous outlook, Alanbrooke. Isn't
attack, attack, attack the essence of all warfare?'

'Depending on circumstances, Prime Minister. There's no
golden rule. Sometimes retreat is called for, as we've just seen at
Dunkirk.'

'Dunkirk was one thing, this is another! The Germans will not
be expecting an attack now, so this is surely the right time to
attack them.'

'By all means, had we but the resources, and any hope of
success ... as you say, the moment itself seems opportune.'

'Resources!' Churchill remonstrates, 'A French Army of some 3
million men! What in heaven's name are you talking about,
Alanbrooke?'

'We saw what happened to the French Army in the events
leading up to Dunkirk.'

'But that was through a German surprise attack, an <u>attack</u>, let
me remind you! And extremely clever tactics by the Germans. It's
no judgment on the French Army, or on our own, for that matter.'

'I have to disagree, Prime Minister. It is a judgment on both our
armies. Dunkirk was a disaster, not some kind of victory!'

'How dare you speak of the British Army and its leaders in that
negative fashion! Are you criticising our leadership, by any

chance? Are you criticising Lord Gort?'

'I'm afraid I am criticising some of our leaders, and Lord Gort in particular.'

'But I'm just planning to give Lord Gort a medal of great distinction. Do you object to that, Alanbrooke?'

'I cannot comment on that, Prime Minister. These things, I fear, are sometimes political.'

'How dare you suggest such a thing! It seems to me you are developing cold feet, Alanbrooke ... 'No resources', for heaven's sake!' 'Had we the resources?' How many more resources do you want?'

'We need a French Army that can fight, and I fear it can't.'

'Well, go over to France and revive the French Army, Alanbrooke! Regard it as your special task. You are much respected everywhere.'

'It is kind of you to say so, Prime Minister, but I fear the French Army, and indeed the French Government, possibly even the French people, are dead. I am not the Lord Jesus, Prime Minister, and I cannot raise the French Lazarus from its tomb!'

'You speak in colourful language, Alanbrooke, but you do not convince me. Cold feet, that's all it is! No spark, no spirit!'

'I have to remind you, Prime Minister, that I do not think with my feet, nor with my solar plexus, but with a cool rational head, in so far as one can keep cool at all in the thick of battle.'

'O well said, well said!' Churchill replies, with heavy sarcasm. 'I suppose you think I'm still fighting the Boer War on the jolly old South African veldt, on horseback, with some sort of cutlass in my hand!'

Alanbrooke says nothing. A rather awkward silence until Churchill resumes, 'What makes you think the French Army is dead? You have only a part of the picture from out there. Who has influenced you, what is your evidence? No, seriously, convince me, I really am willing to listen.'

'Well, Prime Minister, the evidence of the French Army's collapse came from many quarters. I was in communication with many Divisional Commanders. All had the same tale to tell. And where the common French soldiers were willing, their leaders were not. And least of all their Government. It is a very strange political situation ... After all, why did the Anglo-Saxon nation succumb to the Norman invasion in 1066? A whole nation defeated by a mere 5,000 mounted knights and some thousands of foot soldiers. You are an historian, Prime Minister. There are strange precedents for this affair in France.'

'Very acute of you, Alanbrooke. A very interesting analogy ... very thought-provoking. Indeed, indeed. Some collapse of the will to fight, you think, even in defence of their own home territory? Some kind of ... malaise, perhaps?'

'It would seem so, Prime Minister. I report merely what I heard, and what I saw and felt myself. And by one piece of acute foresight I am retrospectively most impressed.'

'And whose was that?' Churchill asks with considerable interest.

'Divisional Commander Montgomery,' says Alanbrooke, but before he can go on, Churchill is spluttering.

'O that abominable little pipsqeak, Alanbrooke! What on earth can you mean? Why only a day or two ago that blighter was telling me how to organize our home defences, and criticising the plans already laid down!'

'Tactfulness is the last thing one would expect from Montgomery, I'm afraid, Prime Minister. It is his one great lack, and I am always telling him so ... You must try to forgive him ... '

Churchill interrupts, 'Bloody little man wanted me to commandeer hundreds of <u>buses,</u> so that he could organise what he called a mobile defence of our southern counties. I've a good mind to give him his buses, and let him get on with it. See where that leads us! <u>Buses</u>, for heaven's sake! The man is cranky, Alanbrooke, and I am most surprised you can't see it, you who are at all times a good judge of men ... or so I am told. You seem to have a blind spot there, I fear, Alanbrooke.'

'Not at all, Prime Minister, not at all. Rather the reverse it is a case of having to look beyond the unpromising exterior, and coming to see the genius within.'

'Did you say <u>genius</u>, Alanbrooke? Am I hearing you correctly?'

'O I know he didn't go to the right school, Prime Minister, and doesn't have the polished Eton manner – but I beg of you to think again, for he is a talented man, with uncanny gifts of perception and foresight ... '

Alanbrooke hesitates.

Churchill says 'Go on, Alanbrooke. I am doing my best!'

'I have known him from Staff College days, back in the 20's. He was, and is, a brilliant teacher, with a phenomenally clear mind and great insight. He seems to have X-ray vision sometimes.'

'These are all generalities, Alanbrooke. Give me something concrete.'

Alanbrooke pauses, then gathers himself.

'In France, Prime Minister, as soon as he arrived, he went on a tour southwards, to look at the French armies. Within two or three weeks he had concluded it was so badly led and organized, and with such low morale, that it could not possibly fight and win.'

'It's easy to be wise with hindsight. Show me that he had foresight, Alanbrooke.'

'He told me his judgments at the time, Prime Minister. We are old colleagues and friends, and very close. If he's got something important to communicate, he will tell me as one of the first.'

'Did you believe him at the time?' asks Churchill.

'I didn't know whether he was right ... I couldn't be sure. But I do know he is in some way almost psychic. Tactless and insensitive though he is, he has a way of getting straight to the heart of things, seeing into people's souls, one could say. Anyway, the real proof of the pudding is that he immediately began to organize his own Division for defeat and retreat. Not only that, but when the retreat to Dunkirk was at its most crucial stage, and when we were threatened with being cut off, he saved the day, plugged a crucial gap with his 3rd Division, moving into position at night, sir, a most extraordinary operation, so that most of us got safely home. I think he deserves a medal for that, since we were talking about medals.'

'I doubt if there'll be any medals for him, Alanbrooke. He's managed to upset Dill as well, our CIGS. Went straight to the War Office after Dunkirk, and told Dill who to sack. Just about everybody except you and himself, it turns out ... A real pair, you are, to be sure.'

'That was tactless, and very unfortunate. But he was probably right in his judgment all the same. Just boorish and insensitive, I'm afraid. I didn't know he had been to see Dill. That's certainly a blow to his career I'm sorry to say. Such a pity. He deserves a serious command fairly soon, and I hope you will support me in this, Prime Minister.'

'I'm not quite sure I will, Alanbrooke ... though I am listening and absorbing what you say about him. However, if a man can't control himself and his outbursts, you yourself will surely admit he is not suited to high command, Alanbrooke! Just a little man on the make, that's how I see him.'

'If that were the only part of the story I would have to agree with you, Prime Minister. But in the thick of battle, where it really matters, Montgomery is the man who is more in control of himself, and of events, than anyone I have so far encountered. He is always fresh, always keen-minded, always ready. He dared to take his 7 or 8 hours sleep at night, when others didn't, and were rendered exhausted. He ate his meals regularly, was sprucely turned out, and always cheerful, goddamit, cheerful! The worse things got, the more he seemed to enjoy it. He seems made for these circumstances ... he enjoys the fighting, and the seeming-chaos, Prime Minister!'

'Why, don't you, Alanbrooke, don't you?'

'No I do not. Most certainly I don't enjoy it!'

'Well, I did, Alanbrooke, I did. I was in my element. What made you a soldier, then?'

'A strong sense of duty. To be there, and exercise a calm responsibility, and, I hope, a humaneness, in the thick of the worst activity man inflicts upon man ... That, I think, would sum it up.'

'A curious philosophy, Alanbrooke. Hardly a warrior's creed. But I take your point. Most interesting.'

'Well, I shouldn't boast too much, Prime Minister, because in the thick of things I could not in the end keep my calm. Something broke in me during those last days at Dunkirk, and I am not sure that I'm not too old and battered now to take up such

a command again. Though many are worse than myself. And ...'
he pauses, 'Lord Gort was the worst of all. Beside himself. And
for one crucial day, paralysed, unable to give orders, or even to
think ... All his faculties just seized up, Prime Minister ... If
medals are to be given for the extent of suffering and mental
breakdown, Prime Minister, then certainly Lord Gort will deserve
his medal!'

'You must not say these things, Alanbrooke. I cannot believe
you. I have the highest regard for Lord Gort, and it is repugnant to
me to contemplate the things you report about him. Some
malicious tongues have been at work here, you mark my words ...
Bitter rivalries, that sort of thing ... '

'Not on my part, Prime Minister. I have no desire for such
command in the field, not any longer.'

'I believe you there, Alanbrooke, and have the greatest respect
for your integrity. But please do not criticize Lord Gort again in
my presence, I beg you. We must agree to differ there,
Alanbrooke.'

'Very well, Prime Minister. But there is just one more thing.'

'And what is that?'

'Am I to organize a complete evacuation from France, or are
our troops to stay there and fight?'

'Bring them all home, old fellow, bring them all home. We'll
have, as you say, to organize and recuperate, and fight another
day.'

A pause.

'Thank you for listening so patiently, Prime Minister. We must
talk again before too long.'

'We certainly must, Alanbrooke. And I'll be looking for a good
post for you at home, now, you can be certain of that.'

1940 – 1942 General Summary

Monty is now in charge of Southern Command, as a Lt.
General, and responsible for training. His training of men
continues to be excellent, and he proposes clear and simple

military ideas. However, his personal lack of balance is shown in several incidents during the years up to his appointment to lead the 8th Army in August 1942. Partly it is his bereavement, and partly his lack of a fighting command, for which he feels better qualified than many of those chosen. He is therefore bitter, restless and provocative ...

Summer and Autumn of 1940, during the Battle of Britain

Churchill is on the phone to Alanbrooke. Churchill is saying, 'Alanbrooke, it's your damned Monty again ... Do you know what he is up to on the south coast? He's sending all the wives of officers away. Back to London, or even further. Won't have any wives at all down there ...'

Alanbrooke interrupts, 'I expect he's concerned about a German invasion, safety of wives and families of officers. And concentrating the minds of the officers on their job ... Monty never does things without sound thought, Winston.'

'Sound thought be damned! He's just upsetting everyone, and enjoying it! How can that be good for morale? Sound thought is no damned good without tact or common sense, is it? Where is this leadership quality that you so go on about? And yet you want me to find him a fighting command somewhere ...'

'I have to agree with much of what you say. His tactlessness is his worst quality ... and in his present loneliness and bitterness it's probably worse than ever ... However, I will venture my opinion again. Had you given him a real fighting command, none of this would be happening. He feels undervalued and underused. That can make him a damned nuisance, I agree.'

'I thought that training men was his forte, Alanbrooke. Maybe he is at his best where he is ... Do you think I am going to be bullied by his insufferable behaviour into giving him a fighting command?'

'No, of course not. He must learn to behave himself. I'll give him a good talking-to again, Winston. He does listen to me. But don't write him off as a fighting Commander, Winston. He has huge talent, even genius ... '

Alanbrooke is lost for words.

'I am hearing you, Alanbrooke. I am not writing you off, or him off. The moment has to be right ... And meanwhile, he must behave ... Churchill suddenly becomes more animated. '<u>Did</u> you know, Alanbrooke, he has not only been evicting whole military families from their houses, but he goes on to <u>blowing up</u> the houses after they've left, without even telling them! Blowing up houses! For some military reason obscure to me and to everyone else!'

'Terrible!' says Alanbrooke. 'He sounds seriously unhinged ... I promise I'll have a serious talk, Winston, I'll read him the Riot Act.'

'Yes, do,' says Churchill. 'And presto! We can't afford many more incidents down there!'

He puts the phone down. We see Alanbrooke put his head in his hands and shake it from side to side.

Early in 1941   Monty is lecturing to a class of officers.

'The first principle that I want to lay down is this. Never begin the land battle until supremacy in the air has been won. Monty pauses, and looks intently into space. 'Never. Never,' he says, firmly and clearly, and then, gradually fading to a whisper, ' ... never ... never ... never!'

A long pause, and then briskly, 'Of course this will mean close co-operation with the Air Arm, and the putting aside of rivalries and silly prejudices. As you know, the Germans, and other nations, are well ahead of us in these things, and we just have to manage as best we can with the antiquated and, as it were, tribal system that we have failed to change.'

He looks round the class from face to face, fixing each officer in turn with his eyes.

'An artillery barrage, however ferocious and sustained, is never quite enough, as we learned, or should have learned, from the last war. There was one episode in particular that should be in all the history books. Gentlemen, we bombarded a German sector for a full week, and then sent our troops over the top, secure in the hope of victory. What was the result, gentlemen? Our infantry was shot to pieces by the German machine guns , as though not a single shell of ours had ever hit its target. And why was that? It was because the Germans at that point were dug in some seventy feet underground, not only safe and sound, but thoroughly enjoying themselves, drinking German wine and eating rump steak, playing music and dancing, gentlemen, dancing! And also secure in the knowledge that the best hospital and medical facilities were close at hand, deep underground also, in the unlikely contingency of a hit by the enemy. These superb facilities were all built years before 1914, in pursuit of the Schlieffen Plan for the rapid capture of Paris and the surrender of France. It says little for our Security and Intelligence Services that these things were not known to us ... However, gentlemen, I digress. We are talking about artillery. I believe in a high concentration of artillery, a massive bombardment at a particular point, rather than a dispersed one all along the line. That, together with air superiority, must be the prelude to any infantry attack.

'Another vitally important principle is this ... always try to fight a battle on the ground of your own choosing. If that sometimes means sitting tight and waiting for the enemy to come at you, so be it.' A pause. 'I will be called a cautious commander for that (if ever I am given serious command in the field again, of course). However, our resources are scarce, our men are scarce and precious. We only just got them out of the Dunkirk debacle. It is our job henceforth to preserve as many of our men as possible. We just don't have the organized might of the Germans, neither in men nor in weapons. We must be patient, and wear the enemy down. Fighting on the ground of your own choosing is the essential thing here, even in a battle of attack.

'In the matter of attack, we must in the end create, or at least identify, a point in the enemy line where we have superiority. When this is certain, we must gather overwhelming forces and make a breakthrough at that point. This sounds very obvious, gentlemen. Am I repeating all the cliches and illusions of the last war? Well, not quite. What we need to bring about such an opportunity are plans of elaborate deception. To make it look, for weeks on end, that the attack is most likely to come in one area, when all along we are really jockeying for a position where the attack can be launched. So, not only dummy tanks and dummy field guns and aircraft ... and their replacement during the night by real ones ... and so on. But much more than that, that is schoolboy stuff. Dummy pipelines, both water and oil, being built over a matter of weeks or months, for instance. And then false plans being found on the dead body of one of our men. This is all good, clean fun, and of course is the province of Intelligence Corps, so very much more professional than of old. If you are in command, pick a good Intelligence man and let him get on with it. Pick good men, then trust them. Do not drive them mad by interfering and controlling at all points.

'Another fundamental principle of mine is to keep tactics as simple as possible so that they can be communicated and understood by all. This is absolutely essential. The ideal is for every man to understand the plan, and to understand clearly his own role within the plan. And indeed, the thing must be so simple as to be understood by <u>word of mouth</u>. Understood and <u>remembered</u>, gentlemen. Cultivate memory, gentlemen, in yourselves and in the men under your command. Minimize paperwork, and bits of paper floating about. Bits of paper are a curse, gentlemen. People are always about to re-read them, so as to <u>really</u> understand, but don't get round to it ... by which time another bit of paper comes in, and one has to re-read the previous bit first. And so on and so forth!'

There are nods of appreciation all round, and smiles. Monty smiles into the smiles, and continues, 'My old friend Liddell Hart must be kicking himself, gentlemen. His revolutionary ideas for mobile tank warfare have been taken up and applied by Hitler in France, to our immense disadvantage, while we ourselves have largely ignored them ... A prophet, without honour in his own country? Well, yes and no, gentlemen. Splendid ideas, yes. The '<u>but</u>' consists in the fact that <u>they</u> are a truly professional army, with NCOs trained to take over officer-responsibilities, while we are not. We disarmed in the 20s and 30s, with the result that we have now a largely conscript army, and not enough time to turn that into an army of the German sort. In these circumstance, gentlemen, we must do the best we can within our limits. And that means simplicity, and everyone knowing his job. We simply cannot, as yet, undertake movements of the subtlety envisaged by the excellent Liddell Hart. His splendid ideas are for another day, as far as the British Army is concerned. Meanwhile, therefore, the poor bloody infantry are still central to our effort, and they need encouragement and looking after, gentlemen.

'The welfare of troops and the morale of troops. Hardly anything is more important than that, as you know, and everyone knows. And yet, it is not always seen to in as comprehensive way as it should be. It is no use having good food if the water is awful, and vice versa. It is no good giving soldiers frequent and short holidays out in the field if their post from home is not arriving, or their own post not getting home in good time. The nurses are always good, and thank God for the nurses, gentlemen, thank God for the nurses! And even a bit of harmless romance and romantic dreaming is a boon, gentlemen. Nothing like making the wounded infantryman feel like a knight errant who must protect his unattainable lady, and die for her and all her kind ... Ah, gentlemen, that is a thing indeed, a thing indeed!'

Monty turns away, to hide the tears coming to his eyes. Then he prevents the tears by going off on another tack.

'However, some of the padres leave a lot to be desired! Is it too much to ask that all our padres should possess genuine spiritual power, and be a source of that power for our fighting men? So that our men feel in their presence that God truly loves them and cares for them, and that death's terrors are only relative after all? To die for a good cause, and for God to fulfill in them afterwards the purpose of His love and their creation ... That is all we ask our padres to convey ... but I feel that many of them do not. It is hard to know what made them become Christian ministers at all, in too many cases. If we can't change things there, then we must somehow strive in our own persons to convey that faith and inspiration ... if we are believing Christians. But we must desist from communicating a dark and threatening and bullying religion, gentlemen. The common soldier quite rightly detests that, and will quickly become hostile. It must be a <u>human</u> religion, gentlemen, kindly, and at the same time supportive of our most sublime hopes ... of fellowship with God in immortality, gentlemen, nothing less. If we can't believe that as Christians ourselves, so much the worse for us.

'I said 'kindly', but I don't mean kindly and <u>woolly</u>, gentlemen. Kindly and human, but full-blooded traditional in all the important ways. What use is mere sentiment, gentlemen, if the Christian hope is not there? Quite useless, gentlemen! Have no truck with the useless. If anyone is useless, he must either be sacked, or found another position in which he can be of use. Preferably the latter, of course, but it is not always possible.

'I was talking earlier about frequent breaks for troops, and that applies to battle-situations as well as to the more or less peaceful interludes. It is one of my firm principles to bring in reserves in the thick of battle, and to retire whole units for rest and recuperation. Two or three days facing fire is almost enough for any man, a week at the utmost. My only fear is that such moves will be interpreted by our politicians as defeatist. We must educate them, gentlemen, by degrees. There is a sound psychology in my principle. It is partly about wear on the nerves in continuous battle, till the man snaps and either goes mad, or into apathy or rebellion. But it is also about the effect on the mind and morale of being taken out of battle at an early stage, in the realization that one has fought bravely and successfully, and yet has survived, and earned a rest. This increases the determination to do even better in the next episode ... and to survive that as well! And the sense that warfare is a succession of short intense episodes of danger, rather than a protracted nerve-stretching that eventually becomes terror, this is of the essence, gentlemen. Remembering yet again that we are largely a conscript army, and must bend our military principles to that understanding.

'Another thing that men need in battle is to be vividly aware of their overall Commander's presence and personality, and even to see him occasionally ... preferably in some distinctive dress. To that end, it is my belief that one's Tactical Headquarters should be near the battlefront. This will also enable the Commander to be in close and constant touch with his liaison officers, and to respond quickly to changes in the situation. A flexible response to changing situations, together with forays into the front line by the Commander himself, who must be easily recognizable and distinctive. These are sound and important practices, gentlemen.

'And to conclude, I feel I must touch on one of the most sensitive issues of all. It concerns the frequent breaks for troops during peaceful interludes. Do not keep your troops hanging about all the time for no reason, gentlemen. Apply for leaves for them. Let them go off to the 'fleshpots of Egypt' and enjoy themselves. To keep them hanging round serving no purpose, just for the sake of discipline ... or to keep drilling them, these only build up resentment and bloody-mindedness. And there's nothing so tiring and so mind-numbing as boredom and having nothing constructive to do. Therefore, breaks and escapades whenever possible. Refreshment is good, and even what I will call 'horizontal refreshment' is necessary.'

The officers are looking a little puzzled.

'I will clarify that,' says Monty. 'I mean a soldier's horizontal refreshment with a lady of his own choice.'

There is a burst of laughter.

'And though in wartime abroad, the lady of a soldier's choice may not be a very choice lady, the principle holds. War, gentlemen, is monstrous and unnatural, and we professional soldiers should be dedicated to the management of the monstrous and unnatural, in such a way as to mitigate these terrible qualities.'

Monty pauses, looks round at each in turn, and continues, 'Just think, gentlemen, if you have not already done so, of the monstrous burden that a large, occupying army imposes on a civilian population. Think of the thousands of peasants in days past, ruined by the depredations of armies, the commandeering of food on a huge scale ... to say nothing of the rape of women. Well, in the case of food at least we have improved. A great part of logistics is precisely the management of food supplies for our armies, without making ourselves a nuisance to the local population. It is high time we did the same with the sexual needs of our soldiers.

'I will tell you, gentlemen, that one of the reasons I am in disagreement with the higher authorities, and have no field command at present, is because I took these matters in hand with our Army in France in 1939 and 1940. I witnessed the terrible consequences of a sexual free-for-all, in the shape of large numbers of our men going down with serious venereal diseases. I attempted to regulate both the women and the men, with regular medical inspections for the women, and with free contraceptives for the men ... What had I done wrong in drawing attention to a very real problem, and attempting a sensible solution? Yet the whole corps of padres came down on me like a ton of bricks, and they were supported by the top brass and the politicians. They all threw up their hands in horror, as though these things didn't go on ... or shouldn't go on ... or shouldn't be talked about or thought about even if they did go on! It is ridiculous, gentlemen, absolutely ridiculous. We might as well try to pretend that war doesn't involve actually killing people, gentlemen! What would you think of Commanders who couldn't bear to be reminded that war involves death and wounding, gentlemen? Would you laugh or cry, gentlemen, or both? It is the same with sex. It has to be faced ... you might think that I, gentlemen, the son of a saintly Bishop, would be the last person to raise this issue. Also, having no great sexual urges myself, that also would seem to make me the very last person to take this question seriously. But it seems that, far from being the last, I am the first! I don't know why, gentlemen, I was not seeking notoriety, I was not just playing games with the higher authorities ... But there it is, authority is blinkered, and I ask all of you to have the courage to raise these matters in the field and to persist in challenging authority. I certainly mean to do so ... and if I am awarded a field-command, I will persist until at least I get free contraceptives for my men, gentlemen. In some things one has just to persist, gentlemen, and to make oneself such a confounded nuisance that in the end one is given the thing one asks for. It is no good expecting always to be liked. If the men under your command like you, that is the main thing. Whether Churchill likes me, and whether the top brass like me, is not a thing I bother my head about, so long as I get my way when I am in the right about something. But it can be a great trouble, in the end, being right about so many things, and having to fight for them, one by one! People begin to talk, gentlemen. One aquires a malodorous reputation. But they will come round in the end, gentlemen, if you are proved to have been right. Some people will even shake your hand, and apologize for opposing you. I'm glad to say I've already experienced that on one or two occasions. It is worth remembering that, gentlemen, when the going gets hot, and one is detested by all and sundry. Bash on regardless, gentlemen, just bash on regardless.

'I've said all I want to say for the present. The military principles I've outlined will be the subjects of our detailed examination over the coming weeks and months. By the time you leave here you will be well-versed in what I consider the absolutely essential things to understand, and will be able to apply them at whatever level you are employed in. I have absolute confidence in these principles, and although they are all simple, they are effective. Do not allow yourselves to be discouraged by those who say they are too simple. Do not allow yourselves to be seduced and distracted by the apostles of the super-subtle, gentlemen. There are still too many of them. Regard them as poison, gentlemen, it is the safest way.

Now we will have three minutes for coughing, and then I will take questions ... And thank you for listening so intently, gentlemen, and for not coughing!'

Later in 1941

Monty is walking along cliff-tops on the south coast. A sign-post there shows Dover. He is accompanied by an NCO from an artillery unit.

'Our big guns can hit France from here, isn't that so?' Monty asks.

'Yes sir,' says the NCO, 'with ease, sir.'

'Pity we can't set something up, then, and bombard them!' says Monty. 'Wonder why no-one has suggested it ... can you think of a reason, Corporal Ellis?'

'Perhaps not to antagonize the French, sir, by killing their civilians?'

'I suppose so,' says Monty, 'I suppose so. However, the French have only themselves to blame for their predicament. We shouldn't let the French hold us back ... what do you say, Ellis?'

'I don't feel I can express an opinion, sir, even as an artilleryman. The problem may be the German retaliation, sir. Perhaps they are quiet only because we are quiet.'

'Doesn't seem very likely to me,' says Monty, 'If the Germans don't bombard us, perhaps it's because they're not in a position to. All the more reason for us to bombard them!'

'Perhaps so, sir,' says Corporal Ellis.

There is a pause before Ellis speaks again.

'Actually, sir, there is a large gun less than a mile from here. Would you like to see it, sir?'

'I most certainly would!' says Monty, 'why didn't you tell me before?'

'It's a little hush-hush, sir,' says Ellis. 'It's Churchill's gun, sir, and can only be fired with his permission, or with Churchill himself present, sir.'

'What!' exclaims Monty, 'The Prime Minister with his own private piece of artillery! What a piece of nonsense! Who in the name of thunder does he think he is? Take me to this gun, Ellis! I can't wait to see it!'

They walk rapidly along the cliff-top and come to a wooded enclosure surrounded by a stone wall.

'It's inside there,' says Ellis.

'Is it indeed,' says Monty, 'Where's the Officer in charge?'

'There's a small building just over there, sir,' says Ellis. 'Hopefully someone will be around ... '

They walk over to a black wooden hut a hundred yards further on. Monty walks up to it and knocks on the door. An artillery officer emerges and salutes.

'Can I help you, sir?'

'You certainly can!' says Monty 'I want to have a look at that gun ... I am Montgomery, Commander of South Eastern Command, by the way.'

'Certainly I can show you the gun, sir,' says the officer, coming out of the hut, and making his way towards it, as they follow.

'It has a most interesting history, sir. Mr Churchill's special gun, sir. His toy, as you might say ... '

'So indeed I have heard,' says Monty sarcastically.

They are shown into the enclosure where the big gun sits.

'This is it, sir. Churchill's gun!' says the officer.

There is a pause.

'Fire it!' says Monty.

There is another pause ... an explosive one.

'What!' exclaims the officer, 'Impossible, sir, I'm afraid. Only to be fired on Mr Churchill's orders ... and in Mr Churchill's presence, sir. Strict orders, sir !'

'What!' shouts Monty, 'Is this some kind of joke? The Prime Minister with his own big gun, tucked away in an enclosure near Dover, on the clifftops, all for the Prime Minister's pleasure when he comes here on some sort of picnic! What nonsense!'

'Nonsense or not, these are my orders, sir,' says the officer.

'And what about my orders! I do happen to be the Commander of the Army in this area, officer! Does that mean nothing?'

'Of course not, sir ... But the Prime Minister, sir ... it's more than my job is worth ... '

'O do spare me that!' Monty interrupts, 'In heaven's name! The Prime Minister must have his little military toy! For heaven's sake, does he have a toy battleship as well, and a toy bomber, and a toy submarine?'

'I couldn't say, sir!' says the officer.

'I could not say, sir' mimics Monty savagely. 'No-one can say, it seems. No-one must breathe a word. What kind of a Prime Minister are we saddled with? Some kind of big schoolboy, by the sound of it! Eh?'

'Obviously I cannot comment on that, sir,' says the officer.

'No, obviously you cannot comment on that either!' Monty rages, 'But as for myself, I will comment, I certainly will. This is the most ridiculous piece of damned nonsense I have ever come across in my whole military career!'

There is a pause.

'Fire it!' Monty snaps.

'Alas, sir, I cannot!' says the officer.

'Nonsense!' says Monty, 'My Army. My gun. I order you to fire it. That is an order from your Commander, officer. Fire it!'

'That will take some arranging,' says the officer, beginning to give in, amid sighs and perspiration and deep shock.

'Certainly,' says Monty briskly. 'Arrange it, then. I and my Corporal will sit here until it arranged. We are in no hurry, but we mean to see it fired. And you need fear nothing from Mr Churchill, officer, I will see to that. I shall take full responsibility.'

'Thank you, sir,' says the officer, enfeebled and close to fainting.

'I will see what I can do, sir' he trails off, as he goes in search of ammunition and artillerymen.

Corporal Ellis is in a state of some shock as well, but gradually adjusting as he paces back and forth along the cliff-top, now they are out of the enclosure.

'Don't worry, Corporal Ellis, no harm will come to you either. I expect you are wishing you had kept your big mouth shut now, aren't you?' says Monty, laughing, and seething with mischief and enjoyment.

'Come on, Ellis, sit over here on this nice bench provided for the purpose! We will sit here and look out over the Channel and dream dreams of England until the gunners arrive!'

Alanbrooke is in his office. The phone rings.

'Alanbrooke speaking.'

'That you, Alanbrooke? Churchill here.'

'Hullo, sir. Is all well?'

'No, Alanbrooke, all is not well!' Churchill pauses to gain his breath.

'I am all ears, sir,' says Alanbrooke.

'It's your damned Monty again!' says Churchill.

'God help me!' whispers Alanbrooke to himself. 'I'm sorry, sir, what is it this time?'

'He's fired my gun!' shouts Churchill.

'Fired your gun, sir? I'm not quite sure what you are saying, sir. What gun is that?'

'What do you mean, 'what gun is that?',' Churchill shouts. 'It's my gun, my big Bertha, on the south coast, near Dover, and never to be fired without my permission, and without my personal presence! I thought everybody knew that!'

'Indeed, sir!' says Alanbrooke, pausing for thought.

'What do you mean 'Indeed sir'?' shouts Churchill, 'Are you some kind of butler, Alanbrooke? Don't you understand my sense of outrage?'

'I am trying to understand, sir, how a Prime Minister comes into personal possession of a piece of artillery ... It has not so far been part of my military experience, sir ... but give me time, sir, give me a little time.' Alanbrooke is soothing, but sarcastic at the same time.

'O, so you are on Montgomery's side in this, are you, Alanbrooke? I can hear it in your tone! You're going to let me down, aren't you? I can just see your face, Alanbrooke , all calm and superior and ironic!'

'Far from it,' says Alanbrooke, 'I am deep in thought and wonderment.'

'Wonderment! There you go again, Alanbrooke! Irony and sarcasm ... you're grinning, Alanbrooke! That's the truth of it ... I can sense your grin from here. It's hurting me, Alanbrooke ... it's deeply insulting!'

'Well, I wasn't grinning, sir, I promise you. But I'm not sure that I'm not grinning now ... It's a bit rich, sir, isn't it? It does have its comic side, sir, you must see that!'

'So you are on Monty's side, Alanbrooke! I knew it ... I can't bear it!' says Churchill.

'Monty had no right to do what he did, anyway, quite apart from your point of view on the matter, sir. But on the other hand, I'm not sure a Prime Minister has a right to his own artillery, sir.

That's what I'm pondering, sir.'

'O don't be such a kill-joy, Alanbrooke! Damned Ulster puritan
– kill-joys all of you!'

'Joy and the killing of joy simply don't come into it Prime
Minister ... The whole thing must be kept quiet, sir, that is my
view.'

So no punishment for Montgomery, then – I just knew you were
on his side! O, I can't bear it!'

'If you were to punish Monty, the whole Army and eventually
the whole country would come to know about your private toy, sir
– '

'O so you call it my 'toy', do you? I just can't stomach your
holier-than-thou attitude, Alanbrooke! Is there to be no <u>fun</u>,
Alanbrooke?' Churchill is spluttering, incoherent.

'In its right place, sir, in its right place ... '

'O God – no-one understands me – everyone deserts me when
I'm down, Alanbrooke – and you're no better. I thought you were
my friend, Alanbrooke ... but when it comes to it ...' Churchill is
on the verge of tears.

'Comes to what, exactly?' asks Alanbrooke.

'O you know what I mean, Alanbrooke! Why are you being
such a prickly old pedant! ... 'Exactly' this, and 'precisely' that.
Show some simple human sympathy, Alanbrooke, for heaven's
sake!'

There is a pause, too long for a telephone conversation.

'Are you still there, Alanbrooke?' says Churchill.

'Of course, sir.'

Another longish pause.

'Well, I suppose there's nothing you <u>can</u> say, in the
circumstances,' says Churchill at last.

'No, sir. It's best that we forget the whole thing, and say no
more about it ... I can't prevent you from holding it against
Montgomery, but I do hope you won't – not in an objective
military sense, at least ... Hate him as much as you like
personally, sir, but do not overlook his great military talents, I beg
you.'

'Humph!' says Churchill, 'I've seen precious little of these military talents ... I've only got your word for it, Alanbrooke!'

'Then give him a serious field command and you will see – Let him prove himself ... Our performance in Greece and in Crete has hardly been brilliant, has it? ... our armies driven out and taking refuge in North Africa ... If we are driven out of Egypt we will have lost the war!'

'How dare you say that, Alanbrooke!' Churchill shouts, 'We shall <u>never</u> lose the war, for the simple reason that we shall never surrender.'

'Nevertheless, one can't run tanks and aircraft and ships and lorries on lemonade! If we lose the oil, effectively we lose the war. That isn't defeatism, sir, it's just plain speaking.'

A series of humphs and grunts from the other end.

'I'm terminating this conversation, Alanbrooke.'

Silence.

'Did you hear me? I said, I'm terminating this conversation.'

'Very good, sir.'

'Stop sounding like my butler,' says Churchill, "As you say, sir!"'

June 1942   The Fall of Tobruk

Churchill is with Roosevelt. Alanbrooke is there, and Marshall. The loss of Tobruk is a crushing blow for Churchill, after the loss of Greece and Crete in 1941, and the loss of Singapore, which we were expecting to hold, in February 1942. Roosevelt is very gracious to Churchill, and softens the blow. They are looking at a large map of Europe and the Middle East.

A discussion of strategy ensues. Does the fall of Tobruk entail a new approach? Marshall believes it confirms his own ideas for a Second Front in Northern Europe, which Stalin has been asking for, and which is popular with the general public.

'I think the fall of Tobruk just about seals it. The battle for North Africa seems to be unwinnable, with Rommel there. You could fall back on Egypt and hold that. Hold the Suez Canal at all costs. And further east ... I agree with Auchinleck, the threat is there. If the Germans break through around the Caucasus there is an immediate threat to the oil fields in Abadan. If we lose that, we can't fight the war. But if we hold Egypt and the Canal, and reinforce Syria and Iraq, and hold the oilfields, we can at the same time launch an attack across the English Channel. That would relieve the pressure on Stalin, and enable him to put more resources further south, in the Caucasus area. Stalingrad and the Black Sea area is surely the crucial area at present, I would say ... How does that grab you, Alanbrooke? Is a Second Front in Northern Europe still impossible for you? Isn't it an open and shut case just now?'

Alanbrooke draws breath before replying.

'General Marshall outlines a most compelling case for his strategy. But there are serious drawbacks, which I must repeat here ... Until we take control of the Mediterranean there is absolutely no chance of mounting a successful campaign in Northern Europe. This is because of the oil situation, which General Marshall is absolutely right to draw attention to. All our oil at present goes round the Cape of Good Hope, at a huge cost in time, and in oil. In that situation, holding the Suez Canal is almost academic ... though we must hold it, of course, precisely for the eventuality of the Med being cleared for our own traffic, when it will come into its own again.'

Alanbrooke pauses, emits a deep breath, calms himself, and then goes on, 'If the key is the Mediterranean, then of course we have to stay and fight in North Africa. President Roosevelt, your help in the Western Desert will be invaluable, if embarked on and persisted in. But will be weakened if you are distracted by premature campaigns across the English Channel, whatever Stalin might think. The best way to please Stalin at the moment, once I have explained to him the insuperable difficulties of a Second Front in France and the Netherlands at present, or the near future, the best present for him, I am convinced, is an Allied success in North Africa. Persistent Allied success in North Africa. That would rejoice his heart, and reduce his clamour for the Second Front, which is impossible before the end of 1943, I would guess. Now that is why American help in Africa would be invaluable,

General Marshall. If your people advance from the West, our battle is won. We will relieve Malta, and go easily into Sicily and Italy, destroy the Italian Navy and Air Force, capture the airfields, and push the Germans out of the Mediterranean. Those are my reasons for continuing to oppose the strategy you are suggesting, General Marshall, and I fear I have to be most emphatic in my opposition! I would be glad of your opinion, Mr President.'

'Well, you know I'm no strategist. Marshall's idea seemed feasible to me, and now you persuade me. I will have to think a little longer and take more advice. But I do feel I am coming round to your way of thinking, Alanbrooke, and I'm grateful to you for setting it out so clearly. But we must keep the Russians supplied with whatever equipment they ask for. It is so important that their vast struggle in the south succeeds. Perhaps we can keep them happy that way, so that Stalin doesn't make too big an issue of the Second Front ...

Churchill now breaks in. 'I think I can persuade Stalin to accept Alanbrooke's view, and convince him of our good faith. That's the main thing. Alanbrooke will come with me to Moscow, if necessary, and we will do the thing together. The one thing that worries me is our string of defeats. I agree with Alanbrooke that a solid and lasting victory in North Africa would do more good than anything. But just what is the matter with our commanders? Why do they keep losing battles? We've had superior odds in North Africa, and yet we lose! I can't keep jumping on our commanders in the field, but they try me sorely. I thought the loss of Singapore was the worst we could suffer. But the fall of Tobruk ... it's enough to break the heart and spirit ... But I deeply appreciate your support on that, Mr President, it is most heartening. With your support, Mr President, we will fight on with new courage, and we will win! But I fear Auchinleck, in North Africa, may have to be removed. I will visit him again, and will remove him if necessary ... and then we must find an agreed replacement. What do you think, Alanbrooke?'

'Auchinleck has all the qualities of a good commander except one ... he is a bad judge of men, he picks poor men as his subordinates. And somehow he does not enthuse his troops. It is all very puzzling. He is a very good man, but somehow the parts do not add up to a whole. Something is missing ... As for his replacement, I think you know my views on that, Winston. I have long advocated the promotion of Montgomery to an important field command, and now is, I think, the time to do it!'

'I will only have Montgomery if I can find no-one better. I am not quite persuaded he is the right man.'

'But for the enthusing of troops, lifting morale, and for the supreme self-confidence that lifts the confidence of others, he is ideal ...'

Churchill interrupts. 'His self-confidence has not had that effect on me, unfortunately, Alanbrooke. It leaves me wanting to hit him with some blunt instrument. But of course I have to take account of your knowledge and your assessment ... My first choice would, I think, be 'Strafer' Gott ... '

'An excellent man, Winston, but somewhat tired at present. Very much needing a rest,' says Alanbrooke.

'Well, I shall talk to him personally, and make my own judgement on that. But whoever we choose, the support of our American friends in North Africa would make me very happy.'

There is a longish silence. Roosevelt then says, 'I can see that, Mr Churchill, and you are very persuasive. As a matter of urgency we will have to see what we can do. Marshall and I will have some urgent talks together ... obviously something must be done ... and decisions will have to be made ... I say decisions, because we also have the Pacific theatre to worry about. '

'And so do we!' says Churchill vehemently. 'You don't suppose I can look with unconcern at the Japanese threat to India, I'm sure. We're already having to divert troops and aircraft and equipment from North Africa to our Empire in the East. It is dispiriting in the extreme for our commanders there – and it makes my plea for your help in North Africa even more urgent.'

Another longish silence. Then Roosevelt says, 'A new chapter in Anglo-American history, I feel. Whatever our divergences of interest, our common interests are surely just as great, and we must not squabble and fall apart, 'that way madness lies'. But much of the American public does not quite see it that way, and I see it as my job to bring them round.'

Chapter 12 – Meeting with Bernard Shaw

July 1942

Bernard Shaw is in Augustus John's studio, sitting on a on the dais for his portrait. Augustus John puts down chair his brushes, wipes his hands with a clean rag, and says to Shaw, 'That's it for today, Mr Shaw. Not a bad session's work, I hope you'll agree.'

Bernard Shaw gets up, stretches himself vigorously, and steps down cautiously from the dais. He is still straight as a ramrod, but is old, in his eighties, and walks with care. He looks at the portrait and leans back, his hands planted on his hips.

'Certainly a big step forward today, Augustus. A portrait of the genius Bernard Shaw by the genius Augustus John, with my genius just beginning to show through ... What a wonderful confirmation of one's view of oneself when a great painter manages to see it and to show it for all to see! Congratulations Augustus! When shall I come again?'

'Ah, that depends on an extra factor, Bernard. There is a military gentleman whose portrait I have just begun, and he has expressed a desire to meet you.'

' Has he indeed!' says Shaw. 'It must be a very remarkable kind of military man who wishes to meet and converse with genius. Who is he? Will we have anything in common, do you think? Is he famous?'

'No, he is not famous, but pretty high ranking, I think. His name is Bernard Montgomery.'

Shaw shakes his head.

'I can't say I care for him myself,' says John. ' As for whether you'll have anything in common, it's very hard to tell. But there is just one thing ... '

'And what is that?' asks Shaw in his crisp, light voice.

'You both have an inordinate vanity that is shocking – or quite amusing, as I find yours. So far I find his somewhat oppressive ... A soldier who has his portrait painted on the assumption that he is going to be famous – although at the moment no-one knows him, is not a particularly attractive type. He has no obvious points of interest that I can see ... a small, rather prickly man, full of himself. Sharp as a ferret, mind you, and about as likeable, I would guess, at close quarters. However, I am not in rivalry with him, and he manages a certain surface charm with me that helps things along.'

'Well, we shall see,' says Shaw, 'we shall see. As I said before, any military man wishing to meet me, must have something remarkable about him, now mustn't he, Augustus?'

'I had noted that you had said it before, Bernard,' says John with a smile, 'don't think I miss these things. But perhaps he just wants to hob-nob with the famous ... to be able to say, in the Officers' Mess, just casually ... 'As I was just saying to Bernard Shaw, only the other day!''

They seize right hands together in a shout of laughter.

'About a fortnight, Bernard', says John, 'leave me a few dates on a piece of paper. I'll fix it with Montgomery.'

Shaw scribbles on a pad, and goes out.

A fortnight later.

Shaw is sitting in a large throne-like wooden chair in an ante-room to Augustus John's studio. The door opens and Monty comes in from the studio, followed by John himself, who is saying, 'We should only need 5 or 6 more sessions for completion, sir.'

Monty looks discontented and bored, but tries to be civil, smiling weakly and nodding at John as he goes back to his studio and says loudly 'Be with you in about half an hour Mr. Shaw.'

Shaw rises briskly from his throne and introduces himself. They shake hands.

'I'm delighted that you wish to meet me' says Shaw. 'It is most unusual for a military man.'

Monty manages a wan smile. He is half-expecting another dose of Augustus John's weary tolerance, and almost regretting the whole venture.

'Mr. John will be some time yet, probably more than half an hour' says Shaw 'Cleaning up, and adding dabs here and there to your portrait, and taking the cloth to it, perhaps even the knife, perhaps scraping off whole areas of paint with a view to beginning more or less from scratch!'

'He might be well advised to do so sir, for I can't say I like it myself as it is now. But then, I know nothing of these artistic things. Though my wife Betty was a good artist, and she did her best for me in that direction. But I remain an ignoramus I fear.'

'Oh I'm sure you're not sir, I'm sure you're not!' says Shaw. 'However, leaving that aside for the moment, please do sit down and tell me about the things you consider you do know! I am myself becoming extremely interested in the tactical questions of war and military planning, but know nothing first–hand, never, thank heavens, having been called upon to serve ... Now, shall we take our seats and will you do your utmost to relieve my ignorance!'

Monty begins to light up, enjoying the energetic exhilaration of Shaw's manner and talk. Shaw goes back to his throne and Monty sits on a small chair at his feet and leans forward, his arms on his knees, his face thrust out and looking keenly at his man.

Monty begins 'I fear you are rather exaggerating your ignorance of military matters, Mr. Shaw. My wife took me along to several of your plays, and I was so impressed that I took to going on my own initiative ... so I am aware of much of your way of looking at the world, and, as I said, I was struck here and there by a most uncanny knowledge of battle, most unusual in a playwright, and almost as though you had been in battle yourself, though as you swear that you haven't I am puzzled. Or perhaps I should say, overwhelmed yet again by your genius. How do you know these things, Mr. Shaw?'

'I think I can imagine which passages in my works you are referring to ... but my genius in many cases is quite spurious! Keep quiet about this, won't you? My 'genius', if you like, consists in doing exactly what I am doing now, that is to say, picking the brains of those who really know, and making sure they do not fob me off with comforting platitudes. I need to know everything. And, in war matters, the horrible truths that you soldiers try to make sure we civilians do not find out ... And that has been the case even after the last horrible war, in which millions of civilians were involved. Only a few people here and there have been telling the rest of us what it was like. As for myself, I just <u>have</u> to know.'

They pause and look at each other, and Monty puts out both hands, Shaw grasps them, and they become conspirators.

Shaw then resumes, 'You see, I had no formal education at all. School for me in Dublin as a boy was a nonsense and a misery. I came to London with my mother and I contrived to educate myself, like Karl Marx, in the British Museum Library, and of course in the London cultural and political scene. That was heaven to me. I learnt at a phenomenal rate. I met great men like William Morris, I saw his workshops and his printing works, I learnt to look at paintings, and, as you probably know, I became a regular music critic under the pen-name of Corno di Bassetto. I also became an Art critic for many years, once I had become sure of myself in that sphere. As I said, I like both to know and also to hold forth on just about everything. Does that make me some kind of charlatan, do you think?'

'Not necessarily Mr. Shaw ... Please continue. All this is precisely what I came to hear.'

'Thankyou sir, thankyou. I am glad I am not boring you. Now I have reached nearly ninety I talk even more unstoppably than ever, and sometimes I even talk nonsense, I fear. I rattle on, and some people say I am like a lot of dry peas rattling in a tin-can.'

'Not to me, Mr. Shaw,' says Monty. 'Please resume.'

'Well, as I was saying to you, whenever my Library learning felt inadequate ... which is to say, much of the time ... I simply collared all sorts of people, high and low, and persuaded them to talk to me at length. Now that itself takes talent of a special sort, you know ... not everyone unbuttons ... it has to be felt as a kind of special occasion in their lives. I make people feel special ... and then they tell me everything they know. And then also I can tell them a few important, mainly political, things, for at these times they will listen to me with interest and respect. Now, where were we?'

'Your education, Mr. Shaw.'

'Ah yes … Well of course the main part of it was practical-political. In order really to understand politics and economics one needs to be practically involved, and, oh heavens that takes time and energy, oh heavens it takes it out of you! Well of course I know H.G.Wells and Sidney and Beatrice Webb, and a whole host of people in that sphere, and I did practical and boring work alongside them for years on end … I was a Vestryman at St. Pancras for a long time, dealing with every practical thing, street lighting, drains, sewage, tram-lines … oh heavens, I learnt a lot. But oh, how it interfered with my personal and artistic life. It was drudgery, but I needed to know first-hand, so I undertook the drudgery. Of course people like Sidney Webb just love drudgery of that sort. Webb is a drudge.'

'Didn't you once say that the trouble with Socialism is that it takes up too many of one's evenings?'

'Ah, you know me well. Yes, I did say that. But it is through learning how things get done that one also learns how things don't get done … and I mean in this case the Parliamentary system, I'm afraid.'

'Is that what led you to support the dictators Mr. Shaw?'

'Certainly. Certainly. I like to see necessary things get done. Poor old Mussolini did good things for Italy before he embarked on his silly Imperialism. Hitler too, for a short while. And Stalin certainly.'

'But the Treason Trials, and the killings! What about all that.?'

'Well I fear I might have been wrong about Stalin. I feel I have not taken seriously enough the corruption that comes about through the exercise of power … there are depths of evil I have not been aware of. I seem in many ways to belong to a bygone age. And it does seem to me now that the Parliamentary system, with all its faults, is the best thing we have. By the same token, we still need you military men, which is something, after the last abominable war, that I could never imagine myself saying. But as for Stalin, well, we all have to button our lips for the moment, don't we? But now I want you to tell me the answers to some of my military questions. It's your turn now!'

'Thankyou,' says Monty, 'But let me first draw your attention to those passages in your plays where you already show remarkable knowledge of military things ... I mean of principles that are my own principles ... things that you said nearly forty years ago that my military thinking has led me to believe are true. I've often wondered how you came to know and understand ...'

Shaw just nods, and Monty carries on, 'Well first of all there is that wonderful scene in 'Arms and the Man', where the soldier, Bluntschli, isn't it?'

Shaw nods again.

'The chocolate soldier!' They both laugh. 'This tough professional soldier has broken into the romantic woman's bedroom, seeking to escape his pursuing enemies in one of the Balkan Wars ... which one doesn't seem to matter, does it?'

They both laugh again.

'In the course of their confrontation in that bedroom the woman says, 'Though I am only a woman, I think I am at heart as brave as you.' And leaving aside the question if the common notion of women's lack of bravery is not itself a romantic myth...' says Monty.

'Yes yes yes,' says Shaw impatiently.

'Your soldier says, 'I should think so. You haven't been under fire for three days as I have. I can stand two days without showing it much; but no man can stand three days. I'm as nervous as a mouse ... Would you like to see me cry?' Well, I swear I did not remember your passage and then apply it, but I also swear that the resting of whole units of men after, at the very most, two days of battle, is one of my most important principles.'

'And now generally accepted in the Army I suppose', says Shaw.

'No, not generally accepted! ' says Monty emphatically. 'Not generally accepted at all. I employ several principles that are not generally accepted. I look after the welfare of the ordinary soldier to a meticulous extent that is unfortunately far from being generally accepted. All sorts of things that I think and do are not yet generally accepted! In that way you have been to me an inspiration. You have had to wait a long time and endure ridicule and anger and contempt before some of your understandings were accepted. I have learnt patience, and partly from you.'

Shaw is moved by this, and lowers his head to hide his emotion. 'But I have been wrong almost as much as I have been right, and now I am having to learn about that.'

'Oh I think you exaggerate where you have been wrong,' says Monty. 'But let me tell you the other passage in which you show real knowledge of battle-situations. It is in your play called 'Getting Married', and what a wonderful comedy that is!'

'What? Marriage?' Shaw interrupts naughtily.

'Possibly that as well, but not in my case,' says Monty. 'For me the love of a wonderful woman was pure bliss.'

'You say '<u>was</u> pure bliss', says Shaw. 'Am I to understand that your wife is…'

'Dead. Yes.' says Monty. 'Died of a mere scratch really. Blood-poisoning.'

'Confounded doctors again,' says Shaw, getting onto one of his hobby-horses, but desisting this time.

'They obviously did their best,' says Monty. 'As for me, I can hardly talk about it. But I sense we have much in common, and that you understand my loss … And what my wife was to me, in the sense of what she made up for.'

'A cold mother, I imagine. Exactly the same in my case. Exactly the same … How remarkable. And that you sensed the same in me. Remarkable. Do go on.'

'Well in your play you have the General talking to one Hotchkiss, who describes himself quite shamelessly as 'Celebrated Coward, late Lieutenant in the 165th Fusiliers.' Then another character describes the incident which led to the charge of cowardice. But the General's response is surprising. In effect he excuses him, saying his military experience has told that the nerve of the bravest man can desert him at times. Everything depends on the situation. And as far as your actual play is concerned, one realises for certain at that very point that your General is no buffoon. If the actor has played him as a military buffoon, then at that precise point the actor is shown to be a fool himself! Am I not right in that, Mr. Shaw?'

'You are absolutely right, sir, and your insight is remarkable. I could not of course direct and control every performance of my plays, so I'm afraid he was sometimes played as a buffoon, so that the passage you refer to came over often making me look like a fool as a playwright, not the actor looking a fool. But it is unavoidable in the theatre. Too many rampant egos. Anyway, go on.'

At this point the door opens and Augustus John puts his head round. 'Have you two done yet,' he asks bluntly.

'No of course we haven't done,' says Shaw equally bluntly, 'we've barely begun, and this is the most interesting conversation I've had for a long time. Be off, Augustus, be off!'

'Very well' says Augustus 'Just knock on this door when you're ready. I've got plenty to do in here.'

'Good.' says Shaw. 'Now tell me what else the General said, if you can remember.'

'Oh I can remember very well. He said that some very honourable men should never go into action at all, because they are not built that way. At the time I was myself shocked by this. But experience of men and experience of battle has taught me better. And I now insist on the principle that it is far better to find a man a job he can do than to force him into something that he can't. When I reflect on the matter, it occurs to me that there are thousands of professional soldiers who should not and do not go into battle, though the Army keeps that a close secret, as you can imagine. Well what is true of the professional soldier is even more true for the poor conscript, is it not? Not every soldier can charge into battle with fixed bayonet and do the dastardly things with bayonets that we are paid to do. Not every man can be a silent killer, killing another in a few seconds with swift punches. I am pretty certain I could not do that job myself, be the enemy as evil as could be. Nor could I creep up on a man and slice his head off with piano-wire, though some, as you know, are trained for just that. Stupid Army Commanders think we are all the same, say so, and unwittingly do great harm to morale.'

There is a pregnant silence. Then Shaw says 'You and I are indeed blood brothers. Our mental processes are very similar, and our conclusions similarly shocking sometimes. People think we are trying to be clever, and to shock, but we are not, are we?'

'Not at all' says Monty.

'But tell me more,' says Shaw at last. 'Tell me more. What I would most like to know is what it is like to go forward into battle, as a group, and that part of a larger group, and so on, with whom communications must be kept intact, surely, throughout the proceedings. Communications of all groups with the main HQ, but also of each group with at least some of the others. I cannot quite see how, amid such a violent and chaotic thing as warfare, communications can be kept intact, and orders made clear at all times. After the first hour or two of battle, for which each unit no doubt has its plan and orders, how can the men be sure if they are meant to go on doing what they started with doing? And if unexpected obstacles appear, the same question must be asked.'

'Mr Shaw, you have hit upon one of the very things it has been my life's work to ponder, and try to solve. I am not reconciled to accepting quite the depth of the 'fog of war' that many of my colleagues accept as inevitable. The senior Officers I have trained are fortunately of my opinion, and in any major Command I am offered I will of course sack those who are incapable or unwilling to adopt my methods, and bring in my own men.'

'But why haven't you got a major Command at the moment, sir? Look at the hopeless mess in North Africa. You would think at the moment that no one could do worse! I am shocked, Montgomery!'

'Partly prejudice, Mr. Shaw ... and partly my own tactlessness. I tend to upset people when I express myself thoughtlessly. For all I have said about my sensitivity to the needs of the common soldier, and to the officers beneath me, I somehow cannot always manage respect to those above me. Especially when I reflect upon the incompetence and heartlessness of the most superior Staff Officers in the last war. Their main principle seemed to be that it simply didn't matter how many men were killed, you just pushed more men forward. And if the casualties were on occasion too many even for Field Marshal Haig, well then he just lied about them. Simple, isn't it!'

'Of course, of course,' says Shaw. 'But a pity you couldn't watch your tongue all the same. Your weakness there has clearly held you back. I wish you more luck, sir, and speedily. Anyway, come back to your principles. Come back to my question.'

'You can assume that all my principles are built around achieving the maximum effect with the minimum of casualties. If one risks too many casualties, morale will suffer ... and perhaps collapse. I cannot see another generation of the British and their Allies agreeing to suffer as the last generation did. We have already seen the collapse of France, partly at least on account of that fear.'

'Certainly, certainly.' says Shaw.

' As to communication between units when an Army is moving forward, I have done my best to improve that, but have been only partly tested, at Dunkirk, and only as a Divisional Commander, but I was the best Commander out there, I think, and there are those such as Alanbrooke who will say so. But I have not yet had the full opportunity, I'm sorry to say.'

'Who or what is the chief obstacle to your advancement, sir?'

'Churchill.'

Shaw gives a deep and prolonged sigh. 'My dear fellow, my poor dear fellow! There was a time when I was in a position to take Churchill by both lapels, put my angry face within two millimetres of his and bellow 'Now look here, Winston, just you listen to me!'

And he damned well had to! That man made so many damnable mistakes in his career, he has no right at all to be high and mighty about other men of genius, even though he is now indispensable, or was, if my reading of the present situation is correct.'

'I hear such rumours myself Mr. Shaw.'

'Well, he has at least done his bit, whatever happens next. But blindness and arrogance is no part of that, and is inexcusable. Unfortunately I am no longer in a position to shake Mr. Churchill up – my star has waned. '

'But I haven't proved what you call my genius, that's the problem. I'm not too sure of it myself at times.'

'I'm glad you only say 'at times', sir. For you must be convinced of it, if you can, at all times. You say you haven't proved it, but I can sense genius, and I can see it in your eyes.

So have no doubts about that. It only needs the opportunity.'

'You are most kind Mr. Shaw, and I am most obliged by your generosity. I am deeply grateful to you. You warm the cockles of my heart, Mr. Shaw.'

'Say no more about it. I will do what I can for you. But please now continue the exposition of your principles in battle.'

'Well, as to communication during battle, you have stated most of my principles already, in your line of questioning. I have tightened up and multiplied the means of communication. Also, I have decided to have a Tactical HQ, separate most of the time from Main HQ, and far nearer to the front-line. in spite of the obvious dangers to myself and my hand-picked Staff there. I feel invulnerable, as a matter of fact. But I cannot explain that to an atheist.'

'Oh I am not quite the atheist you imagine, sir. But never mind. Do carry on, please.'

'In addition to this I will have a hand-picked team of Liaison Officers up at Tactical HQ with me, and I will see them twice a day, and be able to make on the spot decisions – and with a basis of knowledge of the real situation far more accurate than ever before. These Liaison Officers will be prepared to take enormous risks to themselves in order to get their information.'

'And all this, you think, will clear the fog of battle, do you think, sir?'

'No, Mr. Shaw. I might at times have to pretend so … but the fog will still be there. But it will enable me to make better judgments than before. I will know better when to modify a plan, and in time, in time. We shall be saving time throughout. And I will have a Chief of Staff on the Napoleonic principle. That will also speed things up. And in conjunction with another principle, we should do much better in battle than we have so far done in this confounded war.

'My other principle is this. I will try to convey to all the troops, as clearly as possible, the plan of battle, and the place of each man within the plan. Each man must have the clearest possible idea of his own role. Each man must feel himself to be important –as he is, of course – this is not a confidence trick. This clarity of plan, and clarity of role, I will emphasise to the officers at all times. The most complex situations must be clearly understood by the senior officers, and each officer must be able to communicate this to his subordinates in the clearest way. And it must be reducible, in the last analysis, to clear terse orders in the heat of battle. Not to printed missives flying to and fro between offices. I aim to reduce paperwork, and paper orders, to an absolute minimum. All men must learn to remember – and all officers must learn to simplify, and to communicate clearly … I want no clever fools around, if you understand me!'

'Only too well sir! I have had my own bellyful of clever fools. Chiefly Theatre-Directors in my case. But all that you say is just common sense.'

'It is perhaps because humanity has been lacking, that common sense has been lacking. If there had been the motive to save lives, then these principles would have been adopted years ago. The military authorities will say that they knew them all the time, that they didn't need me to tell them, and so on.'

'Of course they will. That is the way the world wags. Yes indeed. My dear fellow, many of them have done the same to me. When I began my career as a playwright I wrote some revolutionary plays with some shocking social ideas. Many of course said at the time that I was just a hothead, and would grow out of it. Others said I was a propagandist merely, and not a true artist. But when I advanced into middle age, and was bitterly disillusioned by the war, and wrote my 'Heartbreak House', the same people – or probably the same people- now they said 'Look, Mr. Shaw has lost his fire. Where are the ideas, the ideals? He is not the man that he was. He has burnt himself out, and is not worth listening to.' And now that I am an old and visionary man, who has written 'Back to Methusaleh' and other things, and who talks too much… who talks more than ever, I am ashamed to say. Well, what do they say now? They say 'We prefer the Shaw of middle age, the man of sound worldly judgment, and of ideas belonging to this world. Now he is just a garrulous and half-senile old man.' And so, at the end of all this, two propositions stand strangely together. The first one is this. 'Mr. Shaw is undoubtedly a man of genius'. And the second is this. 'At no time in his life have his works been worth seeing or reading or listening to.' Now what do you make of that?'

Shaw puts his hands on his knees, and shouts with laughter, leaning right forward and looking into Monty's eyes. Monty lights up and stares back intently and intensely, and then bursts into laughter himself, his express-train laugh.

The door opens, and Augustus John puts his head round again.

'Oh go away Augustus!' says Shaw. 'Can't you hear we're enjoying ourselves?'

'Just checking,' says Augustus 'Take your time.'

'We certainly will,' says Shaw. 'We certainly will....Silly old fool. No common sense!' he whispers.

Monty becomes serious again. 'You had some complex economic ideas to make clear in your 'Widowers' Houses', Mr. Shaw. But all I'm saying is 'Be Clear, and Explain things clearly to your men.' Why should such a thing be so resisted?'

'Now where have I heard that principle before? 'Explain, explain, explain.' Would it not be one Vladimir Ulyanov Lenin sir?'

'Well possibly, Mr. Shaw, if you say so.'

'I do say so sir, explain, explain, and then again explain. Yes, you are indeed the Lenin of the British Army. You are a dangerous revolutionary, sir, and I'm not sure we should be seen talking together!'

They both laugh a little, then both explode into laughter, slapping hands on their thighs and rocking backwards and forwards, and then drumming their feet on the floor.

'You are a splendid fellow Mr. Shaw … I'm just sorry I can't share your politics. I hate the British class-system, it stifles thought and advancement in the Army. But further than that I cannot go.'

'Well we share that particular hatred, and I've lost my dictator-fervour, so I don't think we're now particularly far apart.'

'In some ways we are very close. Why, with the English upper and middle classes, is there such a distrust of clear principles and clear explanation?'

'Oh my dear fellow,' says Shaw, 'the English will never thank you for thinking clearly, they prefer a fog. Do not, whatever you do, expect from upper-middle class England, any thanks for making things clear. They will call you shallow, and lacking in poetry and imagination. And this especially if your clarity requires some change in the system of things. If you cannot see the beauty of their shabby compromises, they will tell you that you have no soul and no imagination, that you are French and logic-bound. They will say that your emotional life is undeveloped ... all because you don't share their peculiar English mentality. I tell them willingly what they know already, that I am certainly not an Englishman. And I'm not sure that you are either sir ... I seem to detect something of the Celt beneath the clipped accents?'

'Certainly, Mr. Shaw. We are from Ireland as a family, with a deeper background in Normandy, I imagine. I think we came over with the Conqueror ...'

'And so I think did we.'

'Certainly there has been something in me that has not gone with the grain of English life as I have known it,' says Monty. 'But that indeed may have been because I was emotionally undeveloped. But my dear wife Betty has helped me there, and I know that my merely logical principles are infused with life and humanity now. I do not doubt that. And in communicating with the men, the common soldier, I begin to find a spiritual bond between us. They are grateful for my clarity as well as for my concern for their welfare and well-being. And their gratitude gives back to me something that I find I need. I love my men, Mr. Shaw, and I believe many of them love me. My wife taught me love, developed me wonderfully, and now I am able to convey it in many ways. I become clear about it, as is my way. But I become a different person. That is a mystery, the change in me. That I cannot explain logically. But when I do become clear about some deep thing and attempt to explain it clearly, then I again come up against an English sort of brickwall!'

'Oh the English love the ineffable!' says Shaw. 'If you ask them if they have any philosophy of life, they will say that possibly they have, possibly they haven't. But that even if they have, people like ourselves cannot hope to understand it, for it cannot be stated in mere words. You can only grasp it directly, without words, or you cannot grasp it at all. And if you do try to grasp directly you will find yourself no further forward. For if you go on to ask, Is this the thing I am supposed to be grasping? If, in short, you ask 'Is this it?' Well, they will say it is quite impossible to tell, for the whole thing is quite ineffable. So there can be no verbal communication whatever about this very important thing we are all supposed to value, this unstateable thing. You cannot know if you yourself have grasped it, because no one will tell you, and you cannot find out if anyone else has grasped it, because these things are not talked about, ever! So that is English life, a comfortable mutual isolation. The Englishman is kind in his own special way, but, by heaven, he does precious little to reduce the gulf between man and man! Well sir, are the important things in life absolutely ineffable, in your opinion, sir?'

'Not at all, Mr. Shaw, not at all. I tell the men, the most important people in the Army are the nurses and the padres, the nurses because they care for you if you are wounded, and the padres because they convey to you, if they are any good, that God cares for you, and will fulfil you, even if you have to die on the battlefield. It is perfectly simple. God in Himself may be ineffable, but his love is not ineffable when you can feel it and see it, in the face of the padre, and often in the faces of comrades around you, including your officers, sometimes. What is ineffable about that? Without what I here describe, how would many of the men fight on, even in a just cause? And why shouldn't I speak as I find it, in the simplicity of my own heart?'

'You are right to do so sir, and it warms my heart to hear your words. Heavens, all good men hate war and the suffering and chaos it brings. Not only wounds and death, but the brutality, the brutal necessity of it sometimes. But sometimes it is unavoidable, and never more than now. But if we must have you military men a bit longer, we must have you human, and giving clear human messages. If we cannot communicate the values that are important, if we cannot give a clear account of them, why should we expect from the common man any special effort, any loyalty? But if we can communicate them, and if we practise them, then I can hardly imagine a limit to what the men will do for us, and for themselves … They will do wonders, and come to know God at the same time.'

'Mr. Shaw, I wish you could come to my Command area in the South of England with me. I would put you on top of my Armoured Car, or whatever, and in front of the men, and I would just say, 'Talk. Talk, Mr. Shaw. Talk about anything you like. Whatever you happen to say on the spur of the moment will be pure gold, and the men will love it. You have the gift of spontaneous utterance, to add to all your other gifts. And you make the most serious things amusing and exhilarating, just as in your plays. As for myself, I have to think and plan everything beforehand, including the exact words I will say to the men.
It is a somewhat tedious business, but that is how I have to do it.

Well I know I have these gifts, sir, but, at many times, the more effortless my brilliance, the more I am distrusted. A few mumbled and groping words, with poor grammar and jumbled syntax, would often have stood me in better stead with the English public. As for my being amusing, that too has often been to my disadvantage. I cannot help being amusing, sir, it is as natural to me as walking or breathing. And because every breath that I venture is scented with humour, the English will have it that I am not being serious. And that is just another reason to them for not paying much attention to what I say.'

'Everything you have said today has been a delight to me, Mr. Shaw, and an inspiration for my own task. It has been a privilege to talk to you, a privilege and an honour'

Monty gets up, extends his hand, and they shake hands.

'I'm afraid I won't stay any longer, delightful though it is,'says Monty, 'for I rather dread meeting that man again today.' He gestures towards Augustus John's studio. 'For to tell you the truth I do not like him, and his presence oppresses me. I like him even less than I like his portrait of me. What is it about him? Something grubby and distasteful – too many loose women around, Mr. Shaw.'

'I entirely agree' says Shaw ' but it all rolls off my back. Since I am never tempted in the direction of his rather grubby women, the situation here does not bother me. So, goodbye sir, and it has been a privilege and an honour for myself as well to exchange some thoughts with you.'

They shake hands again, and Monty leaves. Shaw goes to sit in his chair for a few moments, takes a notebook from his pocket and writes furiously for a while, and is still writing when Augustus John comes in.

'Well Mr. Shaw,' he says 'all is ready and prepared. But I see something has stimulated your imagination. It surely cannot have been Montgomery, can it? What a dry boring limited soul he is!'

'O certainly it was Montgomery my good fellow. A most interesting man.'

Shaw stops writing, gets up, and they walk into the studio.

'A most interesting man,' Shaw continues, 'I'm sorry you find him dry. Might I perhaps be permitted a glance at your portrait of him?'

'Well certainly, if you must,' says Augustus. 'You certainly seemed to be having a mountain of a time together, you two. How you get him to talk, I can't imagine. I could hardly get a word out of him.'

He is going to a corner of the studio, and turns round the portrait of Monty, which had been face to the wall. Shaw stares for a few moments, and says, 'Well I'm not surprised you couldn't get a word out of him. This is not Montgomery at all. This portrait is yourself Mr. John. Did you attempt to engage him on subjects of his interest, Augustus?'

'Well, no. Or rather, he doesn't seem to have any subjects of interest, except his war and strategy, and that doesn't interest me.'

'Then you are the poorer for it, and your portrait is the poorer for it, for in not engaging him in his chief passion you have thereby failed to excite him, and you have failed to see his extraordinary eyes. It is the amazing burning eyes that look right into you, these are the thing. These, and his general comportment. A compacted hank of steel wire. All this spells genius. The man is a genius, just like you or I. And you, my dear fellow, have for once failed in your mission. It is a pity, but there it is.'

'I suppose you are right Mr. Shaw. Too bad, too bad.' he says, pushing the portrait back to its previous position. 'But now let us sit down, and let me resume the task of communicating your special genius to the general public. At least it is entertaining, whereas, as for that man …'

'My dear fellow, he has a wild and wicked sense of humour, but you've missed that too. You've missed that too.'

Chapter 13 – Monty as Commander

<u>August 1942</u>

Alanbrooke is on the phone from his Commander of the Imperial General Staff (CIGS) office in London.

'Hullo, is that you, Monty? Monty, your time has come. You are appointed Commander of the 8th Army in North Africa, and Alexander is to be your boss, based in Cairo.'

'Thank you, Alanbrooke! You have worked things out for me after all. Thank you!'

'No, it's fate that has worked it for you more than I have ... '

'What do you mean?'

'You are Commander because Gott is dead.'

'Gott is dead?'

'Killed in an air crash. Brought down by Messerschmitts over Greece. Plane burst into flames on hitting the ground. All on board burnt to death. Horrible. But there it is. You're in charge. Get over there as soon as possible, as things are pretty desperate. Auchinleck is relieved both of his overall command, based in Cairo, and of his 8th Army Command. Churchill has suddenly lost faith in him.'

'About time, too. Damned silly of Auchinleck to combine the two jobs anyway. Barely capable of doing the one ... Right, I shall get ready. Fancy having dear old Alexander over me. We shall get on splendidly.'

'We all hope so, Monty. We're all hoping for a fresh impetus.'

'Impetus!' says Monty, 'There'll be as many sacked Commanders arriving in London as bloody German bombs ... that's part of the impetus, I can tell you!'

'Steady on, Monty. Don't judge people in advance, and don't create needless pain and resentment! After all, you don't know what's really going on over there. You don't know the details.'

'But I <u>do</u> know what's really going on, without knowing the details. The details I will get to know in about two hours.'

'Yes, Monty, you are very acute. (Did anyone ever suggest you were clairvoyant?). However, do take care all the same ... not too many ruffled feathers ... promise me, Monty?'

'I always listen to what you say, Alanbrooke, and I do my best to keep your words in my head as I sack people. I do try to spare pain as much as possible.'

12th August 1942

A plane touches down at Cairo Airport. It is stiflingly hot. A clock shows 9am. Monty emerges and asks for a taxi to GCHQ, where we see him arriving and entering the building. There is an awkward meeting there between Monty and Auchinleck.

'You know I'm going?' says Auchinleck, a large, craggy man, nicknamed 'The Auk', after some imagined noble bird of prey.

'Yes!' says Monty, whose head only reaches as high as the Auk's medals.

A pause.

'But I'm still in charge of 8th Army till the 15th August. Please remember that. Go down to the 8th for a couple of days, and look around, before taking over.'

'Yes,' says Monty. 'May I see General Harding, please?'

Monty walks out of the office, and waits for General Harding to arrive. Harding is amazed and pleased to see his old colleague from student days at Camberley.

'Monty! What on earth are you doing here?'

'In charge of 8th Army, John. And not a moment too soon! Now, John, can you create a sort of Panzer Force for me? To be held in reserve, ready to strike and move fast at the right moment?'

'I can try, Monty, with the Sherman tanks that will soon be arriving here ... But how soon do you want to know?'

'By six o'clock this evening, John, at Shepherd's Hotel.'

'What!' cries Harding, 'But on the other hand, why not?'

'Right, off you go, John. Now, who is Chief of Staff of Armour round here? Old Freddie de Guingand, isn't it? I shall need to see him too.'

Harding leaves. Monty goes to an office to telephone. He is soon speaking.

'Hullo, Freddie! This is Monty. I'm in charge of 8th Army, and we need to meet. Where are you exactly? Well, can you be at the Alexandria – Cairo crossroads at about 7 tomorrow morning? You can? Good. We'll drive off to Alamein together ... should be there by about 10am. I need to have a good look round, and to pick your brains pretty extensively. Goodbye!'

He leaves the Command Office, walks out into the foyer of the building again, and is amazed to see General Alexander entering it from outside.

'Well, hullo Alex! You here already?'

Alexander is elegant, handsome, self-assured, but sensitive to others and without vanity ... a 'perfect gentleman'.

'Hullo Monty, I see you're here before me. Where can we talk?'

'Shepherd's Hotel,' says Monty, 'Know it of old. Here in early 1930s. Excellent place. Good food, atmosphere, dark corners, privacy, talk without fear. Harding arriving there at 6pm. Got to pick his brain.'

As they talk, Monty leads Alexander out of the building to a taxi. They arrive at the famous Shepherd's Hotel in central Cairo, and enter its voluminous mosque-like interior with awe. They make for a dark corner, and order food and drink.

'I have just asked Harding to assemble a Panzer force for me, Alex. Do you agree with that?'

'Certainly, Monty, it sounds just what we will need.'

'Look Alex, you know changes have got to be made out here, pretty drastic changes ... will you back me up when I make those changes, Alex?'

'You know I have huge confidence in you as a Commander, Monty, and will support and provide anything you ask.'

There is a moment of silence, while Monty enjoys the trust that is placed in him.

'This is like a dream,' says Monty, 'Suddenly I seem to have everything I want, and no one trying to cramp me and fence me in. Nothing like this has ever happened to me before, Alex. Is it real?'

'It's certainly real on my part, Monty. We've both waited long for moments like this. And we surely can't do worse than the poor old Auk in recent months ... I feel sorry for him, he is worn out, but doesn't really know it. The desert seems to be a grave for British Generals, Monty. We can't change the desert, can we?'

'I love the desert,' says Monty, 'I was here in the early 30s, did night exercises in the desert, huge fun. Worked with dear old Freddie de Guingand here ... he was a master of staff work. So I got him into Camberley for Staff Training, and now he's out here too. I'll probably use him ... you like Freddie, don't you, Alex?'

'Very much, and who doesn't?' says Alex. 'Yes, it does seem a bit of a dream. Working with people one <u>likes</u> for a change. Too good to be true.'

'I shall make sure all the people in my TAC HQ are men I like, and good fresh young men who know how to think for themselves, and who don't bellyache, and who also know how to enjoy themselves!'

'Freddie's good at that, isn't he?' says Alex.

'Freddie's the same old wine, women and song, yes,' says Monty. 'I shall probably have Freddie at Main HQ, in charge of everything. He will no doubt be surrounded by men as cheerful as himself ... not bellyachers ... and who enjoy themselves, if not necessarily in Freddie's way! We have to be ourselves even while working together, is that not so, Alex?'

'Certainly, Monty, certainly. What a change that will be! Poor old Alanbrooke could do with a break from Churchill, but he's not going to get it, I fear. What a man, what a man!'

'Who, Churchill or Alanbrooke?' asks Monty.

'Well, I meant Alanbrooke, actually, but of course Churchill as well. Yet what a bully he, Churchill, can be. So damned unreasonable when he feels like it, and so <u>romantic</u>, living in fantasy half the time. Hare-brained schemes. Interfering with well-thought-out plans of his Generals, losing faith in them all the time. Panicking ... well, not exactly <u>panic</u>, no, that's not fair. But impulsiveness, sudden tempers, grudges, and stubborn clinging to things he <u>knows</u> are not true! Clinging to his feelings, his grudges ... a big sulky child sometimes. But with strokes of genius as well. We can't do without him, but I'm so glad I don't have to work there, on the spot, with him. No doubt I shall get several earfuls of him out here in Cairo, but that's not the same as being pestered by the old bullfrog in person every day, and indeed at any hour of the <u>night</u>! Poor old Alanbrooke. Honourable man, tower of strength and integrity. But the strain might break him, and then where will we be?'

'Is 'bullfrog' the right way to refer to our Prime Minister and great cheer leader?' asks Monty with a bright laugh. 'Churchill's grudges I know only too well,' he goes on seriously, 'He's been against me all along. But perhaps we'll bring him round, Alex, perhaps we will.'

'Nothing like a good victory in the field, for that, Monty. Tobruk has broken his heart. Go down into the desert, and defeat old Rommel, and Churchill will become your lifelong 'buddy', as the Yanks say.'

'If you will give me all the support I need, I think I can do that,' says Monty.

'I've already said I will,' says Alexander, 'Can't you believe me?'

'I'm just not used to it!' says Monty, smiling, 'Give me a little time!'

'Give you time!' says Alexander, ' You don't give others much time to adapt, do you Monty? No doubt you will ruffle a few feathers down at Alamein, if I know you!'

'And you will smooth them down again, if I know you! "I rough-hews them, and you shapes their ends"'.

'What's that?' asks Alexander.

'Shakespeare wrote, 'There is a destiny that shapes our ends, rough-hew them how we may!' says Monty.

'Not quite clear to me, Monty. Didn't know you were such a scholar?'

'Betty took me to the theatre quite a lot, Alex. Shaw, Ibsen, Shakespeare. Even T.S. Eliot once. I <u>liked</u> it. I learnt a lot. The man who rough-hews is a hedger, Alex, a hedger with a rough bill-hook. And the other fellow is another hedger, who gives shape and grace to the preliminary efforts. May even twist it in another direction. So I'm the rough-hewer, Alex, and you're the shaper. That's how I see things between us, Alex!'

'You are too modest, for once, Monty. I'm sure it's the other way round,' says Alexander, laughing.

'We can't go on meeting like this!' Monty jokes, 'People will begin to suspect we are up to no good!'

'You're absolutely right, Monty,' says Alex, pulling a nearby curtain half-around his face. 'I must make my way back to GCHQ disguised as a Chinaman, while you wait here for John Harding, as nonchalantly as possible. I suggest you change into civilian clothes and do press-ups in the gym.'

'Splendid wheeze, Alex,' says Monty, as they begin to eat and drink.

General Harding arrives at Shepheard's Hotel and seeks out Monty in the same dark corner. He has hardly sat down when Monty says 'How about the Panzer Corps, John?'

'Yes, that will be done, Monty, but we're still waiting for the Sherman tanks to arrive along the Suez Canal. We should use new tanks, not the old ones. The Shermans will be our best tanks by far.'

'Yes, certainly,' says Monty, 'and thank you ... Now, John, you've been out here quite a while. Tell me everything you know, about our Commanders, mainly. Which ones can we keep, and which ones are useless?'

'Well, I wouldn't describe any of them quite as useless,' says John, 'a bit too strong, Monty.'

'You know my meanings, John. If I can't make <u>use</u> of them, they are useless as far as I am concerned. I shall say to them they are not <u>suitable</u> for work under my type of command. And if they are just worn out by this desert campaign, I shall offer them a rest in England. Or possibly an easier job behind the lines. The same goes for the junior officers. If they are jaded, they must be given a rest, and we must draft fresh officers in. The tired ones can serve again later on. You know my principles, John. Frequent rests and holidays. But, of course, if they are <u>absolutely</u> useless, John, they must be sacked. Their is a crucial distinction between 'useless for the present', and <u>absolutely</u> useless ... which means useless at any time ... wrong outlook, wrong attitude, wrong personality. I mean, 'Chink' Dorman-Smith, for instance!'

'He's already been sacked,' says Harding. 'Only yesterday.'

'Such a pity!' says Monty, 'I was so looking forward to that! A real blighter, that man. Full of himself and his own clever-clever ideas. Had more ideas by noon each day than a cod lays eggs. No-one could implement them, too complex. Yet he couldn't see that. Couldn't see they were failing our men time after time ... losing lives. Damned conceited man. I tore a strip off him nearly 20 years ago, when he was a student at Camberley. Made no damned difference. Some men's conceit is as thick as the proverbial rhinoceros-hide, isn't it, John?'

'Yes,' says Harding, a little gingerly, and suppressing a thin smile that was creeping around the corners of his mouth. 'Yes, indeed,' he says quietly. 'But you seem to know everything that's been going wrong out here anyway. Can't see why you need my help.'

'I know a lot,' says Monty, 'I have my spies! But I need to know more, so that I can act swiftly. So just talk, now, and I won't interrupt unless I have to!'

We come back to the end of this monologue by Harding, with Monty still quiet and attentive, and Harding summing up.

'And that's about everything!' says Harding.

'Very good indeed!' says Monty. 'I'm most grateful to you, John. Tomorrow morning I meet with Freddie at the Alexandria crossroads, and we go together to Alamein to have a snout around, and make some decisions.'

'But the Auk's in charge till the 15th of August, Monty, you can only observe till then.'

'I'm not going to let the Auk cramp my style, John. Who's he to order me around? He's no longer boss in Cairo, so he can't boss me around at Alamein. Poor bugger! Yes, I'm sorry for him too.'

13 August 1942

Monty decides to sleep at Shepheard's Hotel, with orders given to be woken at 5am. Soon after that, he is on the Cairo to Alexandria road in a staff car, being driven through the desert to the Alexandria crossroads. At about 7 o'clock, the car arrives there, and Freddie de Guingand is waiting for them. He gets into their car, and it proceeds north west and along the coast towards Alamein. They talk and jest effusively, and de Guingand is also filling Monty in with all he knows, from time to time.

They arrive at the TAC HQ. A General Ramsden is in charge for the time being, until the deadline of 15th August. As they walk up to meet him, they note the depressing aspects of the site. They are introduced.

'Where is the conference room?' Monty asks of General Ramsden.

'Over there, Montgomery, with the blankets thrown over the wire netting,' says Ramsden.

'Is that it?' exclaims Monty, 'Why, it's full of flies! It's like an ineffective meat-safe! You don't mean you officers meet and discuss in there, do you, Ramsden?'

'We do, Montgomery. We don't actually welcome the flies, but the philosophy is that since the rank and file have to put up with flies all day, we officers shouldn't grumble about a few flies.'

'But if you can get rid of the flies, why shouldn't you, Ramsden? Why shouldn't those who are required to think and plan enjoy a modicum of comfort?'

'I think I agree with you, Montgomery. But what can I do, I've been here only a short while, and I'm due to leave on the 15th, in two days time, when I hand over to you.'

'There's no need at all for that,' says Monty. 'You can leave now, Ramsden. I am in charge here, and I order you to leave.'

De Guingand is a little shocked, but just shrugs his shoulders slightly, and smiles gently at Ramsden.

'Surely that is for General Auchinleck to decide,' says Ramsden. 'We are all under his orders until his departure on the 15th.'

'Nonsense!' says Monty. 'Auchinleck is no longer in charge in Cairo, so no longer in charge here, Ramsden. I am in charge here, and I am sending you home.'

'Very well, Montgomery. I will leave you to face the consequences with General Auchinleck and his replacement.'

Ramsden begins to move off.

'Where is the map room, Ramsden?' Monty almost shouts.

'We don't have a map room as such,' says Ramsden. 'Map details are phoned down from Cairo, and we sketch them out ourselves for meetings in the conference room.'

'The meat-safe, you mean,' says Monty. 'No map-room, you mean. Well, well, well. And where is the Officers' Mess?'

'We don't have an Officers' Mess as such ... ' says Ramsden again.

'What the devil do you mean 'as such'?' Monty snaps, 'Either you have a Mess or you don't!'

'There's a small mess for the most senior officers, Montgomery. The rest of the officers mess in the open air, like the rank-and-file. It's all very democratic, you see.'

'It's the wrong sort of democracy!' Monty yells, 'It's a damned nonsense ... no wonder everyone looks miserable! Well, so be it, Ramsden, and, er, goodbye, Ramsden. Goodbye!'

Ramsden walks away, re-faced and angry, but overcome.

Monty turns to De Guingand. 'Look, before we tour this hell-hole, let's find a quiet, shady place where you can tell me the rest of what you know, Freddie. And let's look at the map again first.'

They find a place in the shadow of a lorry, and set out the map.

Freddie de Guingand points to various places on it.

'You'll see that we have a front here all too similar to World War One ... some thirty to forty miles, north to south, all defended, and no easy way to break through, no flanks to turn. Even if we go all the way south, there's no way of operating in the Qattara Depression ... a hopeless area. So the question is, how do we break through, without suffering too many casualties.'

Monty nods, and De Guingand continues.

'However, at the moment it's a question of how we withstand another Rommel attack, which is expected in about a fortnight. We are in no position to attack, the enemy holds nearly all the rocky ridges' (pointing to Kidney Ridge, Ruweisit, Miterieya and

Himeimat), 'and we have been in retreat for some time, as you know.'

Monty nods again. De Guingand goes on, 'Auchinleck let it be known that it is not essential to hold our present Alamein position. He has plans for a defensive battle here, but if the cost is too high he would fall back on the Delta. His main concern is for the Persian and Iraqi oil, not for Egypt. Very important, of course, we can't fight without oil, but all this retreat, and talk of further retreat, has demoralized the troops. And the Auk is not much known among the men, he's not a hero figure, he doesn't inspire. Reticent, decent, honourable, and conscientious to a fault. Discusses plans at great length with his Generals, and allows their ideas to guide him. Endless discussions, and such a regard for his Commanders and their views, that during the actual battle they come to feel it is their right to interpret orders in their own way ... this is especially true of the Tank Regiments.'

'Tell me about the Tanks,' says Monty.

'Well, partly it's their own tradition,' says De Guingand. 'They see themselves as well above the infantry socially, and in every way. It becomes a bit like fox-hunting. These men have a sort of Shires mentality. Tank warfare, they see as a bit like the hunt. They sally out at great speed, pennants flying, inflict a little damage on the enemy, and then retire at speed, often leaving the poor bloody infantry horribly exposed. The infantry go forward, expecting tank protection, and more often than not, don't get it. Feelings are running high in the infantry units at the moment.'

'I suppose our tanks are simply not good enough to stay out for very long?' says Monty.

'Too true,' says De Guingand. 'The German Panzer guns and the 88mm Anti-Tank Gun can knock out our tanks with one shot, usually setting them on fire. It is terrifying for the crews. There has to be a way of protecting the tanks, if they are to perform their proper role alongside infantry. '

'I'll have to think about that,' says Monty. 'But surely we now have a very large numerical superiority in tanks, if not in quality. Wouldn't it be worth suffering big tank casualties in order to get out there and drive Rommel back?'

'If you can get the tank Commanders to agree, which I doubt,' says De Guingand.

'Hmm! I'll see to that, Freddie, don't you worry.'

There is a pause. De Guingand is troubled.

'However,' De Guingand goes on, 'for the time being we are concerned with a defensive battle. Let's think about that. We at least hold Alam Halfa Ridge ... rocky, and about 300 feet above the plain at its highest point. What could we do with that?' (he points to Alam Halfa on the map)

'We could dig in there,' says Monty. 'A fortnight. Just time. I'll need more troops and tanks from Cairo. But Alex will send me those.'

Monty and De Guingand study the map. Monty points to the sandy area immediately south of the Alam Halfa ridge.

'What's the terrain like here?' he asks.

'Much of it is soft sand,' says De Guingand.

'Do the Germans know it?' asks Monty.

'Most unlikely,' says De Guingand, 'They've never been this near to Egypt.'

'Very well. We'll lure them into a trap there, and then pound the living daylights out of them ... That's enough to be going on with, I think. Slow-moving tanks in soft sand. Sitting ducks for our dug-in field guns, and our dug-in tanks. What say you, Freddie?'

'Excellent! But how do we decoy them?'

'First of all, Rommel likes attacking in a southward curve. Secondly, we will put it about that the sand south of Alam Halfa is very firm. Leave evidence, a map, leave it on a broken-down motor cycle, let that be left near enemy lines. Simple. Thirdly, we will put some advancing tanks facing west in the gap there, just south of Alam Halfa. When Rommel attacks they will withdraw eastward, and Rommel will follow ... couldn't be more simple ... I like to read Rommel's mind. I have brought a portrait of him which I intend to hang up in my TAC Headquarters.'

They roll up the map, and begin to walk away.

'And by the way,' says Monty, 'I'm making you my Chief of Staff ... Berthier to my Napoleon. Your command will be my command to every single unit ... and you will speak for me also in our full co-operation with the Air Force and Navy, whose commanders I will now seek out. They have a lovely HQ at Burq-el-Arab, near the sea. Our HQ will be moved there, close to them, and to some fresh air and sea-bathing. How about that?'

'Thank you, Monty, for the honour. And the sea will be splendid.'

'Who are the Air Chiefs now?' Monty asks.

'Portal and Coningham,' says De Guingand, 'And Cunningham for the Navy, Monty.'

'Right,' says Monty. 'Right. We must get that side of things moving pretty quickly.'

They reach their car.

'First of all we must gather together all the senior officers here. I wish to address them this evening. See to that, Freddie. Meanwhile, I'll go and visit some of the units myself, Force and Navy HQs ... ' he tails off.

Finally the two cars set off, the dust rising behind them as their directions diverge.

Monty drives north and arrives at an Australian infantry unit. He joins a group who are hanging out washing and brewing up tea. Monty is of course casually dressed with no signs of rank, so no one salutes him.

'How can we help you, cobber?' says one.

'Are you looking for the new Commander?' says another, ' So are we! Can't wait to see the new disaster ... the one to lead us to the Delta and then beyond, to the mysterious bloody East. The sooner we get to India and those bloody Japs, the more I shall be pleased ... in a sense, anyway ... nearer home, at least that!'

'Well, I am your new Commander,' says Monty, without emphasis. A deadly silence. They all stiffen and salute.

'Don't worry,' says Monty, 'I like to hear your views honestly expressed. Invaluable.'

'We just can't say how sorry we are, sir,' says the man who had said so much. 'No offence to you personally, sir ... I hope you will forgive us!'

Monty laughs lightly.

'Seriously, I want to know your views on the situation here, I really do. It is most important for a Commander to know. And on the everyday situation as well. Food, billets, water, postal services, leave, medical care, cigarettes ... How are those things?'

'Not brilliant, sir, especially letters from home. Pretty erratic, I'd say.'

'Well, I'll soon see to that,' says Monty. 'You'll see, I'm as good as my word.'

'Yes sir. Thank you sir.'

'I'll do what I can. I'll look round for myself. We must make ourselves as comfortable as possible ... Sorry I can't think of what to do about the flies, they're just terrible!'

'They are the devil's legions, sir,' says one. 'We've tried everything. Even tried eating them, sir.'

'Not a bad idea,' says Monty. 'How do you do that?'

'They get into the flour and get baked in the local bread and the hard biscuits, sir. Nothing wrong with that ... probably quite nutritious, sir.'

'I see you are very philosophical,' says Monty, 'Still, you won't need to be quite so philosophical soon, after we've knocked Rommel for six out of Africa!'

There is an awkward silence, while the Australians fiddle evasively with whatever is to hand.

'Heard it all before?' says Monty, 'I expect so. The difference this time is that I mean to do it, and I know I can do it ... I shall be as good as my word in that as well, just trust me ... Hard for you to trust after what you've been through, I know ... But listen,' says Monty eagerly, 'You won't have long to wait. Just about a fortnight. Rommel will attack then, and we will hold him off, we will defeat him ... you can trust a new man just for a fortnight, can't you? Rouse some new spirit and fighting force for just that occasion! And if we fail, and we are both alive, I will come here and you can call me a damned fool and a disaster to my face. Relieve your feelings as we hurtle towards Egypt and the Delta. Heaven forbid, though! Heaven forbid we do that!'

'You honour us greatly,' says one, ' and we hardly know what to say, sir, we are a tough lot of buggers, and we've never looked for any special favours, sir, and we're not inclined to whinge, and the like.'

'But,' says Monty, for them, 'Enough is enough. I <u>do</u> understand. And I hear you're not mightily pleased with some of the Tank regiments?'

'Not mightily pleased!' says one, 'English understatement, sir! Sir, sometimes we hate them, sometimes we could kill them, sir! They've left us high and dry, and they'll hardly talk to us, sir ... snobs ... <u>English</u> snobs, sir. I'm sorry, but it's true.'

'The trouble is,' says another, ' this whole 8th Army doesn't work as a unit, sir. It's all bits and pieces. There's no one to impose his will and make it work together, sir. In that situation, it feels a bit like every man for himself ... and we don't take to dying and being seriously wounded in the situation, sir ... it doesn't seem worth it ... our spirit is almost gone ... But when our spirit is up, we'll fight and we'll die willingly, sir. It's the lack of spirit and hope, sir ... it's a contagion, sir ... it's like the flies, sir ... it's everywhere.'

'I thought as much,' says Monty, 'But it's good of you to tell me. It confirms what I've been feeling even as far away as London. And my few hours here have provided a sad and further confirmation. I know I don't look much like a big Commander, but I do mean to be one!'

'You don't look like a Commander at all, sir,' says another 'I mean, no proper uniform, casual clothes, and no hat!'

' 'And of insignificant stature', I suppose you also meant to say,' Monty says, and laughs. 'These things don't bother me at all. I'm all for hard training, <u>really</u> hard training, but I'm not for drill and bulling your kit, all that sort of thing. Waste of time. And I won't enforce Church Parades on Sundays, either here or on leave (I'm a religious man myself, but religion should be discovered by the individual, not enforced). But as for training ... well, you men look pretty fit, but you're not quite what I would call hard and tough. Just <u>fit</u>, you know. But hard and tough is what we must aim at. Hard and tough and on top of the world physically and mentally ... and even spiritually.'

'Spiritually!' exclaims another.

'Certainly,' says Monty 'At the level of fitness I aim at a man has spiritual reserves. He can learn to fight and kill, but still has the reserves not to hate his enemy.'

'But how can we fight and kill if we don't hate to an extent?' asks another, 'I find it easier to fight if I can hate. Hatred rouses me. I don't know if I would be roused without it.'

'Too bad!' says Monty. 'Perhaps it will be different for you when you are hard and tough. Then you can be above hatred. I mean <u>absolute</u> hatred. I mean, dammit, you can hate your commanding officer at times. But absolute hatred is judging a man for all time, for eternity, in fact. But most of these crazy Nazi Germans are just deluded and sick ... they have been worked on. It's an aberration. The spirit of Germany is different, something the Germans must get back to. We must defeat them and kill them, but it's not necessary to hate ... certainly not at all times. Our lack of hatred, our enormous good spirits, will impress them. They will realize it is <u>we</u> who are the supermen, not themselves. Just think of that!'

Monty pauses, rubs his hands, looks round and smiles at all he sees. 'Still, as you say, I could do with a hat!' he says at last.

'Have one of ours, sir,' says a tall Australian offering Monty an Australian bush-hat, down at one side, up at the other.

'Sir, it's making you look quite ridiculous! Smaller than you are already,' says one. 'But wear it anyway ... our units will love it!'

'Give me a badge of your unit,' says Monty, 'I will then go round all the Australian units and cover my hat with their badges.'

Monty walks off to his car, gets in beside his driver, lifts his hand as he calls out 'Goodbye!'

'Cheerio, sir!' they all call out, incredulous smiles on most of their faces.

The car moves off, the dust rises.

'Well, well, well!' says one.

'Strike me pink!' says another. 'A character!'

'Can you believe him?' asks another.

'Well, as he says, 'We'll soon know, a fortnight."

'Can't wait,' says another, 'Let's give the bugger a chance. So bloody forthright ... Puts his bloody head on the line ... Let's fight for the bugger.'

'If he fails, we can all line up and call him a disaster to his face. What a prospect ...'

'Unprecedented in the annals of military history,' says another with a solemn smile.

We see Monty's car driving from unit to unit, we see him coming casually to groups of men, and engaging them. We see a badge offered at each unit, for his hat. Finally we see him drive off, hat covered in badges, and make for the area of the Officer's Mess, where he meets with Freddie de Guingand again.

'All set for my speech?' asks Monty.

'In about an hour, Monty,' says Freddie. 'Meanwhile have yourself something to eat and drink, and a bath, sir. You look filthy! Only two or three inches of water, mind you, sir, and in a tin tub, sir.'

'Don't teach me about roughing it, Freddie. I'm quite used to that.'

'And, sir, what is that ridiculous hat for?'

'I'm very proud of it, Freddie. I can't part with it.'

'Indeed, sir!' says Freddie, sounding like Jeeves.

'Indeed, indeed,' replies Monty. 'Do I detect a note of butlerish disapproval, Freddie?'

'You do, sir. Certainly sir. Still, when you see hundreds of men sniggering behind their hands as they listen to you addressing them, you will begin to think differently.'

Monty goes off to clean up.

An hour later Monty, still with his hat, stands up to address the Officers of the 8th Army.

'I think I can see you better without this hat,' he says, having detected grins here and there. He takes it off and lays it on the table.

'I want first of all to introduce myself to you. You do not know me. I do not know you. But we have got to work together;

therefore we must understand each other, and we must have confidence each in the other. I have only been here a few hours. But from what I have seen and heard since I arrived I am prepared to say, here and now, that I have confidence in you. We will then work together as a team; and together we will gain the confidence of this great Army and go forward to final victory in Africa.

'I believe that one of the first duties of a commander is to create what I call 'atmosphere', and in that atmosphere his staff, subordinate commanders, and troops will live and work and fight.

'I do not like the general atmosphere I find here. It is an atmosphere of doubt, of looking back to select the next place to which to withdraw, of loss of confidence in our ability to defeat Rommel, of desperate defence measures by reserves in preparing positions in Cairo and the Delta.

' All that must cease.

'Let us have a new atmosphere.'

' The defence of Egypt lies here at Alamein and on the Ruweisat Ridge. What is the use of digging trenches in the Delta? It is quite useless; if we lose this position we lose Egypt; all the fighting troops now in the Delta must come here at once, and will. **Here we will stand and fight; there will be no further withdrawal.** I have ordered that all plans and instructions dealing with further withdrawal are to be burnt, and at once. We will stand and fight <u>here</u>.

'If we can't stay here alive, then let us stay here dead.'

'I want to impress on everyone that the bad times are over. Fresh Divisions from the UK are now arriving in Egypt, together with ample reinforcements for our present Divisions. We have 300 to 400 Sherman new tanks coming and these are actually being unloaded at Suez <u>now.</u> Our mandate from the Prime Minister is to destroy the Axis forces in North Africa; I have seen it, written on half-a-sheet of notepaper. And it will be done. If anyone here thinks it can't be done, let him go at once; I don't want any doubters in this party. It can be done, and it will be done: beyond any possibility of doubt.

'Now I understand that Rommel is expected to attack at any moment. Excellent. Let him attack.

'I would sooner it didn't come for a week, just give me time to sort things out ... If we have two weeks to prepare we will be sitting pretty; Rommel can attack as soon as he likes, after that, and I hope he does.

'Meanwhile, we ourselves will start to plan a great offensive; it will be the beginning of a campaign which will hit Rommel and his Army for six right out of Africa.

'But first we must create a reserve Corps, mobile and strong in armour, which we will train <u>out of the line</u>. Rommel has always had such a force in his Africa Corps, which is never used to hold the line but which is always in reserve, available for striking blows. Therein has been his great strength. We will create such a Corps ourselves, a British Panzer Corps; it will consist of two armoured Divisions and one motorised Division; I gave orders yesterday for it to begin to form, back in the Delta.

'I have no intention of launching our great attack until we are completely ready; there will be pressure from many quarters to attack soon; <u>I will not attack until we are ready,</u> and you can rest assured on that point.

'Meanwhile, if Rommel attacks while we are preparing, let him do so with pleasure; we will merely continue with our own preparations and <u>we</u> will attack when <u>we</u> are ready, and not before.

'I want to tell you that I always work on the Chief of Staff system. I have nominated Brigadier de Guingand as Chief of Staff 8th Army. I will issue orders through him. Whatever he says will be taken as coming from me, and will be acted on <u>at once</u>. I understand there has been a great deal of 'bellyaching' out here. By bellyaching I mean inventing poor reasons for <u>not</u> doing what one has been told to do.

'All this is to stop at once.

'I will tolerate no bellyaching.

'If anyone objects to doing what he is told, then he can get out of it: and at once. I want that made very clear right down through the 8th Army.

'I have little more to say just at present. And some of you may think it is quite enough and may wonder if I am mad.'

A faint titter and a few smiles in the audience.

'I assure you I am quite sane.'

A delightful pause, in which Monty scours the whole audience with his eyes, and smiles gently.

'I understand there are people who often think I am slightly mad; so often that I now regard it as rather a compliment.'

At this actual laughter from several of the officers.

'All I have to say is that if I am slightly mad, there are a large number of people I could name who are raving lunatics!'

This last is said louder and penetratingly, with Monty leaning forward into the crowd. It works beautifully, for the whole body of officers is now rocking with delighted laughter, which takes a little while to settle. Officers also look round at each other for the first time, and grin and make wild faces.

Monty waits, and grins himself. Might he even break into his express-train laugh? He decides it is not the moment.

He resumes 'What I have done is to get over to you the 'atmosphere' in which we will now work and fight; you must see that that atmosphere permeates right down through the 8th Army to the most junior private soldier. All the soldiers must know what is wanted; when they see it coming to pass there will be a surge of confidence throughout the Army.

'I ask you to give me your confidence and to have faith that what I have said will come to pass.

'There is much work to be done. 'The orders I have given about no further withdrawal will mean a complete change in the layout of our dispositions; also, we must begin to prepare for our great offensive.

'The first thing to do is to move our HQ to a decent place where we can live in reasonable comfort and where the Army Staff can all be together and side by side with the HQ of the Desert Air Force. This is a frightful place here, depressing, unhealthy and a rendezvous for every fly in Africa; we shall do no good work here. Let us get over there by the sea where it is fresh and healthy. If officers are to do good work they must have decent messes, and be comfortable. So off we go on the new line.

'The Chief of Staff will be issuing orders on many points very shortly, and I am always available to be consulted by the senior officers of the staff. The great thing to remember is that we are going to finish with this chap Rommel once and for all. It will be quite easy. There is no doubt about it.

'He is definitely a nuisance. Therefore we will hit him a crack and finish with him'

After Monty has finished speaking, he descends from the podium and walks out of the tent, amid smiles and lively murmurings from the officers. Small groups form here and there as the assembly breaks up, in high spirits. There is a genuine heartiness in contrast to the usual half-assumed one after most such meetings.

'Perhaps this is really a fresh start', says one to a group 'what do you think?'

'It sounds like it, Jenkins ... but then, as you know, I've always been stark raving mad!' A round of shrieking laughter. 'You'd better ask Colonel Llewellyn.'

'This madness is catching,' says Llewellyn, 'I think I've caught it myself! Well, at least if we lose the next battle we shall all die laughing. That's something for the annals ... The Laughing Brigadiers!'

'Pity all the men couldn't be here to listen,' says another, 'How will they catch the new spirit?'

'O Montgomery will talk directly to as many as possible. We'll have to do the rest by telling jokes! A good joke spreads like wildfire.'

'Trouble is, the best joke of all was Montgomery's hat. Good job he took it off. Someone should have a quiet word with him!'

'If he puts any more badges on it, it'll come down of its own weight over his eyes. Won't be able to see us.'

'That could definitely be a nuisance,' says Colonel Llewellyn quietly. Another round of shrieking laughter. 'Do you think Monty has the Lord Mighty in Battle actually under command, or just in a voluntary supporting role?' he continues. More shrieks, as the officers shake hands and break up.

Chapter 14 – Preparations for Battle of Alam Halfa

Preparations for Alam Halfa

Troops digging in on the Alam Halfa ridge. Flies and sweat and cheerful cursing. Officers doing the rounds. High-spirited exchanges between officers and troops. Guns being moved into position in the holes made in the rocks.

Monty arriving at Burg-el-Arab and meeting Portal and Coningham, the Air Force Commanders. Handshakes and smiles, and glimpses of the sea. And later, Portal and Coningham take Monty to the sea's edge, where troops are bathing in their hundreds. A delicious early evening light, with a dustless sky. Serenity.

Stars emerging, brilliant over the sea. The men in their tents, or in slit trenches. Officers doing the rounds. More and more soldiers arriving from the inner desert, and setting up camp, and breathing the purer light and air. Darkness and peace.

Men talking to the Army Officers

'How can the new Commander be so <u>sure</u> of victory, sir?' One asks 'Is he ... how shall I say it, sir ... is he a little bit <u>touched</u>?'

'On the face of it, it all seems a bit 'touched', says an officer. 'But we're disposed to trust it, all the same, and we advise you to follow suit ... It's do or die, isn't it? That's the new spirit ... And of course, if he fails ... if <u>we</u> fail – that's probably the end of his career ... he's sticking his neck right out ... No subtle greys, just black and white. 'The buck stops here', as the Yanks say. How do you find that?'

'As refreshing as a pint of cold beer after a day in this heat and the flies!' says one man.

<u>14 August</u> : The evening kit cleaning after supper. A group of Australians are laughing as an officer approaches.

'Could you just share the joke, you men?' the officer asks.
'It's this little fellow here, sir,' one of them says. 'He just won't stop laughing! It's getting us down, sir, we feel we can't

197

compete, sir!'

The officer stops in his rounds, and asks, 'Would you say he was diffinitely a nuisance, then?'

'Diffinitely a nuisance, sir! Diffinitely!' they all shout. 'Can't you hit him for six out of North Africa, sir, and give us all a break?'

'I think I'd best leave all that to yourselves', the officer says. 'Hit him a crack and finish with him, that's the spirit.'

Huge laughter, while half a dozen men find a large blanket and bundle the little man into it, running out towards the desert about fifty yards, swinging the blanket back and then hurling their burden, as though from a catapult, as far as it will go. Huge cheers as he flies through the air, lands, and gets up, dancing on the spot with his hands in the air.

'He's like the bloody flies,' says one. 'We just can't get rid of him.'

The officer smiles and passes on.

A few days later, still in August

Monty is sitting in his HQ at Burg-el-Arab, which consists of three caravans, captured from the Italians before Monty's arrival in North Africa, but promptly commandeered by him and made efficient and comfortable. One is a general sitting room and dining room, another is a specialist map room, and the third is a bedroom. He is looking spruce and healthy and cheerful.

'What I need is a speedy tank, and someone to drive it for me while I explore the terrain,' says Monty. 'Any ideas, anyone?'

'I think Sergeant Bennett might be your man, sir. I'll get him for you,' says a young corporal, who goes off.

Monty folds his hands quietly, splays his knees, and looks contentedly into the light from the relative coolness of the caravan, which has an electric fan whirling quietly, and an air of calm. His face is not vacant or bored. It never is. Neither is it agitated, but has a quiet amused interest in what is going on around him, and at what is going on inside him, both equally interesting and fertile to his mind. Sometimes, it would seem he drifts or channels himself into withdrawn contemplation, so still is his posture and so serene his expression. He has a Buddha look at the moment, the corners of his mouth slightly lifted in a beatific smile, and his eyes almost closed.

Presently the corporal returns with Sergeant Bennett. 'Sergeant Bennett reporting,' says the young man, with a stiff salute.

'Ah splendid,' says Monty. 'I'm asking you to take me on a tour. Not too many risks, of course, but I need to see the lie of the land, and to follow up a few ideas of my own!'

'Certainly, sir,' says the sergeant. 'The tank is outside, and we can start now if that is convenient.'

Monty picks up his Australian bush hat, and they go to a light-sand-coloured reconnaissance tank, and get aboard.

'We need to get nearer to the front line, where I'll eventually set up my Tactical HQ,' says Monty. They drive south for a few miles, and as they come nearer to Alam Halfa, Monty asks Sergeant Bennett to stop.

'This is where I'd like to get up into the turret and have a look round with my binoculars,' says Monty. 'Give me a minute or two stationary, and then I'll say the word to move off, Sergeant.'

'Certainly, sir ... Do you intend to wear the hat, sir?'

'I most certainly do, Sergeant. Anything wrong with the hat?'

'Not at all, sir ... it's just ...'

'Just what?' says Monty quickly and defensively.

'It's just that once we get moving, sir, it's rather likely to blow off. As you've become aware, sir, this vehicle is quite speedy.'

'Nonsense, Sergeant. I'm sure I'm capable of keeping a hat on and managing my binoculars at the same time at speeds like that.'

'Just as you say, sir.'

Monty climbs up into the turret with his bush-hat on, and spends several minutes looking round on all sides with his binoculars.

'Splendid,' he shouts. 'Now go west for about a mile.'

'Right-ho sir,' shouts the sergeant, 'we're off!'

The tank sets off briskly, and there is very soon a shout from Monty.

'I'm sorry sergeant, could you stop for a second or two?'

'Certainly, sir. Seen something significant, sir?'

'Well, not exactly,' Monty shouts back, and there is a longish pause after the tank has come to a stop.

'Are you all right sir?' shouts the sergeant.

'Certainly, certainly Sergeant Bennett,' Monty says rather quietly. 'It's just that my hat seems to have caught a curious gust of wind, and to have blown off ... I can see it about a hundred yards away, Sergeant. I'll get down and fetch it, Sergeant, no need to drive there.'

Sergeant Bennett below battens down the hatches of his face and replies, deadpan as he can manage, 'No need for that sir, I'll turn round, we'll soon catch it.'

The tank turns, and roars back on its tracks.

'Here we are, Sergeant, thank you very much,' says Monty, a little more boldly.

He gets down, recovers his hat and goes back to the turret.

'I'll be a lot more careful this time, Sergeant,' he shouts heartily. 'West again please Sergeant. Perhaps a little more slowly.'

'Right you are sir!'

The tank grinds along for a quarter of a mile, and we see Monty holding fiercely onto his hat with one hand, and trying to control his binoculars with the other. But a point comes when his interest grows more intense, and he grasps the binoculars with both hands. Soon after we see a gust blow the hat off again, and it scuttles over the desert like a live thing.

'Stop the tank can't you!' Monty shouts in irritation, and as though something entirely different is the matter.

'Certainly sir!' replies Sergeant Bennett, 'Are you sure you're all right sir?'

'I'm all right, thank you Sergeant. It's that confounded hat again. It seems to like going for little walks in the desert.'

Silence from below as the tank stops and ticks over.

'Which way now sir?' calls up Sergeant Bennett.

'Three-quarter turn to the right, then drive about a hundred yards. But be quick please. The damned thing is hopping away like some blasted kangaroo!'

A pause.

'Sorry about this Sergeant.'

'Think nothing of it sir.' The tank roars and turns. 'The hat probably learnt to hop like that in Australia sir!'

A silence, till the tank roars and goes forward at last.

'What did you say Sergeant?' Monty shouts over the noise of the engine.

'Nothing much sir , just one of my little jokes sir, not worth repeating sir,' shouts Sergeant Bennett.

'Can't hear you Sergeant,' shouts Monty.

'Nothing sir,' roars the Sergeant. 'Not worth repeating'

And then, as the engine quietens a little, 'Just my joke sir!'

This gets through.

'Cracking jokes are we?' says Monty 'Can't say I blame you Sergeant. Stop here, Sergeant, stop here. I'll run after it.'

Monty recovers the hat with some difficulty, the hat deciding to jump again just as he reaches it, several times. He comes back holding, not wearing, it.

'You're quite right Sergeant, this hat won't do for this job.'

'Too bad,' says Sergeant Bennett. Then, after a few moments 'Try this sir,' handing Monty an old black beret, with grease-marks on it. 'It's a spare beret of mine sir'.

Monty puts it on and climbs back into the turret.

'How does it look Sergeant?'

Sergeant Bennett climbs into view and looks at Monty. 'Fits like a glove sir … very distinguished sir. A few grease stains here and there, but we can get it cleaned up.'

'But won't you need your spare beret, Sergeant?'

'The honour is mine sir ... and the beret is yours, if you care to wear it sir!'

'Well … this is a moment to remember Sergeant. A moment indeed!'

We see now the Monty that the world soon comes to know. He picks up his binoculars and works them round the landscape slowly.

'Perfect,' he says. 'Comfortable. Secure.'

'And smart sir. Suits you sir. Keep it sir.'

'Right-ho Sergeant ... and thank you very much. Proceed,

Sergeant Bennett ... Tally-ho!'

The tank sets off again, and Monty spends about an hour in exploration. As they arrive back at Main HQ at Burg-el-Arab, Chief of Staff Freddie de Guingand is waiting in Monty's caravan-complex. They salute each other as Monty steps into the compound.

'Much better sir!' says De Guingand. 'Unusual, but much better sir.'

'I'm glad my butler approves,' says Monty, ' For where would I get in life without that!'

A silence, a sudden laugh from both of them, and a handshake.

'Important news for you sir,' says Freddie. 'Mr. Churchill is arriving here tomorrow to see you, and to inspect generally.'

'Splendid!' says Monty. ' We'll entertain him splendidly, and win him over. We must have him on our side, wholeheartedly, or there will be nothing but hitches and glitches and grumbles. Can I rely on you to charm him, Freddie?'

'Certainly sir. But you are charmer-in-chief sir!'

'But he doesn't like me, Freddie! He's made that perfectly clear on several occasions!'

'He requires some degree of deference sir. Perhaps he's only seen your acerbic side ... or your Leveller side, sir. He's royalty sir, royalty. Work on that sir.'

'H'mph!' says Monty. 'Called me a little man on the make once, Freddie. What do you think of that?'

'Typically snobbish sir. But he's learning, he's learning. Good old Alanbrooke is educating him gradually into a proper gentleman. And Alanbrooke will champion you at every turn, as you know, sir.'

'Not quite every turn, Freddie ... I am in Alanbrooke's bad books sometimes, you know!'

'Really sir!' says Freddie, with false incredulity, and stamping hard on his smile.

'Well of course it's success in battle that will win him round in the end. Without that, nothing else will do. And of course of that I am supremely confident, so what ultimately is there to fret about?

So meanwhile we can only do our best in the charm school, and leave it at that. Anyway, you're the sugar and I'm the pill, right?'

'Not quite sir. You need some sugar in yourself sir. See him as a sort of young boy Prince of Wales whom it is your duty and your pleasure to educate and enthuse, sir. Churchill has a lot of the young boy in him, and you love teaching boys ,,, as well as teaching the rest of us. Be the great teacher that you are, sir, and you will bring him round.'

'O teaching!' says Monty, 'That's easy. I thought we had to do something difficult … such as flattery … or showing respect where you don't feel it … and so on.'

'Some degree of respect is surely not beyond you, sir. And to praise his great leadership of the nation, his courage and passion and sensing the public mood ... that's not flattery sir, simply recognizing genius where recognition is due, sir.'

'He hasn't recognized <u>my</u> genius,' says Monty.

'But he will,' says Freddie, 'he will, sir. Now is our chance

Chapter 15 – Churchill's Visit

<u>19-21 August 1942</u>

The preparations for the battle of Alam Halfa are still proceeding, and Monty in his new beret is being shown round. He meets up at one point with some Australians.

'Where's our hat, sir?' they call.

'No offence intended, men, but I'm afraid I found the hat impractical for reconaissance purposes ... probably for other purposes ... Anyway, it kept blowing away, and I was lent this excellent beret, which I intend to keep.'

'O we have ways and means of preventing the hat blowing away sir ... the strap must have gone on yours, sir!'

'I'm sure it is not beyond the wit of man to find a way of preventing a bush-hat from blowing away. But I've come to prefer this unpretentious little beret, and this is how you will all recognize me in future. And as for you Australians, I know you are among the best of our fighting units here, and I have an enormous regard for you. That will not change, for I know that <u>you</u> will not change!'

'Thank you, sir,' say some of them. Then after a silence, one of them brings out 'Among the best, sir? Who exactly is as good as we are, sir?'

'Come come, Corporal! This is not a Test Match! This is not the Ashes Series! It's only war, and therefore we must be a little moderate in our expressions. 'Among the best' will have to do for mere war, Corporal ... as you well appreciate, you are only having me on!'

A burst of laughter, and a loud voice is heard, 'I <u>like</u> that! I really like that!'

Monty walks on. A member of his HQ catches up with him.

'Mr Churchill is due to land at Burg-el-Arab in an hour, sir.'

'Thank you, Corporal. I'll come back immediately.'

An hour later, Monty and De Guingand are at the airport to meet an elderly Churchill. But Churchill is looking very bright and boyish, glad to be out of the office and on a military adventure. He has lost his bulldog jowl for the time being, and takes Monty's hand in both of his and holds it there for a few moments.

'How wonderful to be out here!' says Churchill, 'Away from all the pests in Whitehall. I need a fresh view of things, Montgomery (and by the way, you are now Lt. General Montgomery, partly thanks to myself). Yes, I'm hoping you can enlighten me and take away the blues that I felt on my last visit here. The flies alone nearly drove me mad!'

This is all said while they are walking across the tarmac to the waiting car. Once they are inside, Monty says, 'I think I can promise you, sir, a nearly fly-free environment at our HQ, we make fiercer war on them than on the Germans, sir!'

'You mean Rommel will be quite easy by comparison when it comes to the time?' says Churchill.

'Yes, and I have already made that clear to the officers here, sir, and the rest of the troops are gradually getting that message.'

'Well, we can only hope you are right, Montgomery. We've come to a sort of acid-test, I feel. It's do or die now, isn't it?'

The car pulls up at the caravans HQ. Churchill and his small staff walk round it.

'It's like the school holidays here, Montgomery. Such an atmosphere of fun! Who would think we are at war with the most evil regime the world has known ... You are taking this war seriously, I hope, Montgomery?' he asks, with sudden alarm.

Monty says nothing, but smiles benignly as he ambles around with the group, his arms on his backside.

'Well, well, well,' says Churchill at last, ' And very few flies, as you say. So where shall we go, and what shall we talk about?'

'I'd like to show you the map-room, sir,' says Monty. 'I'm sure maps fascinate you as much as they do myself.'

They enter the Caravan Map-Room, and Churchill is immediately focussed and intense, showing Monty first of all what he knows, and then beginning to ask questions. His small staff melts away.

'What is this great lump of rock?' asks Churchill.

'That is the Alam Halfa ridge, where our troops are even now digging in for our first defensive battle. I expect Rommel to attack in a week to ten days.'

'O, defence eh – you say a defensive battle. What's wrong with attack?' The pugnacious jowl emerges for half a minute.

'We are in absolutely no position to attack at the moment, sir. It will be more than satisfactory if we can hold Rommel off for this time. We need to train and re-train for attack. I need to get our men really fit and hard. The offensive battle, when it comes, will be a prolonged one, sir ... and I fear the casualties may be quite heavy on our side.'

'Don't mind too much about that, Montgomery. Just get on with it!'

'O but I do mind, sir, and in all honesty I must tell our troops what to expect. I'm sure they will respond with courage and endurance, sir.'

'Not much sign of that in recent months, Montgomery.'

'No, sir, but to be fair to my predecessor, Rommel's supply lines were not so stretched then as they are now, and as they will continue to be. We are gradually winning the air war and the sea war in the Mediterranean. And as you know, sir, we are expecting a large consignment of the latest American Sherman tanks into the Red Sea soon, from round the Cape. That will make a huge difference. Our own tanks are frankly not up to the job, sir. It is something of a disgrace.'

'So how soon do you expect all this to happen, Montgomery?'

'Within the next two months, sir ...'

'Two months, Montgomery? That's a devilish long time to wait! O how we need a victory! We've got Stalin still on our backs, laughing at our efforts ... Suppose, for heavens sake, he wins at Stalingrad, but then makes a separate peace with the Germans!'

'Not likely to be caught twice with that trick, sir! Not impossible, but unlikely.'

'Yes, you are right, Montgomery. However, I have Parliament and the country to contend with at home, desperate for good news and pressing me to do this and that ... none of which we can do. I've got that infernal Welshman Bevan attacking me in the Commons, Montgomery, and daring to criticize my whole Mediterranean and North African strategy. Wants a Second Front across the Channel and in Northern France. Thinks we're pleased to sit here and watch the Nazis destroy Stalin and the Communists. Has a great gift of the gab, Montgomery, and is persuading many that I'm a fool ... sees me as some kind of romantic, fighting the last war over again ... Gallipoli and all that. Heavens, they could call again for my head, Montgomery, and then where would we be? I've only recently endured a 'No Confidence' motion in the Commons. We won it, of course, but it is harrowing.'

'Give me the requisite time, sir, and I will save the British and Commonwealth armies out here, restore our reputation, turn the military tide, and save your head, sir!'

Churchill gives himself time to take it in, and to believe it. 'Well, Montgomery, I'm prepared to give you all you want to achieve these things, and I'm coming to believe in you. Heavens, you've made me feel more cheerful already! I've heard this sort of stuff before, of course, and it hasn't cheered me up. But you definitely cheer me up. Now why is that? Are you just a good salesman, or what? But salesmen never pull the wool over my eyes, no, no, no! It's not salesmanship. Are you inspired, by any chance, Montgomery?'

'Yes sir,' says Monty.

'Hmm ... Strange that I've never thought of that before. I confess I feel I have not been quite fair to you in the past, Montgomery. I haven't perceived your true qualities, and I'm sorry for that.'

'Well, sir, I haven't actually done anything yet – but be sure I won't let you down, sir!'

There are tears in Churchill's eyes, and he looks down at the map again to conceal them.

'Tell me where this attack of yours will proceed, Montgomery.'

'There is plenty of time for that, sir, and I'm sure you must be tired after your journey. Go and enjoy some rest first, we've several things to deal with later, and tomorrow.'

'Nonsense. Never felt better in my life ... but a whisky would not come amiss, and a bit of relaxed talk in your shady compound ... What a place of rest, Montgomery! Don't you know there's a war on?'

They walk out of the map-room and over to comfortable seats in a shaded area.

'A double whisky for the Prime Minister,' Monty says to an orderly, who vanishes without a sound.

They sit in silence till the whisky arrives. Churchill clutches at it and gulps down a large portion. He then puts his glass on a small table and reaches in one of his pockets for a cigar, lights it, and puffs contentedly, large puffs into the burning air of North Africa. As the smoke spreads, Monty cautiously moves away and averts his head from the smoke.

'Anything the matter, Montgomery?' asks Churchill.

'Nothing very much, sir. I don't smoke myself, sir, having only one effective lung due to a Great War wound. I tend therefore not to encourage smoking in my HQ, sir.'

'O my dear chap,' says Churchill, all concern and tenderness, 'what a great lump of selfishness I am! I will put this out immediately ... '

'Not at all, sir, for you a great exception is made. Smoke like a factory chimney, sir. I don't have to breathe it, and for some of my staff it will be a great whiff of nostalgia ... of England, of London streets, of romantic winter nights, of fog and damp and dimly lighted old pubs!'

'Exactly,' says Churchill, 'and thank you.' He puffs away. 'Ah, my best days are coming to an end, Montgomery. I feel it myself. My mental faculties are not what they were. This war is tiring. Thank heavens for whisky and cigars to remind one of old times!'

He lifts up his whisky glass, only to find it is empty. An orderly is at his elbow in a flash, on soundless feet.

' Another whisky, sir?'

'Yes please, old fellow!'

'Single or double, sir?'

'Mmm ... double,' says Churchill. 'And neat, this time, please!'

Monty suppresses an incredulous smile. 'I'm sure, for all you say, you are tired now, Mr Churchill, sir. Won't you take a little rest in the Bedroom-Caravan, sir, when you've finished your drink? Then we can go and look at the preparations for the battle of Alam Halfa, and after that we will go to the sea where you can bathe if you wish, sir. I get all the men to bathe here whenever they can. It is wonderful after the flies. After that, sunset, as you know, arrives very quickly and it becomes quite cold. Then we will sit around a camp-fire well wrapped-up, eating smoked fish or some other delicacy and vegetables cooked on the fire.'

'Brings back the jolly old Boer War,' says Churchill. 'Yes, I will take a rest as you suggest, when I've finished the next whisky, and then had one more. They do help to put my mind at rest, Montgomery, they do help.'

Two hours later, Churchill and Monty are going round the Alam Halfa ground together. The sight of Churchill with his cigar and Monty with his beret make an impression on the men that will soon become fixed in their minds, and a standard image on the Pathe News. For the moment, it is fresh and surprising.

Churchill talks easily to the men, and also listens, in much the same spirit as Monty. Fascinated as ever by all things to do with war and battle, Churchill wants to know everything and go everywhere. He gazes at the large excavations that have been made in the rocks. There is already artillery in position in several places. Churchill stands by one of these pieces and looks out.

'Almost due south of us as we look out' says Monty, 'is Himeimat Ridge, heavily fortified by the Germans. I expect part of the attack to come from there. Artillery, bombers, and later tanks. Our first task is to neutralise it. Our current superiority in the air should enable us to succeed. I am in touch with Air-Chief Coningham on a daily basis. I moved our HQ to Burg-el-Arab precisely to be near them, and to plan a thoroughly integrated action.'

'Splendid, Montgomery, splendid!' says Churchill with half his mind, while he took in this and that around him, and dreamed his youthful dreams of action. 'You're almost persuading me of the beauty of defensive warfare with this outfit here. How much damage you will inflict on Rommel will of course depend on how much he wants to take this position.'

'Absolutely sir. And I can assure you he desperately wants to take it … for if we fail here the way is open for Rommel to the Delta and Egypt. Also, if he breaks through here, he will break through from the south in a wide sweep and proceed rapidly north to the sea, encircling us and standing in the way of our retreat. And that will mean our surrender, and the end of the struggle in North Africa.'

'Don't frighten me like this, Montgomery. Another defeat here might be the end of me as well! Are you aware of that, Montgomery?' Churchill is suddenly intense and loud.

'You have had much to bear, Prime Minister, but I can assure you that your worries are over. Rommel's absolute need to break through here will be his undoing. He will not break through, but his desperate need to will cause him to break his armour on our massive defences. He will only give up and limp away when he is utterly broken. It will be months and months before he will be ready to attack again, and during that interval we shall attack him! I am beginning to read his mind, sir,' says Monty finally, after a little hesitation.

'Yes, I noticed Rommel's portrait in your bedroom, Montgomery. Does it really help?'

'I like to think it does, sir. But the less I talk about it the better it works, I think. I need to be humble about this faculty of mine, sir.'

'Dear me,' says Churchill, with a little acid in his voice, 'that must be something of a scourge for you, Montgomery.'

'Good for the Soul, sir, good for the Soul! However, to resume my narrative. Rommel's only chance of a breakthrough is by attacking us during the next week or ten days. And he is not ready for that. We just need another week ourselves, or ideally ten days. After that we will be impregnable, sir!'

'Like the Maginot Line I suppose!' says Churchill.

'Nothing like that folly here sir! Rommel has supply difficulties with fuel now, and we can hang on long enough to make it impossible for him to carry on! Just a week to wait for the attack, and then another week while he wrecks himself on our defences, and then your worries are over, sir. No need to worry about our later attack on him at Alamein. If he fails here at Alam Halfa …

as he undoubtedly will … then he is more or less finished as an effective force in Africa sir.'

'Worry is a terrible thing sir,' says Monty again, 'Don't worry sir.' Monty stretches out his hand, and Churchill takes it, and then takes it with both hands and looks Monty in the eyes for a few seconds. 'Thank you, Montgomery, thank you. I shan't forget this. And I will follow the course of the defensive battle with the closest interest, after what you have said, Montgomery.'

An hour later Monty and Freddie de Guingand are accompanying Churchill in his florid dressing-gown across the beach. Several hundred yards away thousands of soldiers are bathing. As the party reaches the edge of the sea, turquoise and peacock-blue, Churchill stops and looks in the direction of the multitude of bathers.

'Strange,' he says, 'Everyone is wearing white shorts! Is there regulation issue even for bathing, Montgomery? Bit stuffy, isn't it?'

'No sir,' says Freddie de Guingand, 'They are not wearing shorts at all, sir.'

'Not wearing shorts at all,' says Churchill vaguely and uncomprehendingly. 'Ah, I see, I see, De Guingand. Not wearing shorts at all. You mean, not wearing shorts at all. I begin to understand you, De Guingand.'

They all three lean back and laugh, first all together, and then separately, and then all together.

'Not wearing shorts at all!' says Churchill quietly as Monty and De Guingand deftly relieve Churchill of his silk dressing-gown, and guide him towards the water's edge.

'But what about my costume?' says Churchill 'I'm sure I brought a costume, or a pair of shorts or something!'

'Must be in the car, sir,' says Monty. 'Never mind sir. Just as you are sir, in you go sir.'

And Churchill toddles the last few steps to the water like a chubby white baby, splashes with his toes and then sits down and then launches himself into the delicious warm and salty sea, and soon plunges into its depths.

Monty and De Guingand look into the perfect sky and smile. It is a moment of triumph.

'Who is the sugar and who is the pill now, sir?' says De Guingand.

'Oh never mind all that, Freddie, forget all that. The point is, enjoy this. If a man is open and unprejudiced, one can be oneself, that is the point. Churchill has come over here with his mind open and free, and therefore I don't have to try, or put on an act. We are even becoming friends. He is bit by bit dropping his first impressions of me ... which were on the whole prejudices, just prejudices.'

Monty breaks off to wave at Churchill in the water, as Churchill is waving at them. Churchill then proceeds to float on his back.

'What beauty and serenity!' says De Guingand, looking up and around. 'Do you take mental photographs as I do, sir, of moments like these, and put them against mental photographs of very different moments?'

'I know what you mean, Freddie. The contrasts in our lives are almost unbelievable. It is as though all the elements of this world are in restless motion, at war with each other. War is not the only war. Peace is also war. Where shall we ever know peace, Freddie?'

'Where indeed, sir!' says De Guingand. 'Do you think these great moments of peace are no more real than the moments of conflict, sir? Or worse, than the times of deadly boredom and greyness. Are they all on a level, do you think, as the great Heraclitus used to say? Or is peace on a higher level, I wonder?'

'I'm no philosopher, Freddie. I only have my simple religion. And surely we shall have peace at last, in a form that is not tedium. That's my belief.'

'We're all philosophers in places like this, sir, in conditions like this. No wonder at the wealth of Arab poetry ... Iranian poetry ... Greek poetry. These pure colours like jewels. And then the night sky at last, like wine, sir.'

'And then the moon like your latest woman, eh, Freddie?' says Monty.

'Oh don't spoil it for me, sir!' says De Guingand. Even my women say that I have soul, sir. They like the soul in me … though I shouldn't talk about it like this … Soul is the thing in the end, isn't it?'

'Yes, if you can keep it alive in the midst of all the carnage and horror, Freddie. That requires strength, an inner peace ... some kind of certainty.'

'I don't quite have that certainty, sir, as you have. And the presence of the padres only makes me uneasy. I cannot really feel much coming from them that helps me. If anything I feel less certain, less sure of Soul, sir.'

'Maybe your loose life is rebuking you, Freddie, making it hard for you.'

De Guingand winces, and is silent.

'No,' says Monty after half a minute of silence between them. 'It is a complete mystery why some things are easy for some and confoundedly difficult for others. You must check any self-righteousness in me, Freddie. After all, it is not good soldiering. I have to labour at all times to spot the differences between the men, and to use the differences in some good way. No use being censorious because one man can't do a particular job. Find one that he can do.'

A longish silence, till De Guingand says, 'But if you were strictly consistent about that, you would never sack anyone at all, sir … whereas I note that the sackings have already begun … '

'We absolutely must have good senior front-line and Staff officers, Freddie, as you know. And for that objective I am fairly ruthless. But I do try in many cases to soften the blow, tell them they are tired and need a rest (which is often true), or that another kind of job back home would suit them. But often they are, objectively, quite useless. Poor Auchinleck couldn't see that … so that we are lumbered, to an extent, with poor senior officer material. Still, let's not talk any more shop on this beautiful Mediterranean evening. And here's Churchill getting to his feet and wanting his dressing-gown, Freddie. Off we go!'

They walk to the water's edge and into the shallow warm water in order to drape the dressing-gown over Churchill's nakedness.

'Glorious, glorious!' says Churchill, 'Oh what joy, what inspiration! Rejuvenation, my two good fellows! Such a weight is falling off me, It is as though Whitehall and the House of Commons are in another world. Can't you send them a cable, De Guingand, and tell them I've resigned? Tell them I'm happy to lead the troops into battle and to face death or injury, but I cannot face another Prime Minister's Questions in the Commons!'

'You won't be fully refreshed until you stop thinking about it altogether, sir,' says Monty, 'And we shall make that our endeavor at all times.'

An hour later, night has fallen, and Churchill is, as promised, seated around a camp fire. All are well wrapped-up and put their hands towards the flames. Churchill has his double whisky at his side, and all is well with the world.

Orderlies move about in the darkness, helping the company to sample this and that, and to second helpings. Churchill's whisky glass is replenished several times, and he becomes garrulous in his reminiscences ... the Boer War, Gallipoli, the General Strike, his own fall from Tory grace in the 1930s, Hitler, and then the Premiership.

'I thought it had to come at last, my hour!' says Churchill. 'Do you understand that, Montgomery?'

'Certainly, sir. A man of destiny. As I was saying to Bernard Shaw only the other day, sir!'

'You were talking to Bernard Shaw, Montgomery! How on earth did that come about?'

'I requested an interview, sir. I've always rather admired him. And he was certainly not a disappointment face to face. As sharp as a razor, sir, and very amusing.'

'It's a good job he's not a Labour MP in the Commons,' says Churchill. 'I fear he would make me hop and skip about!'

'Try to rest your mind, sir ... and have another whisky, sir. And when are we going to have the blessing of the cigar-smoke, sir?'

'When I'm ready for it, Montgomery, when I'm ready.'

'Then I fear I shall miss the pleasure, sir. It's coming up to half-past nine and that is my regular bedtime, sir. But you, of course, are welcome to sit up as long as you like, there will be others here who will enjoy the late hours, and there will always be an orderly to serve you. We have an all-night staff, sir. And so, goodnight all!'

There are several 'goodnight's'. 'But I thought we might sit up together, Montgomery,' says Churchill, rather sadly. 'So much to go over. But then I understand from Alanbrooke that you always make sure of your sleep. Is it true that you took your sleep as usual during the Dunkirk fiasco?'

'I'm glad you are calling it a fiasco, rather than a great British triumph, sir!' says Monty, 'And yes, I did take my sleep as usual. There was nothing to be served by losing sleep, sir.'

'But what about the night-march with your Division that plugged the gap and saved our Armies from complete ruin? I mean, that's Alanbrooke's story, not quite sure I completely believe it. But at least you couldn't have been sound asleep then, could you?'

'Certainly not, sir. But night-moves are about the only exceptions to my rule. And yes, Alanbrooke was right, I did save the British Army by what my Division did, though it is little appreciated on high, sir!'

'I'm sorry about that, Montgomery, and sorry we can't reminisce into the small hours, but there it is! Get your sleep, Montgomery, and we'll have a good talk about the Alamein Strategy tomorrow, I want to know absolutely everything that is on your mind.'

Monty walks away, Churchill has his glass refilled and the fireside company settles into pleasant talk and laughter.

An hour later the company is thinner, but Churchill is still there, still drinking, and also smoking his cigars

Two of the staff get up and say their goodnights

Finally, there is just Churchill and an orderly. 'Well I mustn't keep you up all night,' says Churchill, 'just show me to the caravan will you, old fellow, hope there's a decent light in there, need to read myself to sleep ... nothing like a bit of intellectual wake-up last thing at night … one never forgets the things one reads at those times.' He says all this while proceeding to the caravan, the orderly in front of him with a powerful torch. 'You'll find it very comfortable Mr. Churchill, Sir. General Montgomery seems to be a strong believer in comforts, and not just for himself Sir.'

'A good thing too!' says Churchill.' No whisky in here I suppose?'.

'We can arrange for a bottle to be sent over, Sir, no trouble at all Sir.'

'Very kind of you, good night then!'

'Goodnight sir.'

The next morning 20 August

Monty is in the compound of his HQ, in the shade and talking to Freddie de Guingand.

'We must build up our team here at HQ, Freddie. We must have a team that is harmonious and can work well under stress. A team of memory-men Freddie, not paper-pushers. Can you think of one or two good men you could work alongside and would actually like to have a round you day after day?'

'Yes I could think of a few sir… certainly, but this means more sackings, and it hurts me to sack those who have done no harm.'

'As few as possible, Freddie ... just a handful, But I can think of half a dozen excellent men I'd like to have here, people who understand my principles and ways, people I have taught and trained at Camberley alongside you, Freddie. We must have Kit Dawnay for a start.'

'Yes I agree,' says De Guingand, 'And for a radio operator and excellent signals and intelligence men there's Major Bill Williams, Sir.'

'Remind me, ' says Monty.

'A history don, Sir. Extremely quick and clever and modest sir. And a hard worker, And the sort that takes pains to fit in. First class man.'

'Good,' says Monty 'We'll have him, Each man must be a mixture of expertise and social grace, relaxedness, good cheer, smiles and laughs, Freddie, we just can't have neurotic prima donnas, and tension and shouting matches, we will all need to like each other. And everyone must have sense of humour and a capacity to switch off and relax when not on duty,'

'You're asking a great deal sir! And on top of all these qualities you will want young attractive men with a certain panache, sir, and,' he tails off.

'And what Freddie?' asks Monty

'Let's say a capacity for hero-worship, sir!'

'As to that, Freddie, pshaw!'

'Not pshaw, sir, but amen, sir. And why not, sir? What could be better?'

After a short pause, Monty changes the subject. 'I've been thinking of gingering up the padres, Freddie, we need a new sprit there as well.'

'Oh not yet more sackings, sir! This is too much!'

'Not necessarily, Freddie, I've already sacked Duncan who's padre for all 8th army, and I'm appointing Llewelleyn Hughes, who's already working here at Alamein in his stead. I've known him fairly well from a long way back, and he is good, he is special. He needs seniority, that's all. Once he's in place, it will be he who decides on sackings, Freddie … He will bring a new spirit. If a man is a real leader he can often bring out the latent, good qualities in his followers, he does not necessarily need to sack a lot of people.'

'Sauce for the goose, sir, is sauce for the gander, if you will pardon my frankness.'

'Fair comment, Freddie, but it remains the case that there are some who are quite useless! They haven't got the imagination to see their own deficiencies, even when these are pointed out to them. How can they change if they can't even see? And some have so fattened themselves on class-privilege since their cradles that they are never going to see. Many of our upper-class officers simply can't communicate with the men, Freddie. They lack the sense of their common humanity. They have lived in their own cocoon too long.'

'Yes I've seen that sir, certainly that's true in some cases.'

'I'm sure you have. Freddie. And also, as you will know, I'm not asking our officers to drop their aitches or to stop their glottals, Freddie. That's absolutely pathetic, the worst way. An officer with the most preposterous Oxford voice can communicate with his men so long as he senses his common humanity with them, that's all. If he feels it himself they will pick it up, no matter by what means, all kinds of curious almost invisible inaudible signals. It's strange isn't it? I've even seen wonderfully successful officers of the complete pansy type, the 'camp' voice and mannerisms, nothing much held back, he can be a refreshing change from the so-called he-men. It enables the men to have insight into another type of being ... a sort of wonderland or fairyland, if you'll pardon the pun, which they will allow themselves to indulge out of a pure curiosity. Just because the officer is genuinely himself and makes no apology for his difference ... and seems to be a good soldier as well. It might even make some of them feel better about themselves, if they imagine some kind of 'difference' has been making them unacceptable to their fellows.

'The straightforward Pansy can be a great healer, Freddie! Have you ever noticed that?

'Now that you say it, sir, I can recall one or two examples. Very interesting.'

They sit together in silence, looking out at the brilliant light. De Guingand sighs deeply.

'What's up, Freddie?' says Monty.

'It's about religion and war, sir. I just react badly when I see them together. War is just filthy, sir. It's fine if good men like yourself are put in charge, and somehow come out of the filth of it not filthy yourself, but bearing a human value which all can see. We have the courage and the capacity, sir, to dirty our hands for the common good, and yet can emerge smelling of roses. It's good that some of us can do that, it's a service to humanity, though, as I haven't been tried very much yet, I am not too sure I can manage it.'

'Oh you will, Freddie, you will!' interrupts Monty. 'I can assure you of that. You are a good man, Freddie, or I would not have picked you for the job. You are wholesome all through, Freddie, wholesome all through. People will see your goodness shine out when we are all under stress, Freddie. When danger and stress are upon us, some of the weaker people will look round and search for faces of their fellow humans, looking for a stable goodness, and an inspiration. They can be struck with wonder at such moments, Freddie, when they see a familiar face still stable and, as they say in the East, one- pointed, Freddie, focused. And even lit up. Is it the observer, in his fright or despondency, who projects this lit-upness into the face of the steady brave reliable man, or is the face actually lit up? I expect a bit of both. The gratitude of the person looking for a leader and finding one, a stable face in a bedlam of noise and fear ... this gratitude itself is a transformation of being and will create illumination around him and inside him. But I'm sure the leader serving his role at the dangerous times is also illuminated, and that's what I want my padres to be, at all times Freddie. To be lit up. not by fanaticism, but genuinely illumined by the knowledge and presence of God. So that the men actually see God when they see the padre! Is that asking too much, Freddie?'

'If I could see God and feel God in the padres, sir, then you will have succeeded beyond your dreams!'

De Guingand is silent for some while.

'But all I usually see is a sort of churchy atmosphere, a sort of churchy face that I know too well from my childhood.Not particularly intelligent, not at all conscious or aware of my condition sir, but only of their own. And how can these people know what war is really like sir? They are excused duty by virtue of their office.'

'Would you have them forced to be killed, Freddie?' says Monty.

'No, no, I'm glad that there are those who are allowed to stand outside ... to stand for the value of peace and fellowship,'

'And to stand for heaven and the heavenly worlds.'

'Probably that's one of my difficulties sir. I can't quite believe that.'

'But your Arabic and Iranian poets have no such difficulty, apparently!'

'True, true … I am not yet established in my convictions, that's the trouble … I am a beginner sir. But I see the problem that other beginners like me have with the padres. We can't help feeling that religion should steer clear of war, even when the war is in a good cause, and that war should not invoke religion to its cause. It feels as though religion is a bearer of death, a procession of corpses, even more than soldiers are. It feels as though religion loves death and corpses, and feasts upon them. It makes some of us feel sick, Sir, and the man in black might as well come to us wearing a pirate flag with skull and cross bones on it!'

'These difficulties are beyond my ken' says Monty. ' But I still must listen and try to understand, otherwise I might look like a bearer of corpses myself, instead of an inspiration … I am listening to you, Freddie, and trying to understand. It is for my own good that I need to extend my imagination!'

'I can't give a rational account of myself, sir, these are mainly emotional reactions, and I could be in need of a re-ordering of my own emotions. But who will teach me that, Sir? I need teaching, as good religious teaching as you gave us military teaching. Feelings are what they are. One can't argue with them it seems, but create a fresh context, and perhaps then the feelings will change.'

'What would constitute a fresh context then, Freddie?'

De Guingand pauses some while.

'Well, Sir, I'm remembering what I'm told about the Great War. Both sides claiming God was on their side, and so on. What crass idolatry, what stupidity, when the best of us know that that war should just have been stopped! Did the Churches call for that, Sir? If so the echo of that call has been rather faint. The churches were bearers of corpses then, that's my impression.'

'But it's different this time, Freddie. Our cause is just, and our enemy are possessed by the diabolical.'

'True,' says De Guingand. 'But its not different enough. <u>We</u> may have a just cause, but most of the churches in Germany seem to think that Hitler and Germany have a good cause. Why are the

Churches always so tame, so stupid, so locked-in to the secular world, so lacking in courage and dignity? I just cannot respect churches and parsons, Sir!'

'You feel more sides of a question than I do, Freddie. I can see easily enough what you say, but my thicker hide prevents me from feeling it, and thus from feeling the inner conflict. And my own religious convictions protect me. I can more easily say quite simply, we are right this time, and they, including some of the German churches, are just wrong. It will be depressing, of course, if when peace come there are no consequences for the German churches. But I rather think they will be generally castigated, in a way that they will never be able to forget. It will never be 'Business as usual' for them when this war is over. Humanity and the churches will have learnt something. That thought saves me from cynicism.'

They look calmly from their shade into the light of the compound, while an orderly brings a tray of coffee to them. The calmness all around gives the impression of a very special holiday abroad, with a perfect staff. The men in the HQ control room are almost non-audible as well as invisible.

'You mention cynicism, Sir. My own cynicism, if that's what it is, springs from a fairly simple root. I find it pretty disgusting that men who are excused from fighting and killing and dying themselves can so brazenly and without blushing with shame, hold out the love of God and the hope of another world to those who have to do these things ... and more especially when they, the parsons, probably don't believe much in God and in heaven themselves. The men will pick that up, won't they, Sir? Even if I were to believe, say, in heaven, I would hate to propound it as a compensation. Especially if I were asking others to test it by killing and dying, while I myself don't have to do so!'

'A really good padre's presence might enable you to feel all these things you've mentioned quite differently. But in any case, you know full well that the padre's life in wartime is by no means soft. Many of them share the soldiers risk's in a battle situation in order to be close to the soldiers, and get killed. And they have to not only bury the dead, Freddie, but help collect the dead from the battle-field. Including body parts and all that grisly proceeding.'

'True, true,' says De Guingand. 'I am prejudiced against them, I can see that. I must look afresh, try to look beyond and behind the churchy face…'

De Guingand picks up his coffee and drains the cup.

'Pretty good coffee, Sir… Pretty good. What an idyll it all seems at the moment. Sir, I'm beginning to get a feeling we should be up and doing something. This experience of protracted leisure is making me uneasy. It's usually a prelude to discovering one has simply forgotten some enormous thing. What have we forgotten sir? It is not like me to forget.'

' No, of course it's not, Freddie. But enjoy this idyll while we can. For today and tomorrow our only duty is to look after Mr. Churchill. Everything else is being attended to by our deputies. We must give the Prime Minister a little holiday, and in doing so, try to take one ourselves. And as Mr. Churchill is still sound asleep in my bedroom, there's not much we can do except sit around and chat. I'm glad he is having a good rest. We must let him sleep on.'

While Monty has been saying these last few sentences Churchill himself in his peacock-pattern dressing gown has emerged outside the compound and slipped quietly into it, shuffling up behind Monty and De Guingand and then standing arms folded and listening with amusement to their conversation.

'Yes, the more sleep the better,' says De Guingand. 'There's still plenty of time for a tour of the troops, and a detailed briefing for the Alam Halfa battle and our coming offensive at Alamein.'

'So glad to hear that De Guingand!' says Churchill, only about a foot behind them.

Monty and De Guingand rise up noisily like a pair of rocketing pheasants.

'O good lord, Mr. Churchill, Sir! What have I been saying? Nothing indiscreet, I hope!' says De Guingand.

'I didn't quite give you time enough for that,' says Churchill.

'Well its good too see you up at last, Sir,' says Monty. 'We didn't see you come from your bedroom, so we assumed you were still sleeping.'

'Of course you didn't see me emerge from the bedroom, Montgomery! I have been up and about for several hours enjoying myself with another swim and then with wandering about exploring, and talking to the men.'

'In your dressing gown sir!' says Monty. 'And without a security guard!'

'Yes to both of those, Montgomery. I had a very good sleep in your most comfortable caravan, woke early and wanted to get up and see the early morning light. I am regretting now that I didn't bring my oil paints and a few small canvasses. It feels as if there would have been time for a couple of painting sessions, morning and evening. I have been here several times now, and I am beginning to see things … It always takes a little time to see properly, from an artistic point of view.'

Monty and De Guingand smile broadly and relax deeply.

'Maybe I can rustle up some paint and brushes and boards for you, sir,' says Monty. 'There are one or two war artists here, they would be overwhelmed with the privilege sir, of providing for you.'

'That would be splendid!' says Churchill. 'Too late for a morning session now, but there is always tomorrow morning, before I leave, and this evening I could sit down after another bathe and before supper. Would that be convenient for you both? I only need about an hour to get something down. I will have some breakfast and some of that delicious coffee now, and then I will be with the pair of you for a detailed map-session … I will just go and change. Ah, this is the life I like, this is the life!'

Churchill shuffles off to his caravan, and Monty and De Guingand disappear into the main office. The compound is empty and the day's heat begins to gather its force.

An hour later all three are in the map-caravan, seated around a large table. Monty is showing Churchill, who is in the middle, a map of the Alamein area.

'You will see, sir, that our frontline is over 30 miles long, in the north it stretches to the sea, and in the south to the Qattara Depression. We cannot break through at either of these points.

The Qattara is impossible terrain for both sides, the sea could be very difficult, so the problem is how do we break a 30-mile line at some point, when it is heavily defended all along? It is a static situation rather like the First World War, and will involve heavy casualties when we succeed in doing it. I can promise no other way, Sir.'

Churchill nods and then says, 'As I have already said, Montgomery, it is a victory we need, and casualties are secondary. We will have the Americans in North Africa relieving our burden, Thank God, so we will be spared to many casualties later on. So now is the time to take that plunge.'

'Certainly, sir, ' says Monty, 'certainly.'

'However,' Churchill says, ' After all you said about a static heavily defended continuous line on both sides, how was it that Rommel broke through several times and led us such a dance, pushing us back to where we are now?'

'Rommel was extremely clever with his feints. He lured Auchinleck into many a false move, thus exposing gaps in our line. Suddenly into those gaps, the Panzers would come, from points in the desert where our men had no idea they were hiding. He had a way of hiding his armour, even taking advantage of spells of funny weather, sand storms and the like, in order to do so. Rommel has a way of sweeping round us southwards and then forcing us toward the sea … That's why we must get him off the Mitereiya ridge as I was showing you yesterday sir. If we don't manage it at the battle of Alam Halfa, we must do it at the Alamein battle.'

'Yes I see,' says Churchill. ' But how are you going to avoid falling into the same false moves as Auchinleck before you, Montgomery?'

'By keeping our line intact sir, by leaving no gaps. Until now we have been betrayed into a mobile warfare for which we are not properly equipped or trained. Our Divisional Forces have been split up into smaller and smaller units, in the illusion that we can inflict serious damage in quick sorties and then safely retire. We can't do this Sir...half the time our small columns didn't know where our other columns were. It's a recipe for chaos sir. It seemed a good idea at the time, but it didn't work.'

Churchill nods and asks again, 'But if Rommel attacks, you have to do something! What will you do?'

'If Rommel attacks again, after Alam Halfa is over, our orders will be to stand firm, sir. We will fight as solid Divisions, and with immense power held in reserve all along the line, we will allow no gaps. We will fight a static and un-adventurous battle. We will take the casualties and fill the gaps caused by casualties and stand firm.'

'Sounds like another defensive battle, Montgomery.'

'I said, If Rommel attacks us, sir. But it is my firm intention to attack first. I calculate that after the huge casualties, especially to his tanks, that we will inflict on Rommel at Alam Halfa he will be in no position to attack again for a long time. We will get in first sir. I have already read his mind on that, Sir.'

'Oh you and your telepathy, Montgomery, please don't burden me with that! Just stick to the facts, Montgomery. Just give me the solid facts, if you don't mind.'

'Just as you wish, sir.' says Monty ' But haven't you, and don't you even now, often work by hunches sir?'

'Yes, I have and I do,' says Churchill, 'but a strong hunch is one thing. Pretending to read Rommel's mind by staring at his confounded portrait is quite another, Montgomery! I get my hunches by detailed studies of situations, and by using imagination when once I know those details … its hard work Montgomery, not cheap magic!'

Monty takes this impassively, but is anxious to move on. Churchill, however is in no hurry. He lifts his head and looks at the portrait of Rommel. They all look at it.

'Well, Mr Rommel what have you to tell us today? We hope you had a good breakfast … Ein Gute Fruhstuck ... isn't that what they call it? And are feeling well-disposed to us? Perhaps, in your good humour, you will give us just a wee clue as to what is in your mind. Or must we,' says Churchill, turning to Montgomery, 'consult a gypsy in one of the other caravans! Is that why you collect caravans, eh! Did a gypsy come <u>with</u> the caravans, eh? Was it some kind of <u>package</u>? If not, it should be easy enough to get a fortuneteller from Alexandria or from Cairo, but I expect you've done that already, Montgomery! Eh!'

Monty bends back and laughs easily, then they all laugh.

'Come on, Montgomery, don't waste our time, tell me what comes next,' says Churchill.

'Good aerial reconnaissance, and our spies will be able to assure us that Rommel is not ready to attack us, and nothing like ready. Therefore we will be able to take our time to prepare thoroughly our own attack. We need not rush into it sir, and I will not be rushed. Our attack will be a night attack and must take place at the full moon. There is a full moon in the last week in September, and another in late October. Our attack will begin at the October full moon.'

Churchill wipes his brow. 'Not the September full moon then? It makes me sweat considerably, this waiting for the perfect moment, Montgomery. Anything could happen in the meanwhile …You must admit that, surely?'

'I admit nothing of the sort sir. We will see to it at Alam Halfa that Rommel will be in no position to attack before the end of October. And of course we can fly sorties during that time to bomb his fuel dumps. Fuel supplies are the key to everything at the moment.'

'You make a good case, Montgomery, lets hope it holds up. However, you haven't told me yet how you propose to break in to Rommel's equally static line. You are assuming a static defensive line on Rommel's part as well, then?'

Yes sir, I have read his mind … er … I've calculated that to a nicety. He will have no alternative. Pitting ourselves against that line and breaking through it will not in the end prove too difficult.'

Churchill allows a weary, surprised look to cross his face. Montgomery goes on, 'I shall want general Horrocks in the southern part of our line. I have already sent for him. Here we will build a strong illusion that our main attack will come from a southerly direction. Dummy tanks and dummy fuel dumps will play a part in this.'

'Oh dummy this and dummy that!' says Churchill 'Who does

that fool, Montgomery? Have you nothing better than that?'

'Unless spies upon the ground get through sir, the enemy cannot afford to ignore these things. From the air they still have no way of telling. But of course it is not our only resource of deception, we have a dozen others, sir, of which perhaps our best will be a dummy pipe line for carrying water all the way from the north coast, we will spend many weeks building that … On top of that I shall actually place large numbers of real troops and armour in parts of the Southern section, where they will remain, until we need them for reinforcement in the last few days of the battle, behind our point of break through.'

'Well if you have a large number of troops in the South, you will need extra water as well, so what about the dummy?'

'Water supplies in the south are already adequate, though the Germans don't know that. When they see the pipe line being built, and then begin to take note of the deployment of troops there, they can hardly dare to ignore the threat, and will deploy their own forces accordingly. So long as they too are thinned out along this 30-40 mile front sir, then we can carry out my plan to break through. Obviously they cannot afford to neglect their defences in the north. They will fear a sudden break through there by us, and our race to the coast where we can cut off their retreat.'

'What about the centre then?' says Churchill, 'What will happen there?'

'The centre is in fact north of centre, sir. Their possession of Kidney Ridge is one of their strongest defensive points, so of course they will reinforce it strongly … look closely here sir, on the map.'

'Yes I see,' says Churchill, 'Most interesting. So where do you plan to make the break through, Montgomery?'

'That remains to be seen,' says Montgomery. 'What I am planning first of all is to send our strongest tank forces into and behind the enemy lines. We need our tanks to sit on the enemy supply line. It's called the Rahman Line. Look here on the map sir. Rommel will be forced to respond. But fuel and other supplies will be denied to him for at least a few days and perhaps longer. We will wait to see a point of weakness in his front line due to shortage of supplies, and can make our break through at that point, either in the north or in the centre. We will not use the line in the south.'

'I like that,' says Churchill, 'It's an attacking strategy. As you know, Montgomery, I am in favour of attack and boldness wherever possible. Very impressive Montgomery. Well, De Guingand, you have said nothing, how do you view these plans and preparations?'

'I am pretty impressed too, sir. I have known General Montgomery long enough, with military manoeuvres in training particularly, to know that his clear-headedness usually works out in practice, sir.'

'Training isn't quite war, is it, however hard you try to make it real? Real war is inclined to create panic,' says Churchill.

'We don't know the meaning of the word 'panic' at our HQ sir, neither myself nor General Montgomery, nor any of our team.'

Churchill sits and ponders for a while.

'I'm well satisfied, both of you. I look forward to the actual battles. Perhaps after all you can take this jinx off us Montgomery … Heavens, I wish I could stay here and be with you throughout. Wonderful! Instead of which I must face the House of Commons and try not to sound a naïve fool while I promise them fresh hope … what pests they are, some of them! And when I'm free of them I have pests in Whitehall to deal with. Perhaps the House Of Commons will next time actually pass a Vote of No Confidence in me! That will free me up for coming here! Think of that, Montgomery!'

'I don't consider we should think of that sir. Life can't be all fun and games, sir.' says Monty with a grim humour.

'Well I try to make it so as much as possible, even in Cabinet, Montgomery. Serious fun, you know.'

'I know exactly what you mean,' says Monty, 'and later this afternoon, we have the serious fun of inspecting a unit of our troops. And for that, I have a preference for you in a suit, sir, not in those pyjamas or that peacock dressing gown. Call me hidebound if you wish, sir. But…'

Churchill cuts him off, thumps the table a great bang, and

laughs from his belly and all the way up.

'Montgomery!' he explodes, 'Montgomery!' And then quietly, 'Are you what is called a wag, Montgomery?'

'In some sense, yes sir,' says Monty.

'I would never have dreamt it, Montgomery! A bit of a wag, eh!'

Monty and Churchill, an hour or so later are inspecting an Artillery unit behind the front-line. Monty looks as crisp and neat as ever and is both intense and smiling as he passes along the lines. Monty has his own way of inspecting troops, which consists of a quick up and down look at the soldiers bearing, and ending with a sudden intense look into each soldier's eyes, with the intention of creating a bond with each man. Churchill is solemn, feeling with his imagination the immense seriousness of what is at stake in the next few months, and letting it show.

After the inspection they return in a Staff Car to the HQ. An orderly comes out of the office bearing a large canvas bag.

'Who's that for?' says Monty.

'It is for Mr Churchill, sir. Brushes and paints and a few canvasses sir. Also linseed oil, turpentine and a nice wooden palette and a camping stool. With kind regards from one of our War Artists, sir.'

Churchill beams.

'This is most kind of you all,' he says, 'perhaps I can do a heat-of-the-day painting as well as an evening and morning one. I can't wait to begin.'

'Will you be painting in your dressing gown, sir?' asks Monty.

'Oh no, of course not,' says Churchill.

'I have got an old one-piece boiler-suit I like getting into now and then. I have brought that with me. I could do with some kind of sun hat. No, no I can sit in the shade. I will sit in the shade of the compound and look out to those date palms, at all the busy hurrying figures and vehicles. I have seen my composition already. I will try not to be in the way.'

'Lunch is being served in about 20 minutes, sir,' says De

Guingand, 'We will sit here in the shade together and you can have peeps at your composition as we proceed with lunch.'

'Excellent!' says Churchill. 'How much do you charge for this holiday camp Montgomery? I hope I have brought enough money with me!'

'You will pay in inspiration sir. Our troops are overjoyed to see you out here again. I am not particularly good at spotting historic moments sir, I always seem to have my mind on something else. But this is surely a historic moment.'

'Certainly it is, Montgomery. And the trust I put in you and your team will I'm sure grow into a steady co-operation and lasting friendship, Montgomery, great things begin here today.'

They shake hands, and Churchill finds a seat in the shade while Monty and De Guingand go into the office.

After lunch Churchill appears from his bedroom in his dark grey boiler suit and with paints and canvasses. He seats himself in the shade, in the compound, and looks north through the gateway. De Guingand spots him a minute or two later.

'Oh Mr.Churchill, sir, you can't possibly paint in that hot old boiler suit out here in Africa! Look.' he says and goes into the office for a few seconds. 'Look what we have found for you.'

It is a white cotton garment, very roomy and very long. 'A native galabaya Sir, ideal for the climate.'

De Guingand goes up to Churchill 'You need wear nothing under this at all sir, so you will remain relatively cool in this furnace heat.'

Churchill handles it 'Beautiful!' he says. 'I will go and change immediately.'

He comes out a few minutes later in the galabaya, and Montgomery and De Guingand and one or two of the office staff come out into the open to have an approving and amused look. Somewhere in the background there is a surreptitious click of a camera, half hidden behind another person's shoulder. The camera is hurriedly stowed away, and its presence disguised by everyone talking at once.

'I'll get to work then,' says Churchill. 'Let me know when I'm wanted, Montgomery.'

'You will not be needed sir. I advise a couple of hours sleep, round about 3.30pm, and then you will be refreshed for your evening session. Any other business we can dispatch tonight, sir, in the coolness.'

'Right,' says Churchill, 'I have an hour and a half till my sleep, I'd better get on.'

They all leave him, and Churchill is soon at work; he roughs in the door of the compound and all the sand coloured canvas that is drooped over the buildings as camouflage. Through the large door he roughs in the desert horizon and a couple of date palms and some low horizontal buildings, also camouflaged. He then paints in the hot bright sand within the compound and the even brighter hotter sand beyond it, and afterwards splashes a broadish shadow across the threshold of the compound. He is working boldly and confidently and with joy. He takes a smaller brush and quickly flips in some lighter shadows of the far buildings and of the date palms. He then takes a broad squat brush, mixes an intense blue with it and pulls the brush downwards and very firmly for the visible section of sky, from zenith to horizon, paddling the brush around the date palms, biting into them a little and then biting into the sand of the horizon.

In the heat all the paint is drying very quickly. He is able to return to the distant sand, nibbling with the colours back into the sky a little and putting another thicker layer of paint onto all the sand beyond the compound, making it light and hot and intense. He flicks tones of orange on top of the violet ... of the shadows, of the date palms and the buildings, and even works a little orange into the shadow across the threshold of the compound. Lastly he puts thicker paint on the sand inside the compound.

He pushes his seat back a foot or two at this point and looks at his painting.

'Not bad at all for a beginning. Damn it I can finish the painting today in one session, in these conditions. If only I keep my courage and boldness,' he continues to say aloud to himself. 'Have no fear!' he says, 'bash on with the big brushes, and a bit of serious impasto in about an hour, just before I retire.'

At this point Monty appears from the office and strolls over to him.

'Mind if I look sir?' he says.

'Not at all, Montgomery, don't be too critical though. I'm a good amateur, but only an amateur all the same.'

'I'm sure I'm only an amateur as a critic, sir ... But I have at least learnt to enjoy good paintings, and I like to see the process of production.'

Monty stands behind Churchill.

'A very bold and colourful beginning sir! You have caught the heat and intensity. Good chunky composition, no fussing at all. Lovely use of complementary colours there, sir,' says Monty, pointing at the orange in the shadows and the intense blue of the sky.

'Well good lord, Montgomery, you talk like an expert!' says Churchill. 'How the devil do you know about complementary colours and all that stuff? But you're quite right, my use of the blue and orange was quite deliberate. One has to go immediately for those bold effects that make a subject exciting.'

'Yes sir,' says Monty, 'and avoid the literal and the lifeless. I know enough now about painting to imagine just what a literal lifeless painting of this subject would look like. Genteel and depressing, sir ... no real colour or passion ... my wife was a considerable painter sir, and she taught me a lot about it. With this heat, even your quite thick paint should soon be dry enough, and you will be able to block in some thick impasto in this session. Your painting could be finished before half past three, sir.'

'Just what I was thinking, Montgomery.'

'Some orange maybe on the canvas coverings of the compound, sir, just here and there, in the folds and half shadows. Lovely against the blue sky, sir.'

'Quite right, Montgomery, quite right ... By heaven, I'm enjoying such blissful peace, Montgomery, you've no idea ... such deep restful satisfaction.'

'For a while, sir, for a while,' says Montgomery, 'until the next painting starts to nag at you!'

'It's only unpleasant if you haven't the time or the energy to do the next one, Montgomery. But here I have both. And I have your stewardship to thank for the opportunity. One needs to be able to rest back on something firm in order to relax.'

'Of course, sir, and we will be that rock. I'll leave you alone now, sir.'

Montgomery goes back to the office. Churchill smiles, looks keenly at his painting, then gets up and walks around the compound for a few minutes. He then puts his painting on the top of the paint-box in the full sunshine to dry, and drinks a large amount of water from a bottle. De Guingand comes out into the compound.

'A cable from Alanbrooke, sir. Nothing to bother you, sir, just keeping you in touch and wishing you well. All reasonably quiet on the House of Commons front, sir.'

'Thank God for that!' says Churchill. 'I do wish they'd pass a Vote of No Confidence, in my leadership, however!'

'Oh sir,' says De Guingand, 'what on earth would you do then?'

'Just give me a Tank Regiment to look after!' says Churchill. 'And my paints of course. Let Bevan lead the wartime Coalition, eh, and direct the war-strategy! Wouldn't that just make him squeal eh!'

'Forget about Bevan,' says De Guingand. 'Just finish your painting and then rest, sir.'

'It needs a good 20 minutes to dry,' says Churchill. 'I'll go and rest my eyes inside the caravan.'

After this interval Churchill emerges, picks up his painting from the ground, and puts it on the easel. De Guingand appears again, and waves a wooden object in the air.

'This is a canvas carrier, sir, as you can see. Will carry 4 wet canvasses of different sizes. You won't want to smudge your work will you?'

'First class, De Guingand! Just place them beside me, will you.'

Churchill squeezes out large quantities of white for his impasto, together with yellow ochre, naples yellow, orange and two blues. He gives himself a fistful of brushes in his left hand, picks one for his right hand, mixes up a hot sandy colour with a lot of white in it and drags it across the sandy horizon. It is like spreading thick butter on bread.

'So far so good,' he says, with relief.

He mixes a slightly darker, yellowy-white, with a hint of orange in it, and drags this across the middle ground in large but broken strokes. The shadows of date palms and buildings now look magical against the intense light.

' Now for this damned camouflaged covering,' he says.

He thickens the paint again to do this, and with yet another brush with a lighter sand colour on it, he scratches the surface in various places to show the reflected light which is jumping around everywhere like a fire cracker.

'We're nearly there,' says Churchill. 'But here's the centre of the honey-pot. Not too pale now, not too pale!'

He puts thick sandy paint on a large brush and pushes the brush around the inner compound.

'Solidity as well as light,' he says. 'Don't lose the solid aspect. The painting needs bread somewhere. Can't live on ice cream. Brown bread on the foreground, honey in the middle ground, ice-cream in the background … that's it … and now a bit of butter on the bread.'

So saying he risks dragging a thick splodgy intense light yellow across the sand of the compound.

'Stop now!' he says. 'That will have to do, Winston.'

Churchill gets up, packs paints and chair and easel into a shady corner, and takes just the painting with him to his bedroom.

'Blissful sleep,' he murmurs.

There is no-one in the compound for some time. The afternoon blinding sun beats down, gradually moves westward and throws a growing shadow over that section. It is about 4:30pm and the heat is ebbing a little when a padre enters the enclosure and puts his head into the office.

'Llewellyn Hughes here,' he announces. 'Monty wants to see me.'

He moves into the shade and waits. He is the type of stocky, dark Welshman, with a slightly florid complexion. His eyebrows are thick, irregular and alive. Dark blue eyes dart about far back under these thickets. It is the restlessness of quick humour rather than of impatience. He looks capable of being endlessly diverted by his own thoughts and reflections and memories. He is sturdy and composed.

At last Monty appears and they shake hands.

'I'm trying to get so much done before our big attack, Llewellyn!' says Monty. 'I have to make a number of changes very swiftly and rather ruthlessly. Come over here into the shade, Llewellyn, I don't want Freddie De Guingand to hear too much this time.'

They walk over to the deep shade of the western side and sit down.

'Now then Monty, what is it?' says Llewellyn Hughes.

Hughes has the air of one who is seriously cheerful and at the same time cheerfully serious, without affectation. He gives a solid rock-like impression.

'You know something of my principles, Llewellyn. Now I am going to be able to implement them with a free hand, being more or less in charge for the first time in my life, in a field of war. Now you know that one of my requirements is that every soldier, padres included, (in their own way), must have a clear idea of the coming battle, and an idea just as clear of his own role in the battle. You, I know, will have reflected on this, for we have talked before, in peacetime and in war time. What, on reflection can the padres offer us?'

'It's not so much about preaching, these days, Monty, though I will do that where I feel it is appropriate. It's partly about sharing my beliefs with those who genuinely want to know them, for their own support ... that does help sometimes. It's also about dispensing creature comforts, and just being <u>there</u>, Monty, on the eve of battle ... But for these to be effective, and especially the last (being there), all we can offer is spiritual power, visible and genuine, no shams will do, as you know. And we need that power for collecting and burying the dead, Monty. The power to be moved ... and the power to embody solace and consolation. What more can I say?'

'There's no need to offer any more than that,' says Monty. 'It's exactly what I was hoping from you. The men need to be able to see and feel God when they see the padre, that's all really, isn't it? But of how many of our padres can we say that, Llewellyn?'

'I cannot judge that directly Monty. Who am I to be able to say who will be capable of arousing that trust and feeling of solace? It's something I often have to find out indirectly, like a head master in a school having apparently casual conversations with the boys about their lessons. He talks about the subjects, and the boys will reveal the quality of their teachers, Monty. That's how it usually works. Though of course there are some padres I have chosen whose spiritual quality I know for myself.'

'Yes,' says Monty, 'and are there also padres whose lack of spiritual power you know for yourself?'

'Well, that too,' says Llewellyn reluctantly.

'And do you know quite a number of padres back home whom you would willingly appoint in their place?'

'I know quite a large number of very good padres, yes. But as to sacking the one and appointing the other, that's not been my way, Monty. I haven't had the authority ...'

'But now you do have the authority. I have made sure of that for you. Llewellyn, we need to raise the moral tone of our Army for this war. The men need a very clear idea of what they are fighting for and what they are fighting against. Of course many of them have a good idea already, but it needs to be made central, it needs to be talked about ... and it needs to be put in the context of a Christian forgiveness ... A deep Christian understanding that is fully aware of evil, but also of forgiveness ... The long view, Llewellyn, the looking beyond the war. This also is a concern of spiritual power, surely?'

'Yes indeed, Monty.'

'Some of our Anglican padres are quite unsuitable for the job in my view, Llewellyn. They are padres for the Tory Gentry, some of them. They cannot communicate with the common man.'

'It's much better than the First World War, Monty. We have made progress.'

'But is it good enough, Llewellyn? Will it do? Don't be shy, and don't be too humble, old boy. Come on, will it do?'

'It could certainly be improved, Monty.'

'Then improve it, Llewellyn. Every good padre you know or have trained in England, bring him over. Bring them all over … I'll deal with the touchy business of sending people home, just identify some of them for me and I will do the rest.'

'A bit cowardly of me to let you do it, Monty.'

'We will do it together, Llewellyn … We will work together.'

'I suppose being brutal sometimes is part of my job, Monty. I shouldn't shirk it. Oh, but it's hard, Monty, it's hard.'

They both get up, and Monty puts his arm around Llewellyn's shoulder. Llewellyn does likewise and they walk across the compound towards the office in this manner.

'Freddie!' shouts Monty.

De Guingand appears.

'Meet my friend Llewellyn Hughes, Freddie. Llewellyn, this is my Chief of Staff, Freddie De Guingand. A most excellent fellow, Llewellyn.'

They shake hands.

'I see you have managed to have a good tête-à-tête,' says De Guingand. 'Or what skulduggery is Monty up to now padre?'

Llewellyn Hughes is taken aback and embarrassed by this. He doesn't know how to take a Chief of Staff, speaking in this way of his Commander. He freezes over and smiles a frozen smile.

'Don't worry,' says Monty heartily, 'De Guingand is a sort of licensed jester here, Llewellyn … Mind you, so are all the young staff here. I've instructed them all to give an honest opinion, and to correct me if they think I'm going over the top, and I sometimes ask myself, now what would my wife think here? Or better still, Llewellyn, what is my wife thinking now?'

They all smile and go into the office.

'Tea and buns all round,' Monty shouts.

Soon Churchill emerges again from his caravan, still in his galabaya, and looking rosy and cheerful.

'Any tea going, Montgomery?' he shouts into the office.

'Tea and buns all round,' Monty shouts again. 'Come in sir, come in.'

Churchill paddles into the office.

'This, believe it or not, is the Prime Minister, Llewellyn.'

Llewellyn is this time equal to the unusual atmosphere.

'Overwhelmed to meet you, sir,' he says, shaking hands.

'Good to meet you too, sir,' says Churchill, and goes on, 'The reason for my strange appearance is this,' he says, addressing Llewellyn and all the company, 'I have absconded from Britain and the House of Commons and these good people are hiding me here for a few days, dressed as a native. In such guise I will shortly proceed to Alexandria. I will then take a boat to the Lebanese coast and strike east into Northern Syria, a long camel ride will take me at last to Samarkand. The Golden Road to Samarkand, you must all have heard of it. I will join the camel traders and travel the Great Silk Road as a trader. In politics, no more will be heard of me. When the British government can spare the man-power they will send out an expedition to search for me, but they will never find me ... False sightings will be reported, 'fat bald man seen in laundry basket in Aleppo', and so forth ... But I will elude them. And meanwhile I appoint my deputy, Montgomery, as soon as he has dealt with Rommel here to rule in my stead. A good dose of Cromwellian military government! Bevan will be sent to cool his heels in the Tower of London, and all will go on famously.'

There is good cheer all round as this story is unwinding and the tray of tea-cups and cakes arrives. All sit and relax till Churchill at length gets up.

'Get ready for our inspection, Montgomery!' says Churchill. 'I'm off now to begin my second painting, gentlemen. 'Evening Shadows in the Desert', it will be called.'

Churchill paddles off. Llewellyn also gets up to go.

'Very good to see you again, Monty, after a long separation. We will work closely together as you suggest.' He leaves the office briskly.

Monty and De Guingand are still seated. Monty suddenly gets up and goes speedily after the departing Llewellyn Hughes.

'Ah Llewellyn! One very important thing I forgot to mention. No more compulsory Church Parades on Sundays please! It's absolutely the wrong way to get a good message across … and also, the delicate subject of our army's sexual health and its protection.'

'I know what you are proposing, Monty. It's very difficult for me with the padres and religious superiors, but I do agree with you. I haven't the courage, however to propose it. You will have to go over my head and implement it yourself …'

'Very good Llewellyn, I will do that,' says Monty, and they shake hands, and Llewellyn is off again to a waiting car. 'By the way!' he shouts from the front seat, 'We padres could do with a few more cars and motorbikes, Monty!'

'It shall be done,' says Monty, and the car pulls out of the shade and goes off, in the still brilliant light. Monty spots Churchill in his smart suit, ready for the parade. He smiles and goes back to the office. De Guingand has news for him.

'Several of your new hand-picked HQ Staff arriving tonight sir, in the plane that will take Mr.Churchill home tomorrow.'

'Good,' says Monty. 'We will have a little reception party, here in the capital HQ compound. How delightful it will be! Who are they, Freddie?'

'There's Kit Dawnay, Sir. Also, a great liaison officer, John Poston, and a handful of other liaison men.'

'O, dear old John!' says Monty, 'It will be so lovely to see him again. I will put him in charge of the liaison work, Freddie. He and his Liaison men can report here twice a day.'

'What about your forward Tactical HQ sir?'

'I've come to the conclusion we are near enough already to the front-line, Freddie. We won't need a Main HQ and a TAC HQ. We will combine them here and everyone will know what is going on. (I can't promise that will always be the case, however). Being here will also keep us in constant contact with Connigham at Air Command. It's ideal, Freddie.'

An hour after the inspection, Churchill appears with his painting and equipment.

'That's all I can do today. Just a start this time. Finish it in dear old Blighty. Any chance of another swim, Montgomery?'

'Certainly, sir! We will come with you, Freddie and I, as before. I'll just order a car, sir.

All three are soon off in a large open car, Monty's own choice for himself, in which he will be able to stand up and wave to the troops. Churchill is ushered into the sea as before and floats on his back, relaxed and blissful.

'Well, well, well!' says De Guingand. 'Mr. Churchill is all smiles for us, sir. What a lucky turn of events. Our prospects look rosy to me. He and Alanbrooke should now become a harmonious team, and we should have nothing to worry about ... with General Alexander in Cairo one of your chief fans, Sir, and willing to give you whatever you ask for.'

'True,' says Monty. 'But Mr Churchill is too emotional, Freddie, too temperamental. And also worn out by his huge responsibilities, carried on over two and half very difficult years. He has had to swallow down too many tragic defeats, too many bitter disappointments. He has reached that stage of incipient nervous collapse, where the slightest delay or hitch, the smallest reverse or bit of bad news will set him fuming and raging and hitting out at the nearest target ... which is poor old dear old Alan Brooke in the first instance, and then me, unless I do wonders, Freddie!'

'But you will do wonders, sir!' says De Guingand.

'But it will not always be enough,' says Monty, 'when the nerves are stretched to that extent, only continual wonder will suffice to soothe them. As I say, the slightest reverse will set off his alarm bells again, he will hit out, and we will need our tin hats on, as they say! He is like an exhausted soldier, Freddie, who has seen too much battle and needs a good rest, out of the front-line. Unfortunately there is no-one who can replace him, so he has to soldier on. And he takes refuge in more and more alcohol, as you can see.'

'And in humour. I like his humour and it's doing him a lot of good. But the alcohol could be a problem.'

'He obviously has a tough constitution, and in ordinary times a full tank of alcohol would do him little harm. Perhaps he actually thrives on it. But where a continual clear head is needed, it is worrying. Alanbrooke will have to shoulder that burden, I fear. If only we can make a break-through here, and begin to see the end of this war!'

'Oh, it's going to be a long weary route, unless the Russians can turn the tide at Stalingrad. Perhaps they can.' says De Guingand.

'They will have to if we are to have a chance, otherwise we will be fighting this war for another ten or twenty years, even with American help.'

Monty steps forward to the sea's edge, as Churchill is waving to them and calling for help.

'Bit of a quicksand here, Montgomery!' Churchill shouts, as he disappears nearly up to his knees in the soft sand. They pull him out and hand him a large towel. They all three undertake the job of drying Mr Churchill and then lift the full-length galabaya over his head.

Back at the HQ orders have been given for the meal for the expected new officers.

'Some of my new team will be arriving tonight, sir,' says Monty to Churchill.

'Good,' says Churchill, 'I will be happy to meet them.'

'Thank you sir,' says Monty. 'Once again, sir, I cannot avoid expressing a preference for a suit as your evening wear, sir. But once again I have no wish to impose ...'

'No wish to impose, I should think not Montgomery! I have come to love this galabaya, Montgomery, and in it I shall appear tonight, to meet your officers, they will be delighted to see it, and it will help them in a more speedy acclimatization here.'

'Just as you say, sir,' says Monty.

'Just as you say sir!' imitates Churchill. 'There's the butler again. You won't be short of a good job, Montgomery, if you choose to retire early from the army!'

Monty winces a little and then smiles. Churchill goes off to his caravan.

21st August

Churchill is up early, dressed in his galabaya, and has a car take him again to the sea, where he sets up his easel. The car stays with him as he works.

'No drawing involved today,' Churchill says to himself, as he looks out to sea from a position a mere 20 yards away. 'Just a decision as to how high to put the horizon line. Quite high I think. I want to give myself plenty of space to record these sumptuous sea-colours. All I need to do is to <u>record</u> them. No frills, no fancy tricks. The painting is ready made …'

His canvas has a pale violet background colour on it, already dry. He squeezes out a few colours onto a palette, and begins with a small firm brush, dipped in indigo. He drags this brush slowly across creating the horizon-line. Straight, but not too crisp.

'Horizon is blurred a little into the sky,' he says. 'It's very strange,' he said aloud. 'All the colours in the sea completely reverse the rules of aerial perspective. The darkest is that incredible indigo on the horizon ... a band of indigo, deep and dense.'

He thickens the indigo line, pulling it down into the sea. 'And as we get nearer to the beach the colours get paler and more blue … And then turquoise and then cabbage-green and then a wilted-lettuce yellowy-green, and lastly, a beautiful, pale, sandy green in the shallows, and a furl of white breaking on the creamy sand. Nothing could be more simple.'

He mixes up a thin mixture of ultramarine and sweeps it over the sea with a large brush, coming all the way to where the waves break. 'A good base, a good base. A bit of thwack in it. An undergirding.'

Then he looks at the sky. 'Not blue at all at the base, but a broody purple - quite dark and thundery that sky. Very strange.'

He mixes ultramarine and crimson, adds some white, and washes this thinly over the sky, working from the base-line of indigo with a large brush and pushing the paint upwards.

'Give this broody old sky some uplift,' he says. 'Some

aspiration, some hope.'

He then works ultramarine and white into the apex of the sky, and blends it into the purple below with a dry brush, which takes off some of the paint and eases the transition from purple to sky-blue.

'Now for the jolly old cloth,' he says, and takes a clean rag and begins to wipe the lower area of sea, taking off most of the ultramarine, but not all.

'There's <u>enough,</u>' he says, 'and there's such a thing as <u>too much</u>! I have taken just enough of that blue off, and left a glassy blue there. Just enough for the lighter blues and the greens to bite into.'

He sits back and surveys his work so far. 'Just a little ochre for the shallows and the beach.'

He mixes Naples-Yellow and a little white and draws this thinly across the foreground, taking a dry brush again and blending it into the ultramarine.

He gets up, stretches and walks across to the car.

'I'll leave all that to dry thoroughly for about 15 minutes,' he says to the driver. 'I'll take a nice stroll along the beach. No need to worry about me, Corporal.'

'Please don't go out of sight, sir,' says the corporal.'

Churchill walks slowly along the beach about 100 yards, and begins paddling in the shallows as he walks back. Every now and then he stoops to the sea, fills his hands and splashes the water over his face and neck. He comes slowly back to the car.

'Anything much in the headlines, Corporal?' Churchill asks, as he notices a newspaper. 'Read me out a few passages, will you? I mustn't be completely out of touch when I get home.'

'It's mainly about Stalingrad, sir. Quite hopeful, sir.'

'Interesting and thank you corporal. I will get back to my painting now.'

At his easel Churchill tests the paint with his finger. 'Oh that will do,' he says, 'dry enough. Now for the fun.'

He thickens the paint on the sky first with purple, and then with the sky–blue, pulling it down into the purple and blending it with a dry brush. 'Good enough,' he says.

Then he thickens the ultramarine on the distant part of the sea and then introduces a different blue altogether for the middle distance, with a beautiful layer of cobalt, mixed with a little ultramarine and white, a slightly lighter blue.

'Lovely,' says Churchill, 'That cobalt blue makes my soul sing. That is the heavenly part of the painting. I just mustn't lose that. Now I need bottle-green.'

He dips a brush into a viridian. 'Viridian, not too thick,' he says. 'Semi-transparent, but plenty of body also.'

He mixes some turps into it. ' Just right!' .He works the viridian into the section under the cobalt, and blends them together at the joins.

'Splendid,' he says. 'Now for this extraordinary <u>soapy</u> turquoise. Quite disgusting really, quite disgusting, but it has its place.'

He mixes viridian with cerulean blue and with white. 'Not too heavy, and not too much of it. And now a layer of viridian again. Or rather splashes of viridian here and there, thin lines of viridian, inter penetrating the blues and greens and sickly turquoise.' He does this to his satisfaction.

'And now a very thin viridian.' He comes closer to shore with this washed-out layer of viridian, looking beautifully glassy and transparent. He mixes viridian with Naples Yellow and a little white. 'Now for the cabbage green section.' He paints this in. 'And now for the wilted-lettuce colour. Whoever would have though wilted lettuce could look beautiful!' He puts more Naples Yellow into the viridian mixture and washes it thinly over the next area coming forward. 'And now for the pale sandy green! More Naples Yellow into the mixture ...'

Excitedly he puts this layer on, and then a thicker layer of creamy Naples Yellow and white for the dry sand. Then he takes a brush with white on it and drags it irregularly over the foreground for the furls of the small breaking waves.

'Hallelujah, hallelujah, it's worked!' Churchill says loudly. 'How often does a painting go exactly according to plan, and so quickly? Hardly ever, hardly ever!'

He goes to the water's edge and paddles again, goes further in up too his knees and splashes his face and neck with the cool water. Then he goes back to his easel, sits down and takes pleasure in his painting and in the perfect clear air. He gets up, signals to his driver, who comes over and helps him to pack up.

Churchill arrives back at the HQ, proudly carrying his new painting past the entrance. 'This is a feast of colour, gentlemen! Perhaps my swan song. I can't see myself getting another chance to paint for a long time. And then I will be too old and tired.'

'Nonsense, sir,' says Monty, 'you must come out to North Africa again, when we have driven Rommel out. Then you can pick your spot. Where do you fancy, sir?'

'I have always liked Morocco best of all, and Tunisia,' says Churchill.

'Well, just give us all a few months, ourselves and the good old Americans, and Morocco and Tunisia will be available. I'm sure we can have a breathing-space once Africa is under our control.'

'There's always the problem of the French in Africa and their loyalty to the Vichy, Montgomery.'

'Oh we will make short work of that,' says Monty. 'Don't think the French are going to stand in our way, sir.'

'But I rather thought it would be part of my job to deal with France in Africa, Montgomery. Wouldn't you say so?'

'I'm just saying I will give you full backing in that job, sir,' says Montgomery hurriedly. 'I hope you don't think I have got political ambitions, sir!'

'Well I am not so sure … You take a bigger interest in politics than is perhaps good for a professional soldier, Montgomery. You look after your side of things and we will look after you. That's the agreed arrangement in dear old Blighty, and we should keep it that way.'

'Yes, sir. And by the way, sir, our War Artists Department has produced a splendid kit for carrying several wet paintings together without mess or smudging. I've got it here for you.' He goes into the office and produces it.

Churchill beams, thanks him, and adds it to his burden, plodding off to his caravan like a happy boy. A few hours later, he is getting into his car, with Monty beside him in the back seat, and all at the HQ are at the entrance to salute and wave him goodbye as the car sets off to the airport.

Chapter 16 – Final Preparations for Battle of Alam Halfa

It is late afternoon in the HQ

'Cable from General Alexander in Cairo, sir,' says De Guingand.

'Read it out, Freddie,' says Monty.

'It's about welfare arrangements for the troops, sir; says he will be happy to provide all the extras you've asked for. Food to be improved immediately – cigarette ration to be doubled – and arrangements made for providing more frequent periods of leave for all ranks, sir. And postal difficulties to be looked into immediately and with emphatic kicks up various backsides, sir. Oh, and as to the delicate matter, sir…'

'What delicate matter?' says Monty sharply. 'They're all delicate matters.'

'Well for some, the delicate matter of the dangers of venereal disease, sir, and protection against … That will be treated seriously and action taken. Inspection and licensing of cafes and their personnel, sir, and provision of "contraceptives for those requiring them."'

'For all,' says Monty. 'For all. Just emphasize that, will you, in your reply. Anyway, thank him profusely for everything, Fredddie, and tell him he's taken a large weight off my mind. We shall also need more troops, however. At least, after the Alam Halfa battle is over. I'm sure he is working on that, even if he doesn't mention it.'

'I expect they will arrive with the new Sherman tanks, sir.'

'I fear the Shermans will be a last minute thing,' says Monty, 'Very last minute. We'll have to work like fury to get our men into those, and learn to use them before Alamein, but we will need the extra troops weeks before that.'

The day after Churchill's departure, Monty begins his tour of all the units, wearing the beret and standing up in the open car and saluting groups of men he passes as they salute him. This tour goes on for several days, and on each day he takes a different member of his new HQ team with him, and introduces each one to the troops. He repeats several of the things he had said in his address to the officers some 10 days ago, and especially emphasizes the need to stand firm whatever the pressure, and not to have the idea of a possible retreat at the back of their minds. In spite of his slight stature and foxy look, the talks go down well, and an atmosphere of hope and excitement begins to build up.

He visits also the Alam Halfa ridge and the smaller rocky ridges and outcrops further west, where the digging in is proceeding.

'Some of these rocks are so hard,' says an officer. 'They resist dynamite. I fear that we won't be able to make room for all the guns and armour that we'd envisaged, sir.'

'Just do what you can,' Monty says. 'We can always pull back some of our armour into a safe place, and send it forward again when extra fire-power is needed and the danger is less. I'm looking forward to this encounter ... and I hope you are, officer!'

'If we are well prepared, yes sir,' says the officer. 'But there's so little time. If Rommel were to attack tomorrow ... '

'I don't think he's ready, officer. Our spies are out there. We'll probably get another week.'

Monty passes on, chatting here and there, and looking relaxed and cheerful. For all one could guess from his demeanour, the preparations are for some grand and bloodless Sports Day, on which prizes will be awarded all round and a feast for all sides will be held in a grand pavilion. But the men do not resent this, as they might with some Staff Officers who are all hearty smiles, and who will be well behind the danger area themselves when the fighting begins. Monty exudes a serious consciousness of the price that must be paid alongside his cheerful manner, and beneath that is humanity and concern about these losses, all of which are transmitted to the men.

The communication of subtleties of this order depends on more than words. The listening men hear the words of encouragement, and at the same time rivet their eyes on a face, seeing either a conventional assumed face that does little or nothing, or a face that registers touches from the depths of a man's being which are overwhelmingly convincing. These convey fellow-feeling, and also a sense of the depths of the existence common to all.

Gradually common existence can be transformed by the suggestion of mysteries beyond what it usually contains. The common sense of existence is not <u>annulled</u> as these mysteries come into view, it exists side by side with them. Gradually men realize that family, and the birth of children, and the deaths of grandparents, are all extraordinary events in an existence whose strangeness has not been sufficiently felt by them until this moment.

A degree of reconciliation to death is engendered when its universality is brought into view again by the deep eloquence of a gifted and transported speaker. For along with its universality are brought touches of magic which take it beyond a bare factuality and a grim stoicism required of them.

Monty is at one time insisting again that he will not throw away their lives, and later on_is thanking them for being willing to die for the cause, and in that thanks is perceived a mystery and a consolation and an opening to new realities beyond their own means of expression. It is beyond the actual words of Monty himself, which are plain almost to a fault. But from the way a look in his eyes or a tremor in his lips or a movement of his jaw is conjoined with his words, there comes a flash of compassionate insight, sometimes rising to joy. The compact between them is sealed. They are on a mysterious journey together, and the companions of life will be the companions of death and of what lies beyond. It becomes evident that something does lie beyond it. <u>That</u> is in the quiver of Monty's lip, or even in the way he gives rotundity to a phrase by shaping his mouth in a special way once in a while. The 'beyond' is even in his faint lisp, reminding us that neither mental nor spiritual nor physical perfection is of the essence in this matter. The men will ridicule the lisp, and begin to love it, and its owner, at the same time.

'Here we will stay and fight, even if we must die. Our families at home will understand us and what was required of us,' Monty is saying to a group.

'Families' echoes in the men's minds, and sounds wonderful and brings the beginning of tears. And the knowledge that they might die out here and not get home to their families is sensed, as an extension of the term 'family' again. The family of man, both in extent and in depth, is felt as extending beyond a street in West Ham or in Manchester or in Glasgow. There is nothing, it is sensed, that can actually separate a man from his family, or from his larger family, the dimensions of which are only now beginning to be imprinted on their extended consciousness.

'And let me remind you of the wonderful words of St. Paul, "neither death nor life, no angels or principalities or powers, neither what is present nor what is to come, no force whatever … will be able to separate us from the love of God, which comes to us in Christ Jesus our Lord." The love of God will enfold us, whether we live or die here, and the more we can bring ourselves to believe that, the more conscious we will become of it. Let us entrust ourselves to God, therefore, and to the Lord Mighty in battle(s), who will deliver us the victory.'

Some of the officers, those from a Public School background, are uncomfortably reminded of Speech Day by Monty's addresses. 'Pi-jaw' was what it was called by the pupils, a phrase whose withering contempt should surely have made all such pompous occasions impossible to hold, but for the pompous self-belief, the pompous inability to sense the presence of silent criticism, among some of those who had come through Public School themselves. These were the few hard remains of pompous and impervious, truly believing in the upper class pieties, mistaking them for Christianity and true patriotism. And these were collectively the sap that rises to the top. But the cynical officers present begin to question their own Speech Day cynicism as they hear Monty, and saw his effect on men who had never been anywhere near a Public School. Most of them had been only to Elementary School, and had left at 14. Some had hardly been to school at all. But it was not really unfamiliarity with pi-jaw that held these men riveted to Monty's words and face and eyes. It is an experience of charisma, and chiefly from the concentrated fire of the eyes, which each man feels as looking uniquely into his own soul. Monty has eyes that in sweeping over all could seem to enter into the eyes of every individual present. Monty does not, except on parade inspections, actually look into any individual's eyes as he sweeps his own eyes back and forth and across the whole company. What happens is that each man, as it were, 'steals' Monty's eyes as they are journeying, and directs them at himself, with his own eyes. Such is the power of Monty's glance. Each feels himself seen, and judged, with no possible secrets, and at the same time forgiven and encouraged.

Monty's power over Australians, New Zealanders, South Africans and other 'Colonials' was extraordinary. Finding in him none of the snobbery, or imagined snobbery, of the British Officer Class, or even the snobbery of the British other ranks, the 'Colonials' found in him a unique Britisher, not only to 'redeem' the British generally, but far more importantly, able to speak inwardly and deeply to their condition, even to those who knew their usual condition to be of a Caliban-like roughness.

When Monty salutes and waves goodbye to a large group of men, a tremendous cheer gathers slowly and spreads out in its volume well beyond their area. Soldiers in another unit half a mile away can easily sense that something unusual is happening. Some are reminded of the sustained cheering for their local big football team at home by a large crowd, when it reaches the stage of appreciative roar, without words and without malice towards the other team. It is a surge of energy, and it happens at all the units Monty visits, except for some of the specialist tank units, where he voices sharp criticism of their attitude towards the infantry they are supposed to work with.

'We have to work as a team,' he says, in the cliché of all Speech Days. 'If we don't work together, we will sink together. I will have no exclusivism in my Army. Every one has a particular job to do, and no one is more important than another. And this applies to units as well as to individuals. Units as well as individuals will take my orders without question, as relayed to them by my Chief of Staff, De Guingand, who is standing by me now. Get to know his face all of you.'

And all look at De Guingand, with his handsome face, and when he relaxes a little and smiles his slightly gap-toothed smile under his little black moustache, his charm is evident. And if it is Major Bill Williams who is with Monty, even his lugubrious long face, with his tiny round black glasses is reassuring, exuding the boffin intelligence that all can admire and rely on in these special times. And when he too relaxes and smiles, it is something of a hoot to see such a thing irradiating his suppressed depths and glooms. And if it is Kit Daunay or Johnny Henderson, it is lovely to see relative youth and fresh good looks at the helm, as though it is a vitally important cricket match that is at issue.

Monty goes unrelentingly on, in his determination, day after day, to make himself and his staff visible to every unit under his command. His beret is already being commented on, and his slight figure standing up in the car as it approaches them is being impressed upon the memory. Some of the men wonder already if this is hubris, and whether such a sight will be seen much longer, if Alam Halfa or Alamein after it, turns out to be a disaster.

'Remember that little mad general in the beret?' they envisage asking each other in later months, if they survive, 'Bit of a character! Fat lot of good it did him, or anyone! Still the little bugger had a go, tried to rouse us. Where is he now? Back in Blighty, demoted I suppose. Doing the officer–equivalent of spud-bashing. And yet, and yet,' they surmise, 'perhaps not, this time, perhaps not … '

Monty returns invigorated to his HQ after each round of visiting, sensing that the atmosphere has definitely changed for the better, if only in the stoical and fatalistic almost-pleasure that the men are beginning to take in the stance of defiance unto death. This is the mood that is catching on. Death with Honour. And glimpses of the possible Life with Honour, Survival with Honour, fighting another day, with honour pocketed and secure. There is a beginning of a kind of exhilaration that in later years, for those who survive unscathed in body or mind, comes to be remembered as the happiest and most creative period of their lives, with comradeship and good spirits in a state of permanence, awaking the energies during the day, and ensuring profound and peaceful sleep at night, inspite of the cold and the flies and the strictly rationed water. 'Why can't our peace-time jobs be like those days and weeks and months in the desert?' they say. 'Why can't our homes and streets be like that?' they say. 'We can't make it happen. We are tired, we have suffered a reaction, we cannot resurrect that wonderful spirit. But why don't the others do it for us all, the ones that weren't there? Why is everything so dreary and whey-faced?' Or, 'Why do people moan so much about rationing? We all had rationing in those joyful and heroic days. Even our water was rationed. What harm did it do us? We learnt to value everything we had! What is the matter with people now?' and so on.

Before and after each day of visiting the units, Monty sits quietly, either in his bedroom caravan, or in a shaded part of the enclosure, gathering himself, and talking under his breath to his Betty. 'Dear Betty,' he murmurs, 'dear Betty ... Betty my love. Give me your inspiration! Lend me your spirit, love, to add to my own. Let my love for you, and my longing for you, be in my face and my manner when I speak to the men. It is through you, dear, that I come to love the men. And the men will love me also, for what I have shown them of you. Dear Betty, you are with me always. You are my guiding star, you give me my words, your star is in my eyes as I speak. That is what the men see, Betty, it is you they are seeing , you dear, dear creature!'

He sometimes has to hide the tears that come to his eyes. The refreshment is wonderful and the concentrated practice that had in fact been proceeding for several years now, was giving him the aura of a quiet and dignified asceticism, and giving to the HQ and its enclosure a monastic atmosphere. To Monty's normally unflappable demeanour was added a spiritual peace that was absorbed by sensitive visitors.

'The still centre of the turning world,' says one of these to Monty. 'I'm glad you find it so,' says Monty. 'But there is much turbulence to come, and we shall have to see how we will manage then.'

28th August onwards

On his last round of visits, before the battle begins, Monty is able to distribute free cigarettes, going round every unit just for this purpose. A very large consignment has just arrived via Cairo thanks to Alexander's jollying things along. He waves from his car, and the men cheer.

On arriving back at HQ Monty is given a letter by De Guingand. This is from Alanbrooke. Monty walks out of the office and into the enclosure to read it.

'Yes, yes,' says Monty to himself, then to De Guingand when he goes back inside. 'The right people in the right place at the right time, that's what it is!'

'I hope so, sir,' says Freddie. 'What is concerning you at the moment?'

'This good letter from Alanbrooke, Freddie. Full confidence in us all. Alexander in Cairo and me here at Alamein ... and I'm sure he means my team here as well. You, Freddie, and Kit and Bill Williams and Johnny Henderson, and the two or three still to arrive, and John Poston our chief Liaison Officer, such a splendid young man. And, we have to add, Alanbrooke himself, and Churchill himself, when at his best when listening to Alanbrooke! It is so marvellous to have you wonderful young men, with no envy or ill-feeling, just prepared to do a job to the best of all your considerable abilities. Why, we are even getting on well with Portal and Cunningham at Main HQ. This must be the first time all three services have worked together and long may it continue. It's unusual Freddie ... a gift ... a splendid concatenation of circumstances!'

'There is a tide of the affairs of men,' quotes Freddie, and then pauses.

'Which taken at the flood,' Monty adds.

'Leads on to fortune!' says Freddie.

'But which ... ' says Monty, forced to stop. 'Ask one of the others, will you? Freddie, how it goes on? Bill Williams should know.'

Major Bill Williams sitting in a far corner, has picked up the conversation and completes the sentence.

'Not 'but which' sir. It goes 'leads on to fortune. Omitted', sir,

'Omitted, all the voyage of their life is bound in shallows and in miseries."

'Well, well!' says Monty. 'How wonderfully appropriate, and how clever of you Bill!'

'I played Brutus once in our school play, sir. Remember most of it.'

'Does it go on?' asks Monty.

'Yes, sir, another three lines in that speech. 'On such a full sea are we now afloat: and we must take the current when it serves, or lose our venture'.'

"On such a full sea are we now afloat!" says Monty, in wonder. 'So indeed we are. What is the situation in the play, Bill? What exactly are they talking about? It's 'Julius Caesar' I presume.'

'Yes, of course,' says Bill. 'Brutus and Cassius are discussing military tactics in the latter part of the play. Cassius has one view and Brutus then expresses his own.'

'Curiouser and curiouser!' says Monty. 'Ahhh!' he sighs.

'What is it, sir? Is it 'Would I had followed the Arts', sir?' says Bill venturously. 'Yes and no to that,' says Monty. 'But doesn't Brutus' plan fail, Bill? Doesn't it fail? Does my poor learning deceive me?'

'No, your learning does not deceive you. Brutus and Cassius are crushed and Octavius Caesar triumphs.'

'Oh dear!' says Monty. 'I must watch out for 'hubris', I know. And you men here must warn me. You must speak plainly and sincerely to me at all times, you must not flatter me, not be frightened of my flares of bad temper. Is that understood, everyone? Bring them all in Bill, we must talk about this now!'

'Sir, they are very busy and the rest of the team are not yet here. I think we should leave it for now,' says Freddie. 'We understand, and we can also make it clear to the others.'

'It shall be as you say, Freddie.' says Monty.

There is a return to silence, and they all turn to their work and then into the silence, Bill's voice.

'In any case, it is Churchill who should beware of hubris, sir, it is Churchill who has urged us on and on, 'Attack!' and so fourth, as though we were right now at the flood of the tide when we are not.'

'Quite so,' says Monty, 'quite so. You have taken a weight off my mind. I'll re-phrase it, On such a full sea, we are _not_ afloat. But come the full moon at October's end,' he goes on, 'When sprites and goblins from earth's crevices' ...

'Do tumble forth and wail upon the air,' says Bill, and goes on, 'and presage grave disasters for all those … ' and stops.

'For all those,' repeats Monty, 'for all _who_, Williams? Do go on!'

'I am not quite sure,' says Bill, 'when I can get the scansion, I shall get the words, sir, for now, it eludes me'.

'A plenary curse on you Bill Williams for leaving it like that!' says Monty. 'Anyway, who wrote those lines?'

'Why I did of course, sir. Like you, impromptu!'

'Clever of you Bill, clever of you,' says Monty. 'I wonder why they gave you the part of Brutus, though. I do hope you didn't wear those glasses then, did you Bill?'

Bill turns full face to them all, from his corner.

'No the glasses were a bit later!' he says. 'I was picked for Brutus for my solemn dignity and honour, sir, my sad chops, as it were.'

'Appropriate,' says Freddie, 'and yet, somewhere, something comical about it.'

'It was a hoot from beginning to end, Freddie ... I refused any further part in school plays!'

They work in silence for a few minutes, till De Guingand says,

'At last! A cable saying John Poston, and several liaison men of his choosing, arrive tomorrow, sir!'

'Splendid,' says Monty. 'what are the omens for the journey, Freddie?'

'Oh it's back to omens, is it?' says Freddie. 'Beware the Ideas of March, is it? Well, we're in the dog-days as you know, the dog-star Sirius. A beautiful clear glassy star sir, so white that it looks blue or green at times.'

'Stop talking about Sirius, Freddie, and tell me the weather over Europe,' says Monty.

'Stormy. Late summer storms, I'm afraid,' says Freddie.

'Hmm,' says Monty, 'not too good. Still, if it's very bad they won't try to fly, I hope. What sayeth the soothsayer, Freddie?'

'He sayeth sooth, forsooth!' says Freddie.

'That's good enough, Freddie,' says Monty, 'we can hope for the best and sleep in peace tonight.'

29th August 1942

John Poston and his fellow liaison officers arrive safely about noon. Monty greets them effusively, picking them up from Burg-El-Arab airport, and taking them back to his HQ, where they meet the rest of the team.

'You're just in time, John,' says Monty, 'have a rest and a meal, and drink some water, then I'll show you over the areas you and your team must cover. The trouble is, Rommel may attack any moment, and before this side of things is properly organised. Still, it is at Alamein later on that we shall really need you. We shall be fine here at Alam Halfa.. We're having to improvise as it is. We only need to defend and hold on, there's not much need for you to go far forward. Anyway, you go and rest, I urgently need to see Cunningham about air support for the coming battle. That's my priority. In fact, take today off, I'll see Portal today, and we'll show you around tomorrow. Yep, that's it. Tomorrow, John, tomorrow.'

Monty signals to a driver, and they set off for Cunningham's HQ, while the rest of the team welcome Poston and his colleagues and chat merrily.

30 August 1942

Monty's reconaissance tank, the Grant, driven by Sergeant. Bennett, has John Poston in the observation turret as it tours the Alam Halfa area, with Monty below, shouting information.

'What we see due south of us,' he shouts, 'is the Alam Halfa ridge, where our main defences have been dug in. Rommel will, we hope, eventually attack the ridge from the south with his Panzers and artillery, hoping to break through. He cannot possibly succeed, because we are so well entrenched. But it is his last chance, as he will see it, to get to Alexandria and Cairo - which he has promised his army he will do. So he will persist, and eventually be slowed by the soft sand as he comes nearer, and we will pound him with our guns. Meanwhile his fuel supplies will begin to run out, and he will have to withdraw. He will not be able to do much damage to Alam Halfa from the air, as we already have decided air-superiority. Right, we will now proceed further west, to the first line of our defences.'

A few minutes later Monty speaks again. 'We're now west of the main Alam Halfa ridge, and south of us again are some lesser ridges with tempting gaps between them. Here Rommel will have tried to break through before coming to Alam Halfa itself, seeing his chance of victory here. But we are fortified and hidden here as well, and he is unable to penetrate - sorry John, we are doing this in reverse order - having failed here, Rommel will proceed further west, trying to find a way round the main Alam Halfa ridge to the south – and then top speed to Alexandria … and so on. Once he is fully exposed south of Alam Halfa, we will open fire full blast from Alam Halfa itself. He will then find it necessary to stop racing eastwards, and to attack the ridge itself, as I've already described. How's that so far, John?' shouts Monty.

'Fine, sir, fine,' says Poston. 'The reverse order is not troubling me.'

'Now we will go even further west, to the limit.'

The tank rumbles on over the dry, rough ground for a few miles, and comes to a stop. Monty climbs out and sits on the top, close to John Poston.

'You will be aware that north of us we have a solid north-to-south line of defence. Rommel will not touch that. He wants to circumvent us in the south. He will line up his forces south of Himeimat ridge, there in the south.' They both take binoculars, and focus on Himeimat, and Monty says, 'He will charge at us from there and will then want to turn east, which we will encourage him to do, by having a fleet of our tanks turn tail suddenly and lead the way into the trap we have laid for him!'

'Beautifully simple,' says John, 'But will he do it, sir?'

'He is so passionate about getting to the Delta that he will not be able to resist it, John. He also thinks that by breaking through from the south and then proceeding to the coast he will have succeeded in trapping our entire army in a pincer. For of course he has considerable reserves up in the north and centre opposite our north-south line of defence.'

Monty is pointing at a simple diagram here, and John Poston studies it.

'And he will perhaps think that from our lack of serious resistance at first that we are at a low ebb in ground forces, though in the air of course we have a massive superiority.' John Poston nods.

'To conclude, when once we open up on him from the Alam Halfa Ridge, and his forces begin to get terribly bogged down there, he will turn tail and seek to escape, going westwards at full tilt. At that point, our guns will open up on him from these lesser ridges, where up until now they have been silent, and our bombers will come into use again. Also our New Zealand division will attack southwards from the same point and try to cut off his retreat. He will depart with his tail between his legs.'

John Poston continues looking through the binoculars for a while, then says, 'Not a great deal for self and colleagues to be doing then, sir?'

'Oh yes there is, John. Only there is not quite as much <u>danger</u> as usual, which you should be grateful for, but of course I will need reports regularly, in the usual way. Twice a day at my HQ, John, once after breakfast and again at supper. I will give my orders after you have reported. Even a vain and arrogant man such as myself realizes, John, realizes sometimes, that things do not go <u>exactly</u> according to plan! Otherwise I would hardly need you and your good friends to be risking your lives daily. Good heavens that is obvious, isn't it, John? I mean, constant fine adjustments are necessary ... and sometimes a big adjustment. We must at HQ be on top of events. That's why I'm bringing my TAC HQ so close to the battle. It's worth the extra risk. It's worth it, John.'

'I'm looking forward to this,' says John. 'Whatever the risk.'

'Splendid, John! So am I. If we can succeed in this defensive battle, morale will be shooting high. We will all be eager to see if we can win the offensive battle, and turn the tide in this war, John, actually turn the tide! What a prospect ... I hardly dare believe it!'

'A wonderful vision, sir,' says John.

'And I will then need a larger beret!' says Monty, taking his beret off as he climbs back into the tank. 'Home James,' he says to Sergeant Bennett, and the tank roars, and sets off eastwards.

Chapter 17 – Battle of Alam Halfa

31st August 1942

Rommel's attack has begun. German tanks advance from the south-west and the south. Allied bombers set out for the armaments hidden in the south behind Himeimet; tanks, artillery, trucks and fuel supplies. There is some German resistance in the air, but not nearly enough to prevent the bombers getting through and doing damage. The battle proceeds roughly as described by Monty to John Poston. German tanks get a long way, even on the first day of battle, finding a gap between Alam Neyil Ridge and Alam Halfa and chasing British tanks into it. The Allies on the next day, 1st of September, bring up reinforcements from further north, and fight them off.

2nd September

Churchill, bowed and hardly able to keep his eyes open, is pouring out his woes to Alannbrooke. 'I am <u>deeply worried</u> about Rommel's penetration of our defences! Don't you understand, we can't take ... <u>I can't take</u>, another defeat! We knew Rommel was preparing an attack, why didn't that man attack first! Always waiting, waiting till they have the advantage. You must tell him it won't do!'

'Sir, you have to trust him just a little while longer. Rommel is doing just what Montgomery wanted, pushing into the 'soft sand' area where his tanks will bog down. Believe me, they are being dealt with, and their line will be pushed back in a day or two.'

'Can't we speed up the communications, then, so that I am not stretched on the rack till I can't do anything at all?'

'I'll have a memo brought to you the instant it I hear from Cairo. Meanwhile, you must rest, sir, it is going to be all right.'

By the 6th of September Rommel's forces are retreating and are bombed from the air as they do so, and harassed by Allied mobile forces.

At about 6:30pm on that day, Poston, and other liaison men, gather at Monty's HQ to give their reports.

'Come into the shade, young fellows,' says Monty, beckoning them into a shaded area of the enclosure. 'And bring yourselves a drink.'

Monty sits down and the Liaison officers join him, one by one, drinks in hand, sitting or standing. 'We're nearly there,' says Monty. 'I think we can relax. Rommel is on the retreat, and some of his forces are finding it hard to get out. Well done, everyone. Hardly worth risking your lives now with further sorties. Those Stuka dive-bombers can materialize from nowhere. Very nasty.'

The men smile, and drink the water with huge relief.

'I take it your observations accord with mine?' says Monty.

'Certainly sir,' says John Poston. 'What a victory!'

A long grateful silence, quiet smiles, and some of the young officers shaking hands unobtrusively, or putting an arm round another man's shoulder.

'Well, all of you can have a bit of a holiday now,' says Monty.

'Do some sea-bathing. As for myself, a lot to do. I'll need you all in about a week for reconnaissance for the next battle, the big offensive. So use your time well. Thank you again, and I'll say goodbye.'

Monty gets up and goes into the Office.

Two days later, on the 8th of September, Monty begins his tours of the units again, this time to congratulate all those who had fought in the battle.

'Very well done, all of you, we have saved Egypt,' says Monty, standing up in his car. 'And that will be an enormous relief to our War Office! And our heroic Prime Minister and to the people of Britain. Their relief and gratitude will be felt here, it will find its way! And my relief and gratitude also, I send out to you, for your response to what I asked you to do. I made my plans and my wishes clear to you, and you have performed them splendidly. We only need to proceed further in this spirit, and we will triumph in the larger battle that is coming soon. But for that we will need hard, very hard training. You all look fit but there is a point beyond ordinary fitness which is exhilaration, which will give you enormous mental and physical reserves in an arduous situation ... and that point I intend you to reach within the next few weeks. I have made improvements to all your necessities and luxuries here. Food is better, I'm sure you've noticed, posts more regular, leaves are more frequent and cigarettes more plentiful. So train hard, men, and in the intervals make yourselves as comfortable as possible.

We must think also, and especially, though, of those we have lost over the last week ... some 1,100 wounded or missing or dead. Let us give thanks for their sacrifice, grieve for them, especially if they were our comrades, and set ourselves to live up to their example. Every single casualty I regret, and it is my earnest wish to win battles with the minimum expense of lives. But it cannot always be planned like that, and I fear that in our coming battle with Rommel we will not get off lightly, for the simple reason that Rommel knows that if he loses the battle he has lost Africa, so he will not give up easily, it will be a real slog to defeat him. But I promise you that if we do defeat him at Alamein, it is all up with him. We will chase him one thousand miles across North Africa, and he will not then come back and chase us here again. I promise you that this is the last time you will race what is called out here The Great Benghazi Handicap. It will be the last time that that music-hall turn is played. We will chase him all the way to Tripoli and then into Tunisia. Our job here will be done. Thank you, and good cheer to you all.'

His car moves off towards another unit and as he raises his hand there is a huge clapping and cheering and brilliant smiles from the men.

Chapter 18 – Preparations for the Battle of Alamein

The next day at HQ

'Generals Horrocks and Leese due today, sir, from England. And Brigadier Kirkman of the Artillery,' says De Guingand.

'All my hand-chosen men,' says Monty. 'And you will have known some of them from Staff College, Freddie, I think. Thank heavens we've got rid of Corbett and Dorman-Smith, Ramsden and a few other pieces of dead wood.. Old Auchinleck may have been a good honest soldier, but he certainly had no idea how to choose a good team of men to run the show!'

'He did seem to know how to delegate,' says De Guingand, as charitably as he dared.

'No good delegating if the people you delegate to are absolutely useless!' says Monty, heating up as expected. 'A total disaster delegating battle-plans to that clever fool Dorman-Smith.. I shall never forget him from my Staff College days!'

Monty is making notes and drawings at his desk as he talks.

'So you have said before, sir,' says De Guingand, trying to calm him down.

'So I may well have said before,' says Monty as hotly as ever. 'For heavens sake, have you had time to study Auchinleck's plans for this great battle we are now preparing for? I don't expect you have. But it has the mark of Chink Dorman-Smith all over it! Damnable cleverness. Damnably stupid cleverness! How I detest that sort of boffin!'

'Did I hear the word 'boffin', sir?' says Bill Williams from the other end of the room.

'I'm not against boffins as such, Bill,' says Monty. 'You know that perfectly well. But I just cannot stand the sort of person who will make the most simple thing complicated, just in order to show off, and to make good people feel stupid if they find they can't apply what they are being told! And if he can't even keep a simple thing simple, what in heavens name will he do with something quite complex! It is my practice, as you all know, to try to bring simplicity to complex problems so that staff and men can keep it in their heads, and don't deluge each other with endless bits of paper.'

There is a silence while the room continues to do it's work. But Monty breaks it at last.

'The thing about Chink Dorman-Smith was that he was incorrigible, unteachable. I told him all the things I am telling you now at Staff College. I told him he was too clever-by-half and therefore a damned fool. And what does he do? He goes on being a damned fool in precisely the same way. And gets promoted for it! Fools them all. And was on the brink of leading us all into a great military disaster here at Alamein! It's hard to credit the stupidity of some of our military, the ones that do the selections and promotions! That's partly why I resent Auchinleck so much, good man though he is.'

Silence again, with Monty breathing rather heavily as he continues to work on his diagrams.

'I mean, what is the point of having a brilliant teacher, such as myself, if you aren't teachable! And what's the point of being corrected, time after time if you are in fact incorrigible? No, no he wasn't a boffin at all, Bill, just a damned fool who knew how to talk himself up the ladder of promotion. I suppose no-one dared to say they couldn't actually understand his complex ideas. Each person probably assumed that other people did understand, and he got promoted due to moral cowardice all round. That's the only way I can explain it to myself. As for yourself, Bill, you of course are genuinely brilliant. You've helped crack the German codes and helped to create our Ultra system which will win us the war, so long as we learn to do the right military things..'

Another longer silence while the work goes on.

'As to delegation, this seems a good time to say it to you all. Each one of you has my complete confidence. I have picked you precisely for that reason. When I delegate to you, I will never fuss you. Once you have understood what is required, I will leave it entirely to you, not look over your shoulder or check up on you at all. Besides, I won't have the time to do so, if I am doing my part of the job properly. And you must not fuss me with detail. Just do your part of the job, sort out the detail yourselves and make decisions. That is how we will operate.'

Silence at last is dominant.

'Just one last thing,' says Monty. 'Cultivate memory, and avoid bits of paper. I will be doing the same. And don't ever say to me you didn't have an order in writing, as an excuse for having forgotten it.'

Generals Horrocks and Leese arrive, and are welcomed into the company.

13th September

Monty goes off on his own, and is seen pacing up and down by the palm trees. He is away for several hours, and enters the compound at about 11 in the morning.

'The battle plan is ready,' says Monty to de Guingand in the office. 'I will explain it here at TAC HQ tomorrow to the chief commanders. It will not be passed further down the chain until a week before battle, and to other ranks just a day or so before. Everyone must know. But it is a tricky balancing act.'

De Guingand nods.

'I have been recommended General Lumsden to lead the Corps De Chasse, Freddie. I don't know him personally, but he comes with the highest recommendations.'

'I rather thought you were giving that role to your good friend General Horrocks,' says De Guingand.

'I also thought so, but I've changed my mind. Horrocks is splendid, but perhaps not quite ready for that role. We need special experience here and I'm told Lumsden has precisely that. We shall welcome him here in a couple of days, I hope.'

14 September

Monty is summing up his address to the chief commanders on his battle-plan.

'So here it is again in brief. We appear to commit ourselves most heavily in the South, with General Horrocks in command. All our deception plans are aimed to create that impression, with Rommel's defences spread out, and him expecting a left hook in the southern sector. It should not be too difficult to get our best tanks, our Corps de Chasse, out and through the enemy lines ... to sit here, on the enemy supply lines ... the Rahman Track. As that is being established, our infantry and the rest of your tanks will begin to move forward, making two break-ins, one to the centre here, and another south of centre.

Rommel will still be thinking that our main break-in point is to be further south, so he will not move up reinforcements to these more central break-in positions. And here we will begin to slog it out for a few critical days, perhaps even a week. Meanwhile our Corps de Chasse will be denying the enemy its supplies. If Rommel turns his attention to that too much, we will have the advantage, and we will be able to move forward further from our break-in positions. At a point of my choosing, we will make a thrust in the north, and towards the west. This will be a job for our Australian troops. At that point two things should happen. Rommel should decide that our southern plan was a mere feint, and begin to bring his troops up from there to meet our new moves. At the same time he will have to deploy some of his troops from the central positions to meet the threat along the west road. That will weaken his position at the centre, and we will throw everything we've got at the central break-in point, to take Kidney Ridge here,' he points to his key position, 'and then proceed beyond it, driving a wedge between his forces before his reinforcements from the south have arrived.

'At the same time our own southern forces will be moving northwards to reinforce this colossal blow that we are striking at the centre, and deal with Rommel's forces from the south, which will be racing up as soon as he realises where the main strike is falling.

'Our forces will pour through the gap and then fan out trapping huge numbers of enemy troops and completely dominating their supply lines. And that, gentlemen, will be that. Any questions, gentlemen?'

A long appreciative silence.

'I slightly worry about our Corps de Chasse, sir, out there on the Rahman line. If they are going to be exposed they will need to be very good tanks, and will they have anti-tank gun support?'

'They will be our latest tanks, and they will be mobile and fast. I don't think we need to worry too much about them. We will also have our first-rate artillery, directing massive fire at any force that tries to engage with them. I perhaps need to emphasize again the absolutely vital role of our artillery. The battle will begin with the biggest artillery barrage in modern warfare ... together with heavy bombing.

'This will do huge material and psychological damage to the enemy and will make it easier for our sappers to go in and defuse the minefields, both our own and those of the enemy, at the break-in points. We shall also use darkness, of course, for we will begin in the darkness, at 9:30pm, and we will use smoke screens as well, to protect the sappers.

'Once the sappers have done their job, we will have another huge artillery barrage while, and before, the infantry go in along the cleared mine-lanes. We will deploy a creeping barrage, coming quite close to our own position. The enemy will be forced to keep his head down and keep his sanity, while our infantry go in and establish strong positions well into enemy lines.

'At this point, artillery will prepare the way for our tanks to go in along the cleared mine-lines. We will send up tank defences, anti-tank guns, while the creeping barrage goes on.

'All this is the establishment of the break-in. It will be as Churchill has said to me, not the end or even the middle, 'but <u>the end of the beginning</u>!' We will succeed in establishing a position so strong that Rommel will have to respond to whatever we do next, and we shall never have to respond to what he chooses to do. We will set the terms of the battle from the outset, and with such solidity and strength that we will never lose our shape or our battle plan. It is vitally important in battle, gentlemen, never to lose your shape or balance, and to stick to your battle-plan even if things do not go strictly to plan. Is that clear, gentlemen?'

Nods of appreciation, murmurs and smiles.

'It only remains then, gentlemen, to train your troops for the tasks described, good hard training, gentlemen, both technical and physical. Physically we need hardness, more than just fitness, as I've explained many times. And technically we need familiarity to the point of ease and quickness.

'We have the time, gentleman, all we need now is the resolution. Thank you, gentleman, and good night.'

Monty walks out of the meeting, but the officers stay on, in a mixture of excited hope and puzzlement mingling together and buzzing with talk.

'Is this some kind of dream?' says one.

'Well at least if we all die here together, we shall die with hope in our hearts. If we dare to believe what we are hearing, that is.'

'We've got no choice really. If we don't dare to hope we shall have to accuse ourselves if things go wrong. Perhaps that's what Monty is up to ... giving us no choice.'

'Clever. But he clearly believes it all himself. It's not a posture, is it?'

'Not unless he's a very clever actor.'

17th September

De Guingand goes over to Montgomery, who is in the map caravan, studying maps laid on a large table.

'A long cable from Alanbrooke, sir.'

'Important, I suppose?' says Monty without looking up.

'I'm afraid so ... '

'Well go on then,' says Monty, pushing his maps away, and sitting back in his chair, all attention.

'Politics again, sir. Mr Churchill erupting again. Stafford Cripps has resigned, there is the chance of Churchill losing a vote of confidence in the House over the conduct of the war. He feels at the end of his tether.'

'Distressing,' says Monty, 'but there's precious little we can do about it here. Why do they bother us while we try to get on and do our job? Why do they, Freddie?'

'The trouble is, Churchill thinks there is something we can do to help him.'

'And I can guess what it is,' says Monty.

'He wants us to attack at the September full moon, in just over a week from now, instead of at the October full moon as planned. And it is because he needs a military victory now, this moment, in order to save his political career.'

'Exactly,' says Freddie. 'And of course you will want to say why on earth should we adjust military strategy for purely political reasons.'

'Of course I will and I do say that,' says Monty, flaring up. 'Politics, politics!'

'But we can't just ignore politics, sir. It would be a moral catastrophe as well. Surely you can see that, sir.'

'Yes of course I can, Of course I can. What I can't see, however is why Churchill himself doesn't stay calm in the situation, and wait for us here to deliver him. Also, Attlee is a perfectly good deputy in the war cabinet. The business will go on if Churchill has to rest a little.'

'Attlee is, by all accounts, an extremely good deputy and in matters of the rapid dispatch of business, considerably superior to Churchill. But you know perfectly well what is the nub of it all.'

'Churchill's personal vanity is the nub of it all!' says Monty, interrupting him, 'Sheer bloody vanity, that's all it is! Who would have thought that a vital military strategy should hang upon we men's vanity?'

'Well of course we know nothing about vanity here, do we, sir. It's not in our vocabulary,' says De Guingand equably and without a flicker of a smile.

At this point Monty uncharacteristically covers his head with his hands and arms and howls like a wolf. Then he bursts out laughing, and thumps the table to punctuate his train-tunnel laugh.

'Vanity of vanities, all is vanity,' he declaims. 'Oh damn Churchill's vanity, and damn my vanity. The question is, what on earth am I to do? If I accede to Churchill's request, we shall lose the battle, and then Churchill will fall anyway, so what good will that have done? If I refuse his request, and wait till late October, he will probably be voted out of office, and everything you fear about morale in the country will ensue. It is an impossible position. We are damned if we do and damned if we don't!'

'And its worse than that, sir,' says De Guingand.

Monty takes this in. His face is now far from its usual practical calm. There is anguish there.

'Tell me the worst then, De Guingand,' he says.

'Churchill <u>is</u> at the end of his tether, psychologically and physically, sir. He is close to a mental and physical breakdown. He has had too much pressure and too many disappointments. There comes a point when even little things, small obstacles and worries, produce mountainous negative reactions ... and Churchill seems to have reached that point. He needs a victory, and he needs it now. There seems no escape from that, sir.'

There is a long silence, Monty sighs deeply, then says, 'He would probably have a breakdown anyway, if we fought now and secured, by some miracle, a victory.'

Another silence.

'Often the worst of an illness of the stress sort floods in when the crisis is over,' Monty says again.

'I have heard of such things,' says De Guingand. 'However, if we were to secure a victory, the morale of our country would survive despite a Churchill breakdown.'

Another silence.

'True, true,' says Monty quietly. 'True.' Another silence. 'But however,' says Monty loudly and firmly, 'we cannot deliver a victory now, and that's that. Another defeat here would not only end my career, but it would cause a breakdown in morale and order. The 8th Army would go to pieces. We would lose Egypt, and lose control of the oil-fields. And that would be that. And only a huge victory by the Russians in the Stalingrad area would be able to save the day for us.'

A silence again, till De Guingand speaks.

'We look to the Russians for deliverance. And the Russians look to us. We must not disappoint the Russians.'

'True, again true,' says Monty quietly, and there is again silence.

'There is another worry in Churchill's mind,' says De Guingand at last. 'He is afraid, unless we secure a victory very soon, that the Americans will go back on their commitment to a landing in North Africa, and will transfer their resources to the war against Japan.'

Monty holds his head in his hands again. He then relaxes and smiles.

'If only we could have Churchill out here for a month or two.

Bathing and painting! Perhaps they could meanwhile install a dummy Churchill in the House of Commons, and for BBC broadcasts.'

They both beam.

'Never in the history of this country,' intones De Guingand, 'Has there been such a great commander as Montgomery,' continues Monty.

'In him shall we put our trust, and in his splendid 8th Army,' continues De Guingand.

'And his decisions shall be as sacred to us as is his person!' says Monty.

'And never shall I, a mere Prime Minister, attempt to contravene a decision made by the inspired of God, the holy me!' concludes De Guingand.

They both bend double in laughter and fling themselves about.

'Oh Freddie, Freddie, what a good man you are, and what a comfort to my soul' says Monty at last.

'I endeavour at all times to give my best, sir,' says Freddie.

'Thank you, Jeeves,' says Monty. 'Thank you indeed. But let me see ... I have it now, Freddie. This is what I shall do. I will sit down and write a cable to Churchill. Not angry or defiant or anguished, but quiet and resolute. I will simply say that if an attack in September is an order, then I must proffer my resignation now, for my military integrity is at stake, in that I know defeat will be certain. But I can promise, absolutely promise, that a battle at the October full moon is a sure guarantee of victory. Churchill must somehow hold out till then, Freddie! He must find ways to persuade Parliament that more time is essential, he must just hang on, and insist that political pressure on him now will be prejudicial to our military strategy. Let him by all means cast the responsibility on me. Let him sack me if I fail at Alamein ... and so on.'

'It is possible that Mr. Churchill is exaggerating the political threat in the House of Commons, sir, in order to put pressure on you, sir. I had previously understood that the Parliamentary threat is over. It is the Americans and Torch that really worries him.'

'That's it,' says Monty. 'Meanwhile his health must also survive, and I hope my letter to him will also help towards that. I just wish I could see him again personally ... my mere presence has been known to buck people up, you know, Freddie!'

'Indeed it has ... and it will,' says de Guingand, 'And your presence, or some of it, will come over in your letter, I'm sure. So put your hand to the plough, sir, and I'll meanwhile do what I can, with Alanbrooke on our side as always, and Alexander also. If both Alanbrooke and Alexander speak for you, as they will sir, as they will ... then the job is done. What a boon it is to have a few friends who believe you in totally, sir!'

'O Freddie, it is, it is, and you are not the least of them! What would I do without you, my dear, dear boy?'

Monty stands up and extends both hands and grips both of Freddie's hands in his own and holds them there.

'Comrades in arms, till death us do part,' says Monty.

'Comrades in arms!' Says Freddie. 'How we shall regale our grandchildren, sir!'

De Guingand goes out and Monty sits down at his table again, takes up pen and paper and begins to write his letter to Churchill.

A few minutes later De Guingand puts his head round the door and says 'Oh I forgot to tell you sir. General Lumsden arrives later today.

'Ah, the Tank Man,' says Monty.

'Yes indeed,' says De Guingand, 'But he will not have heard the battle plan and the pivotal role of his Corps de Chasse sir.'

'Put it to him will you Freddie, I'm too busy at the moment,' says Monty, 'and put it over rather strongly if you won't mind, Freddie ... plenty of vim and optimism.'

De Guingand withdraws and Monty resumes writing.

4th of October 1942

De Guingand walks across to Monty's map caravan and puts his head in the door.

'More trouble from Churchill, sir, I'm afraid.'

'But he's accepted my battle plan for the October full moon. He's said so ... what on earth is it now?'

'Yes, sir, he's accepted the date, albeit reluctantly. But he's even more at the end of his tether, as I gather from Alanbrooke, than before. He just can't rest.'

'Well, it won't be long now, thank God, it won't be long. Get him to hang on ... pity he can't take a holiday.'

'Travelling certainly takes his mind off things, sir. He loves gadding about, seeing fresh sights and faces and talking with fresh minds. But he has the Americans too much on his back at the moment, and Stalin's impatience as well. And he's not in a fit state to travel. It's touch and go for him at the moment.'

'Well what is his concern, specifically, Freddie?'

'He's been studying your battle plan, for Alamein, sir, and he's voicing some doubts about the 'Corps de Chasse' and the dash for the Rahman Line sir. He feels it's too risky for the tanks, and could de-stabilize the rest of the plan.'

'Too risky indeed! I thought Churchill of all people would approve of 'Attack, attack attack!' What's go into him?'

'Perhaps his extremely fragile state of health has induced a caution into his responses sir.'

'Well we shouldn't project his delirious fears onto my good plans, Freddie, and someone should tell him. Someone should tell him that!'

De Guingand nods, and clears his throat.

'What's up with you, for heavens sake, Freddie? Never once have you cleared your throat in my presence! You know what I think of coughing and clearings of throat by now. If you continue in this mode I shall be forced to get rid of you!'

'I beg your pardon sir, I was merely preparing to tell you something you will not like to hear sir ... you have told us always to be honest and straightforward with you.'

'Yes I have, you may tell me what ever you like, but don't on any account clear your throat before doing so! Speak plainly like a man, don't snuffle and mumble and cough like some silly old hen of a woman! What is it?'

'Well sir, it appears that Churchill's fears in this precise respect are shared by some of the tank commanders themselves.'

'Do you mean Lumsden?'

'Yes sir, Lumsden among others.'

There is a pause.

'Has Lumsden been going to Churchill behind my back, Freddie?' asks Monty, his anger rising.

'Certainly not, sir.'

'But you are aware of Lumsden's views on this, and I am not. How did that come about? Why did Lumsden not come to me with his doubts?'

'Well it appears he is actually frightened of you, sir. I must say I have noticed it when you are conversing together. He freezes up like a rabbit in the presence of a stoat or a ferret, sir,' says De Guingand, somewhat tentatively.

'Are you calling me a stoat or ferret, De Guingand? If so, repeat it like a man, and don't stand there mumbling and whimpering like that!'

'I wasn't aware I was mumbling, sir. General Lumsden has shared his doubts and concerns with myself ... as a prelude to sharing them with you, sir ... at your convenience.'

'Very well then. We will have a conference of all tank commanders, and we'd better have the other commanders as well. This is what I call 'bellyaching' however, and in North Africa we've had too much of it. Didn't I make that sufficiently clear at my opening talk, De Guingand?'

'You did sir, but it is felt that here we have a matter of substance, and that it is better to thrash it out beforehand than to experience a refusal to obey orders during the heat of battle, sir.'

'Very sensible, Freddie, yes, I am all in favour of that, and if I am persuaded I am wrong on this point I will surrender gracefully. We will meet together on the 6th of October. Dismiss, Freddie, dismiss!'

De Guingand turns to go.

'Ferret indeed!' mutters Monty. 'Stoat be damned! And who'd have a rabbit for a tank commander? Not too late to get somebody else. Not too late at all. Stoat indeed! Ferret be damned!'

6th October

Monty and his staff, together with the tank commanders and others, are gathered in a large mess tent. Monty has pinned up a map with the battle plan on a blackboard and is pointing at it with a long cane.

'So there it is, gentlemen, I've been through you with it again. Now what seems to be trouble? It is part of my orders that the Corps de Chasse will, at a particular point, pass rapidly through enemy lines and patrol the enemy's supply-lines, wreaking havoc there and making it difficult for the enemy to concentrate fully on the destruction of our infantry and other tanks. What fears do you have about that? General Lumsden, what are your views?'

'The Corps de Chasse will simply not go through sir,' says Lumsden.

'Do you mean will fail to go through, or will disobey an order to go through?' says Monty.

There is a longish pause.

'The latter sir,' says Lumsden at last.

'Refuse, eh?' says Monty, 'So my diatribes about bellyaching have been to no effect. Are you fully aware of the possible consequences of not obeying an order, General Lumsden?'

'Fully aware sir,' says Lumsden, and after a pause, 'But even more aware of the disaster that a thrust to that point by our tanks will be. We will be sitting ducks as we proceed there, and sitting ducks when we arrive, sir.'

'But you are a mobile unit, and you will have the best tanks that we have. You are the key to our victory.'

'We do not have the confidence in the quality of our tanks, sir, to make victory possible by this means. We cannot be sure that even the new Shermans from America will be up to the job. There is nothing as powerful as the German 88mm anti-tank gun, sir, and this is no mere fear or fancy. I myself have been through the mill in North Africa. My experience at Gaza will always stay in my mind, sir. Pure terror and sheer wastage, sir.'

Monty is listening intently and sits down on a chair beside the easel.

'I gather that others of you besides our friend General Lumsden are of this view. Is that the case, gentlemen?'

There is a general mumbling of assent, and a few hands are raised gingerly to support it.

'Then I feel I will have no alternative but to adjust our battle-plan, gentlemen, and I have to thank you for having had the spirit to come forward and tell me of its deficiency. I always like to be told in a straightforward way. However, when we have made the correct adjustments it is imperative that orders are obeyed from then on. I hope I have made myself clear.'

There is a shuffling of chairs and a new air of concentration as Monty gets to his feet and points again at the blackboard.

'This is what I have decided. Everything will go forward as planned except for the early use of the 'Corps De Chasse'. I will leave the 'Corps De Chasse' as an element to be used in the last stage of the battle, in the break through and expansion, and not in the first stage at all. And I will revert to an earlier idea, and put that Corps under you, General Horrocks, in the southern sector. That will have the added advantage of deceiving the enemy by yet more evidence that our main attack will be in the south. Is that clear, gentlemen?'

Murmurs of assent.

'You, General Lumsden, will be part of our tank thrust in the early and middle stages of the battle. What we have got to do is to get forward sufficiently to form a strong defensive line in enemy territory. We need first of all to take the long Mitereiya Ridge, and then to press forward to the other side of it, dig in in hull-down positions for the tanks, and with small artillery and anti-tank guns alongside our tanks, to form a powerful defensive line, rather as at Alam Halfa.

'But the difference from Alam Halfa will be this: we will have made an offensive move into enemy territory. To both sides of our two break-in points there will be enemy infantry. We must therefore hold our defensive position firmly while we proceed laterally to as it were 'crumble' the enemy infantry there. We will also go a little forward of our defensive position, and engage and 'crumble' the infantry there. We have the capacity to do all this, but there will be heavy losses on our side as well. It will be a real slogging

'But when Germans see that we are destroying their infantry behind our defensive position, they will come charging at it with their tanks and anti-tank guns. But our defensive dug-in hull-down positions will be a match for everything they can throw at us, and we will positively welcome their advances. We have a vast superiority in the air, and in artillery, and that bombardment will never let up once they become visible attackers, and not merely dangers lurking in the mist and in local sand-storms, as has been Rommel's practice with his tanks, and their sudden menacing appearances out of nowhere! Since our defensive position will be both massive and static, there will be only so many tricks of that sort that Rommel with his Panzers will be able to play on us. We will not be charging about in our tanks as at a foxhunt in the Shires, gentlemen - whoever conceived that ridiculous idea of dashing about the Rahman Line like a set of flamboyant huntsmen?'

A pause for laughter. There is not only laughter but a stamping of feet, and some cheers.

'Thank you, gentlemen. Yes, we will welcome their direct onslaughts on our defensive position - for then we can sight them and outgun them, and outbomb them and outshell them. Rommel will have to attack, he will have no choice. And we will therefore make Rommel dance to our tune, until we are ready for the break through.

'And all I have to say about the breakthrough, is that you, General Horrocks, will proceed from the South to the Central position at the appropriate time, so that the Corps de Chasse will play its not inconsiderable part in that. Are we now all clear?'

Murmurs of assent. 'However I calculate that our casualties will be some13,000 killed wounded or missing so this is no picnic gentlemen. And it will take us 13-14 days. Naturally it is too late to make any further changes to our plan. Explain the latest to your officers, and I will make sure other ranks know it shortly before battle. Thank you for your frankness and kindness to me, and I hope I have restored your confidence in the ability of 8th army to carry this through. Now, shall we mingle and talk, and wait for our supper?'

21 October 1942

Monty tours some of the fighting units, while their officers explain the plan of battle to them. His appearance anywhere raises a cheer and applause, and each officer in charge hands over to him to say a few words if he chooses to. Monty, when he speaks, emphasizes again that this is a turning point of the war, and that the battle will be long and bloody, with heavy casualties on both sides. When he finishes, there is a solemn and feeling silence, and then a huge cheer goes up. Monty raises a hand of acknowledgement, and goes on his way.

All the while there is the sound of British bombers going over. There are four days of bombing before the battle itself begins on 23rd October.

Chapter 19 – Battle of Alamein

23 October

Monty tours some of the fighting units again, and speaks his last personal message to them before the battle. He instructs officers to read his words to units he has been unable to visit personally.

9.00pm – Full Moon

Monty in his TAC HQ at Burgh-el-Arab is holding court to the Staff, and giving his last orders. He is saying goodbye to John Poston and the other Liaison Officers.

'Remember, John, I shall expect your presence here with any news at 6.30am. I shall have studied today's reports again over a cup of tea at 9.30am for about an hour, and then meet you all to discuss them, and to give fresh orders. After that I shall expect your further reports early in the evening. I will need a little time to digest them, and to give you further orders before I retire to bed at 9.30pm. All of you must take your rest and sleep when you can, You are doing an essential job, and a highly dangerous job, and you must stay fresh.'

Monty shakes hands with John Poston; John then leaves with his companions, to find their motor cycles and cars for the first battle patrol. There is an enormous sound of revving and moving off.

Monty turns to Freddie de Guingand. ' I will turn in at 9.30 as usual. The artillery bombardment begins at 9.40, I know, but that will not bother me. I shall be asleep by then. Please do not wake me before 6.30, unless the situation is really desperate. I know I can rely on you, Freddie, to hold the fort, and not to fuss me unnecessarily. How are you feeling, Freddie?'

'A little anxious, sir … but it will pass.'

'I'm sure it will. Goodnight, Freddie. You must sleep in the early morning.'

'Goodnight sir.'

Monty walks out of the office and towards his caravan-bedroom.

Ten minutes later the Allied artillery bombardment begins. This is the most overwhelming bedlam of noise ever heard by man. The pressure of the noise is not only on the head and ears, it is like a heavy body leaning on the body of each man, with no way for any man to escape it, except by movement and action.

'What the hell is going on, sir?' says one of the new Highland infantryman to an officer. Most of the Highlanders are new to battle.

'It's a concentrated artillery attack, one of Monty's new ideas,' says the officer. 'Think how the enemy must be feeling about it. I understand Monty himself calls it 'The Full Monty'. 'Give them The Full Monty, Kirkman, and keep it going!'

'Do we ever get a break from it, sir?'

'Few and far between, I would guess. We shall have to see. Don't count too much on it. Just keep yourself moving as much as you can.'

'How will we ever sleep, sir?'

'It shouldn't be so bad down in the slit-trenches, with planks over them. We'll have to manage. This is a crisis. We have to survive the crisis, look towards the end of it, keep that in your mind.'

The infantryman and the officer now look to the front, and see the patterns in the sky made by searchlights, gradually adjusting until an apex is formed over their immediate frontage. It is an extraordinary sight, searchlights and full moon beaming behind them, and faint stars.

'That is our line of march marked for us and for the sappers,' says the officer.

Suddenly the artillery barrage stops. The officer looks at his watch. 'Ten o'clock!' he says. 'We'll see how long this first break lasts.'

As they speak, lines of sappers go forward on their front, and at various points to their left and right, followed by lorries carrying a few men and a load of equipment. There is also a bevy of special infantry, to assist the sappers in defusing the Allied minefields first, and laying markers to show the safe lanes that the infantry must follow.

The infantry, guided by sappers, simply stick their bayonets into the mines, and twist. Most of the mines are there to de-stabilize and arrest the tanks, but there is an occasional vicious anti-personnel mine, and these have to be spotted in time, and take longer to deal with. Once in the enemy minefields, the anti-personnel mines will be less known, and the task will be longer and more dangerous. A cool head and patience, and unfailing courage are all needed, all of the time.

As it is several miles, in all, that have to be dealt with, it is a big job, and as well as laying down tape to mark the lanes, the men also put poles in the ground, with small lighted lamps on them, for night-guidance. The lorries containing these follow slowly behind the sappers and the infantry. The men work in whispers.

After only a few minutes, the Full Monty artillery barrage is resumed, and everywhere men steel themselves to bear it. As well as the searchlights there are huge fires in the distance, where fuel dumps or ammunition dumps have been hit. Soon it seems the whole of the lower sky is lit up.

'It's extraordinarily beautiful,' says the officer. 'I've never felt such beauty in my life ... all for blood and guts ... aren't we just idiots?'

'Yes, sir,' says the corporal. 'It is a sight ... what are we to make of such things? We're mostly new out here, we've never seen or heard anything like it. And soon we have to move on and kill Germans, sir. Methodically, one by one, the whole bloody lot at this stage, no prisoners, nothing, sir.'

'Absolutely,' says the officer. 'That's the job. We can't deal with prisoners at this stage. One trick too many. It'll be hard enough getting our own wounded and their wounded off the battlefield. However, I doubt if many of the German front-liners will be thinking of surrendering at this stage, they are fanatical fighters, don't care if they die for the Fuhrer and the Fatherland. Don't expect they see the beauty of the night either. No margin left in them for that sort of thing. Madmen, lunatics ... but still human beings in the end, somewhere, somehow. Monty's very good on that! Bring them back to their senses. But chiefly by killing them in large numbers.'

'Yes sir,' says the infantryman. 'However, I don't altogether fancy sticking my bayonet into someone with his hands up. I don't have that degree of violence in my nature, sir.'

'You can just wound him and disarm him then, corporal. That's the best. The stretcher-men will see to the rest.'

A long and momentous silence between officer and NCO ensues, while each gathers up inside himself whatever will be necessary for the coming ordeal.

'It's nearly time to be moving off, Corporal. Here come some of the Lieutenants who will lead the way.'

Shortly afterwards some junior officers, each at the head of a unit of infantry, move off along the cleared lanes, well in front with a lighted pole raised high to show the way. Fire from the enemy is not yet serious, but is sporadic. There is some exhilaration as the small columns set off, and further away, to the right of their position, one Highland Unit marches into battle with the pipes playing. It is an extraordinarily unearthly sound, as though some of the ancient gods have lent themselves to the battle, to lift and encourage the mere mortals under their care. What might seem banal and repetitive on a parade-ground or at a summer fair, registers to the men under command as the most thrilling inspiration from strange worlds which sometimes give utterance to their emotions, and their intentions. The men go forward as in a high dream of Romance, steady and sure-footed and as though invulnerable, and armed with charms and wisdom in addition to weapons.

The officer and his corporal are at last called upon, and move with their unit, the officer again at the head, and taking a lighted pole from a sapper as he moves forward to the cleared lane.

'Here we go then, Corporal. Forward!' he says, almost laughing.

The Full Monty continues, above them, behind them and in front of them. It is less oppressive now they are moving forward. But all of them long for the next break, which in fact comes before they have reached the enemy minefields. But then the British bombers take over, and there are more flashes and fires a few miles in front of them, a continuous line of bonfires punctuated by huge explosions, as further segments of the fuel or ammunition dumps take fire. Some of the explosions are further back, where the big guns and their large contingent of live shells are occasionally hit. The big guns are fractured and twisted into crippled shapes, while most of the men there are blown into fragments, unknown soldiers, all of them, monuments already to the better times that must surely come. Many minds cannot contain the horrors that they imagine. On top of it, they try to stamp the personal, the known, the good, the everlastingness of all good things. The goodness of all good and simple things becomes crystal clear. Many feel that if only they had appreciated these more, terrible things would not be happening. Many see things of home transfigured ... a room, a window, a mild sunlight playing on the white window-frames, magically blue shadows, an armchair, a fireside. The air outside breathes deep and sings. The sun becomes a God, and the wife or mother or sister coming into the room the most beautiful angel. And 'Why can't we be with the angels?' comes storming into some minds, and words escape them, whispered but clear, 'O my dear – my darling – my angel!'

Before midnight the infantry of all sectors come to the end of the Allied minefields. In the northernmost positions the Australians are now coming to a halt, then the Highlanders, and then, in the second break-in area a few miles further south, the New Zealanders led by Generals Freyberg and Leese are manoeuvering for position on the No-Man's-Land that precedes the enemy minefields. Still further south, General Horrocks is with the South Africans who have moved forward. Still further south are the Indian regiments, which have also moved forward, and south of them the Free French await action.

As the infantry on all these fronts eventually move forward again, field guns are being towed in the British lanes behind them, and also lorries full of ammunition. Behind these the tank units begin to organize themselves and to rev up, but their move forward will not come for several hours.

The German firing intensifies as the venture over No-Man's-Land continues. The sappers and infantry often drop to the ground and crawl some yards. When another smokescreen has been created for them, they rise, stoop low and run as fast as possible forward. Many are impeded by the spades they have to carry for digging further on. It is a clumsy and lumbering run, but at least the night is cold and fresh.

As they reach the German minefields they lie low for some while, and another Full Monty of British artillery fire is discharged. This is a creeping barrage, creeping nearer and nearer to the Allied positions, but keeping German front-line heads low, and inhibiting their fire. After a few minutes the barrage creeps westwards again, and right back to the German tanks and big guns in the rear. And then at last it creeps back eastwards, and to the German front line, frighteningly close to the Allied front line.

At this point the lorries carrying poles and lamps arrive at the Allied positions, and the same touchy procedure of de-mining and lighting the way forward is resumed. This time units of infantry have to get further forward in order to provide better cover for the sappers and others. Smokescreens are again created to make the work easier. But German machine-gunners rake their fire across a wide front and back again, and casualties occur. The wounded must lie there until the stretcher-bearers arrive. One, a sergeant, has trodden on a mine and is screaming and crying for his mother. A soldier goes to sit by him and the others nearby struggle with their feelings as the work goes on. Many are new to battle, not only in the Highland regiments. The Full Monty goes on above them and in them and through them.

Once a long-enough clear lane has been made, the officer leading the group takes his lighted pole again and presses forward, with smokescreens protecting. But all along the wide front of the two break-in areas, many of these officers are killed or wounded. It is one of the most dangerous jobs, and reserve officers have to be ready to take their place. The upright heroism of these young men, most of them upper-class and public-school boys, impresses itself on the infantrymen so strongly that the experience of common humanity is felt, often an entirely new experience.

At about half-past midnight the Allies come near to the German forward positions, and then the real battle begins. In spite of their nearness to the Germans, the pipers in the Highland regiments continue to march forward behind the officer with the lighted pole, playing their pipes. Several of these are also shot down, but the brave piping continues behind them and to each side of them. Those new to battle receive their first taste of the heroism of defiance, and pride stiffens them even as tears come to their eyes. If it is a 'performance', or a 'melodrama', it is an absolutely necessary one, it is felt, even to those who see through their own tears and the extraordinary emotions that nearly choke them. They also feel an iron power possessing their bodies, a capacity for endurance they could never have predicted.

All around them, as well as the noise and the fear, there is the spiritual atmosphere of comradeship, a palpable knowledge that they will not suffer or die alone, not even if they are left stranded on the battlefield. Fibres of love spread across the gaps and bind them together. And as with their lovers or wives, or sisters and mothers and brothers at home, they are astonished that such fibres have been so little felt before.

Well behind all the Allied infantry and sappers, the stretcher-bearers of the Royal Army Medical Corps and the Friends Ambulance Unit move to pick up the wounded from the Allied mine-lanes. The dead will have to wait for another party, though they are moved to the side to allow the tanks to come through.

And as this is happening, the real battle at the front begins. Even while the sappers are still clearing the lanes, groups of infantry can now spot German positions not too far away, with their field guns, and their machine-guns swivelling from side to side with their terrifying fire. Allied infantry get down in small groups and return fire, with bren-guns and rifles, as their own field-guns and ammunition are gradually brought up behind them, with mortars and mortar-bombs.

As they proceed closer to the German positions, some of the small groups, with a smoke-screen to cover them, creep forward rapidly, go to the far side of the dug-out, to avoid the gunner out front, and come close enough to launch hand-grenades into them. There are explosions and screams. The chief German machine-gunner, if still capable, swings his gun furiously on the attackers, who dive to the ground, or scuttle rapidly behind a smokescreen to disappear into the night. The attackers scatter in all directions to reduce the target.

Even as the German positions are fiercely attacked, the Allied casualties mount, for the Germans rouse themselves and defend every compass-point of their dugouts. Each Allied raid is more dangerous for a while, until the German strength in each one is gradually reduced. There are some small rock formations and areas of broken rock in this part of the desert, and surprise at this point of the battle can be achieved through Allied infantry hiding there for a while. Their comrades make feint-raids from more exposed positions. As these retire, the hidden infantry go in rapidly and hurl more grenades into the dugout.

Few of the dugouts are completely silenced, but the chief Allied task on this first night is to get forward to agreed positions as quickly as possible. To the left and the right of them, up to two or three miles away, are whole complexes of German defences that will not be dealt with tonight. The purpose is to go through, and for the tanks to come through behind them, later to join them in a defensive position, called The Oxalic Line, by dawn. In the 'central break-in area' this means climbing the Mitereiya Ridge, and then going down the forward slope of it, facing the German guns. This is the task mainly of the New Zealanders. Himeimat Ridge, furthest south, is for the Free French to take.

In pursuit of these objectives, only the Axis positions immediately blocking their way have to be dealt with. The lateral positions are to be dealt with by the so-called 'crumbling' operations, and only after a solid break-in has been achieved, with tanks and tank-guns at the front to fend off and destroy Axis forces further west. This is the Plan, and, as Monty has said, the Plan must be adhered to.

Further north the Highlanders have been instructed also to proceed to the Oxalic Line, the route to which is punctuated with rocky points named after various Scottish towns. But partly due to inexperience, and partly to the naturally irregular course of their own terrain, the Highlanders end up by mistaking their eventual stopping point for the Oxalic, when in fact, as they learn the next day, it is some 3000 yards short of it. The Australians, however, (according to Monty, the finest of all the 8th Army infantry), do reach their correct position by dawn, after some fierce fighting in the north. They stand facing Hill 28, one of their next objectives.

Some tanks also get through before dawn to cover the Australians. The Highlanders' mistake as to their own position meant that they fail to provide cover for some of the New Zealanders further south. When the promised tanks begin to go forward to join the New Zealand infantry on the Oxalic Line, German tanks and the deadly 88mm anti-tank guns open up and knock out six Sherman tanks in a few minutes. At length their Commander, General Lumsden feels forced to order them to withdraw.

Further south, about a third of General Gatehouse's tank units get to the top of the Mitereiya Ridge, but when they attempt to cross the Ridge and go down the further slope to protect the infantry, they too are met with deadly fire, and soon withdraw behind the Ridge. The other two-thirds of Gatehouse's tanks have hardly moved at all, but are instead blocking the lanes that were to bring up food and fresh ammunition for the forward units. There is much swearing and bad feeling there. The same old thing has happened as under Auchenleck. For the umpteenth time, the infantry are furious with the tank brigades for not turning up as planned. At dawn, the scene along the Allied from is a long way from what Monty had planned and hoped for. In fact, it is chaotic. Even those tank brigades which have gone down the further slope of the Mitereiya Ridge to join the New Zealand infantry, finally choose to withdraw again behind the Ridge after being hit by withering fire.

With no tanks to challenge them, the Axis forces are even laying fresh mine-fields only a short way from the Allied positions. The Plan had involved the beginning of both lateral and forward 'crumbling' operations by the infantry, with the tanks dug-in and providing a defensive line while the 'crumbling' went on. This needs to happen on the first day or the Plan itself may 'crumble'. The Axis forces could even be planning a counter-attack that would drive Allied infantry back.

Good outcomes are strongly in Monty's mind, and the chaos

that liaison officers and several commanders of units report to him as daylight floods El Alamein on the 24th of October are of course not to his liking. There are the false optimistic reports from Major General Briggs, reporting progress that has not been achieved, and presuming to use Monty's own language, such as 'forcing the enemy to fight on ground of our own choosing,' and the like. Monty is not fooled by that, for it becomes a truism that Monty cannot ever be fooled, even by a Commander seven or eight miles away. Out of sight is never out of mind, as far as Monty is concerned.

However, Monty listens quietly to his Liaison Officers, and does not get ruffled or bad-tempered. His sole concern at this moment is to get as clear a picture as possible of the situation on the ground.

'Spare me no detail, however chaotic,' he says to John Poston. And there are no interruptions and no sharp intakes of breath, just the occasional question.

'Have you spoken to Lumsden and Gatehouse?' Monty asks.

'We have tried several times, sir. We just can't get hold of them.'

'I see,' says Monty. 'We must of course find them, or contact them, and insist that the Plan is followed through. In fact, some of you can go on that errand now, and give them my Orders, and insist that they speak to me if they have difficulties to discuss.'

John Poston details a group of his Liaison Officers to do this, and after a few more minutes talking to Monty and receiving his questions, they leave.

Generals Lumsden and Gatehouse are finally located and told that Monty insists on the Plan being followed. Poston reports back to Monty.

'Well, gentlemen, this is a terrible day,' says Monty, 'The tanks are not in the positions required by the Plan. Why not?'

'Sir, General Lumsden says that on the ground, the Plan may in some circumstances be unworkable ...'

'Tell me those circumstances.'

'The Generals say that the funnels the tanks were supposed to advance down, are clearly pin-pointed by German 88mm guns. They feel it would be too costly to advance along that line.'

' But I have told them that heavy casualties in the break-in have to be borne – we have plenty of tanks in reserve. The infantry have done their job bravely. Are they to get no protection because the tanks will not do theirs? Please warn the Generals that the Plan hangs in the balance. If the Germans make a serious counter-attack today, and our infantry are driven back beyond the Ridge, the whole battle could be lost! Can't they understand that this is the decisive battle, that could be the turning point in the war? Risks have to be taken, and casualties endured. What are a few tanks, and a few dozen lives lost, compared with the success or failure of the entire campaign, the loss of Egypt, and humiliation and disgrace? Please tell them they must move, and there is no time to lose.'

When the messengers come back, they tell Monty that the two Tank Commanders finally said they would make another attempt, perhaps by a slightly different route, but that this would take several hours to organise.

By the evening of the 24th, no further tank movements by Lumsden or Gatehouse have been reported, except for one armoured division ordered up by General Leese to support the Highlanders. 'Our gingering up had some effect, then,' says Monty.

Monty tells his Liaison Officers that evening to report it as an Order to Gatehouse and Lumsden to bring forward their tanks, or to face the dismissal of their Commanders Briggs and Fisher. After giving this last order, Monty goes to bed as usual at 9.30pm, and falls asleep as usual. Faced with a possible disaster, he clearly cannot afford to lose a good night's sleep.

But between 2am and 3am , De Guingand reluctantly wakes Monty, to report the most serious crisis. Monty gets up quietly, and does not complain or appear ruffled. De Guingand arranges a Conference at TAC Head quarters for 3.30am, with Gatehouse and Lumsden to come in person.

3.30am   Freyberg, Leese, Lumsden and Gatehouse arrive at TAC HQ, and are directed to Monty's lorry, where Monty is sitting studying a map pinned up on the wall.

'Good morning, gentlemen. Perhaps you could in turn point to this map, tell me your current positions, and give me an account of your difficulties.'

Gatehouse is the first to go up to the map. He takes a stick and points to an area about half-way down the Mittereiya Ridge. 'We had to come through on this funnel, sir, quite a narrow funnel, and therefore very easy for us to become a fixed target for the enemy's 88mm guns. However, even before that happened, we suddenly found the minefields almost impossible. The regular pattern is here superseded by a veritable patchwork of mines, and we lost several tanks even before we'd attempted to cross the Ridge.'

Gatehouse pauses a while, and looks at Monty, who is benign and impeturbable.

'Carry on, General Gatehouse, please.'

'I'm not saying that the tanks can't be repaired, of course. Tracks blown off, merely, and no lives lost. But when we tried to cross the Ridge we lost several tanks to the 88mm guns – I presume, and I calculated that we could not possibly get down the further slope to a secure position without too many tanks being set on fire, and tank-crews killed. It is utterly appalling knowing some of our tank-crews are being burned to death. I thought we had to retreat at that point, re-group, and think again. That is our position at present, sir. Also, the German crack Panzer Unit 21 is facing us there, sir.'

'But I happen to know that that Unit is facing Horrocks down south. But thank you, Gatehouse. I can see your dilemma, of course. But we have plenty of tanks in reserve – far more than the Germans have, now that our bombers and artillery have done their job. It is terrible to suffer casualties in the form you describe. But are you aware how many casualties the infantry have suffered in the first day of battle?'

'I have an idea that the number is quite large, sir.'

'I'm glad you have that idea,' says Monty, a little acidly. 'Our infantry have lost 3,000 plus, killed, wounded or missing. If we have casualties at that rate over twelve days of battle, that makes 36,000 – whereas in my head, our <u>total</u> casualties for this battle, infantry, tanks, artillery, the lot, is some 13,000. ... we just cannot afford to lose infantry at that rate, Gatehouse.'

'Yes, of course, sir,' says Gatehouse, 'However, as you have explained, we were expecting the heaviest casualties for this break-in phase ... it will hardly proceed along those lines for the rest of the battle, sir.'

'True,' says Monty, 'But we were expecting the tanks to take their share of casualties in this absolutely crucial break-in phase. There is no point in suffering these large infantry casualties in the break-in operation if we don't in fact <u>break-in</u> properly at all. We need tanks and field guns and our own anti-tank guns down there on the far side of the Ridge, Gatehouse – the tanks doing their bit, and suffering along with the rest.'

'I can see that, sir,' says Gatehouse, 'but it did not seem either wise or humane to push forward in that situation – our losses could have crippled us for the next part of the battle ... there's the tank morale to consider, sir, as well as our battle-plan.'

There's little need to talk about the importance of morale, Gatehouse. What do you suppose is the state of the morale of our New Zealand infantry cousins now, down there on the front-line, under fire, without armour support, and seeing the Germans sowing fresh mines? The initiative is being lost, and they know it. The success or failure of this whole battle rests on these first two days. Our infantry 'crumbling' operations should have begun yesterday morning – with your tanks providing a screen for them. Only the Australians, God bless them, have begun the 'crumbling' operations, and the Highlanders too, and with a minimum of tank support. Can you imagine what is being said about your British tank-men down there among the New Zealanders? Our Commonwealth cousins have come to our aid, they are shedding their blood for the parent-country, but our true-blue Englishmen of the Shires are holding back!'

'The circumstances are unfortunate, sir, and I would hate that impression to be substantiated ...'

'But it is nothing new, Gatehouse,' Monty interrupts. 'This unpleasant thing goes on. I must say I begin to have sympathy with Auchinleck. He had this Shire stubbornness to contend with all the time, and their <u>snobbery</u>, Gatehouse, snobbery!'

'Sir, that is too strong,' says Gatehouse. ' Our tank-units have their proper pride in their traditions, and their own 'esprit de corps'. But 'snobbery' is too strong, sir.'

'You do not persuade me, Gatehouse. I have my ear to the ground, and I know this unpleasant thing exists. If even I cannot overcome it, no wonder Auchinleck couldn't'.

'I'm sorry sir,' says Gatehouse, ' I can only do my best with the material I have to hand.'

'Well, we needn't have a row about it, Gatehouse, but I really must insist that another effort is made to get your tanks over the ridge and to the front. Do we all realize that this battle could now be lost? What will become of us all then? Defeat, humiliation, and then the humiliation of further defeat and possible surrender ... Come on, gentlemen, feel with me the absolute urgency of this present moment, this present wonderful opportunity to turn the tide of this whole war! ... What do you think, Freyberg?'

'I'm absolutely with you in all you have said so far,' says Freyberg. 'I can hardly describe the bitterness and anger of our New Zealand infantry. The air is blue down there, sir. Also, we have managed to get some tanks forward in the north, to help the Highlanders and Aussies, sir. So why not down here? But even with the Highlanders the tanks were slow – though we could see no particular difficulties getting through at that point. They could have come through sooner.'

'What do you think, Lumsden?' asks Monty.

Lumsden, handsome and moustached, is of the type of effortless superiority. He is stylishly turned out, with a silk scarf neatly arranged around his collar. But he seems numbed into silence at present, rather than confidently superior.

'I can see the urgency of the situation, of course – but also the seeming impossibility of doing better than we are doing. We urge and urge, sir – but urging men forward is not going to silence the German 88mm guns, sir … '

There is a silence.

'I have witnessed some appalling scenes in the tank wars in this desert, sir. We have been subjected to decimation – and horror, sir, horror. It was not Aucninleck's fault, and it was not our fault. It is the reality – our tanks, the physical structure of our tanks, are not up to the job. Even the Shermans are not quite up to it. Perhaps we should be fighting a different kind of battle, but don't ask me what, sir. The Mittereiya Ridge, with its patchwork of mines and its cruel exposure, is perhaps beyond our powers.'

'It's too early to conclude that, Lumsden. I have the strong impression that the tank effort has simply not been sufficient. You must try again to get forward, yourself and Gatehouse, and take the casualties … Heavens, you all know I hate casualties, gentlemen – I have a horror of them! But I never promised that this particular battle would be easy. We have to break the stranglehold that Rommel has had on us, and in this battle we can do it. Once we have done it, the rest will be easy. Please, I beg you, and remind you, look at it in that light, consider the larger picture, the ease after the bloodbath. What do you think, General Leese?'

'I too am absolutely with you, sir. But I accept that Lumsden has had bitter experiences out here, and that it is far from easy for him to push the tanks through willy-nilly.'

'But we must have one more effort,' says Monty. 'And I can't say, 'take your time, gentlemen'. It has to be soon! However, you have your own sappers, and your own field guns and heavier artillery to protect you. Tackle the mines, get on with that, and use your artillery to get the German 88mms, and then get down to the front-line with the infantry. That is my final word, gentlemen. I have listened to you, but my opinion remains more or less the same. Our 'crumbling' operation with the New Zealanders must begin at some point today. Is that clear, gentlemen?'

They all nod in assent. Monty then says 'And now I must get some more sleep. We will confer by telephone at about 10am, gentlemen.'

Monty leaves the lorry and makes for his bedroom caravan. He lies down, and is soon asleep.

De Guingand is with the Generals. 'I'm sorry, sirs, but this seems to be the crunch. The old boy is quite immoveable on this!'

'We will do what we can,' says Lumsden, taking Gatehouse' arm and moving off. Leese and Freyberg also go off together towards the cars. 'Goodnight, Freddie,' they call out.

'Goodnight, sirs, and good luck to you all', says Freddie.

There is a revving of engines, and then departure. De Guingand looks up at the stars, and goes inside his office and bunk-house, and says to his orderly, 'I must get some sleep too. Wake me at 8am, please.'

25 October – 6.30am

At the front, at the foot of the Mitereiya Ridge, a figure can be seen crawling along in the sand. It is sun-rise. The figure props itself up on its elbows, and holds binoculars to its face. After a prolonged scanning, it rises, and walks and runs, around clumps of rocks, and eventually finds another position higher up, on some rocky ground, and stands up, looking around the horizon in a 180 degree arc. It is the young John Poston, chief Liaison Officer for Monty, and he is finishing his surveillance before returning to base.

He descends from the high position, and makes for a place about a quarter of a mile away, a narrow defile. Shots ring out, and John Poston drops to the ground, stays still for a minute, and then begins again to crawl towards his goal. As more rocks appear, he is able to crouch and run from one to another. Shots again sound, and whistle by, but Poston feels he is winning, and continues his crouching run. At last he reaches his defile and is able to hide himself safely while surveying the German positions with his binoculars.

Having done this, he makes his way up to the top of the Ridge, takes a water-bottle from his pack, and drinks deeply. He then descends on the safe side of the Ridge to more rocks where his motor-cycle is hidden. Revving up, he sets off, following the hard surfaces of the faint track wherever possible, and hoping there are no further mines to worry about. By 7.30 he is back at Monty's TAC HQ.

De Guingand's orderly speaks to him. 'Sorry, sir, but both Montgomery and De Guingand are asleep. Precious sleep, sir after a disturbed night.'

'I was aware of some crisis, corporal. Hope it's resolved by now. I'll sit here, then, for a while. Cup of strong coffee would be most welcome, corporal.'

'Immediately, sir', says the orderly, and goes off.

Poston sits on a canvas chair with arm-rests in the shade of the compound, and falls asleep sitting up before the coffee arrives. The orderly taps him gently on the arm.

'Coffee, sir.'

'Many thanks, corporal.'

Poston sits up, swigs the coffee in large gulps, and stares into space. Bill Williams puts his head out of the Office.

'Welcome home, dear old John. What a night it's been!'

'Glad to see someone's awake,' says John Poston.

'Everything will be stirring soon,' says Bill, and goes inside.

As 8 o'clock arrives, both Monty and De Guingand appear, De Guingand looking slightly the worse. He is used to missing sleep, but the prolonged crisis has had its effect. Monty is, however, as bright as a daisy, though quiet with it, aware of stretched nerves around him.

'Hullo John, what a delight to see you safe and sound as usual. You are a good deed in a naughty world, John.'

'Glad I seem so, sir ... feel more like a wet dishcloth on a Monday morning in rainy Manchester.'

'Well you must take some sleep, John. Use my caravan by all means.'

'Thank-you sir, but you'll want my report?'

That can wait an hour or so, John. Things are being resolved here, I'm glad to say.'

John finishes his coffee, and limps off to Monty's caravan. He too is a rapid sleeper. He lies down, and is as though dead in about two minutes. Sharp motor-cycle bangs and stuttering soon after tell the arrival of other Liaison Officers, who walk into the compound, and then seat themselves in the office. John Poston sleeps soundly through the noise.

Monty talks to the other Liaison Officers in the office. 'John Poston's asleep,' he says, 'and the rest of you can also take a rest for a while. Get some sleep, and I'll call for you later.'

They file out and make for their tents.

'Well then, Freddie,' says Monty, rubbing his hands and smiling, 'peace at last! And this is it, eh? Today is it!'

'Yes, sir, it is indeed.'

'Well you could just check up with Leese and Freyberg, and find out how Lumsden and Gatehouse are getting on. I'm sure the Liaison Officers would have said immediately if the position is serious ... but just to be sure, eh?'

De Guingand goes off to the field telephones, while Monty attends to his breakfast.

'What would you like for breakfast today, sir?' asks the orderly.

'Everything that is available, corporal,' replies Monty. 'Cooked porridge ... then a cooked breakfast with plenty of eggs and sausages ... then some fruit ... and then toast and good strong coffee ... The Full Monty, please, corporal, The Full Monty!'

'It shall be done, sir. The Full Monty, as you say, sir.'

The orderly goes to the field kitchens. 'Full Monty again for the Monty,' he says.

'Full Monty again!' shouts the chief cook. 'The little man doesn't get any bigger, does he? Goes straight to his brain ... gets used up pretty fast ... what a man!'

'Brain-food for the big chief,' he says to the other cooks. 'And look sharp. Strong coffee on the hob.'

Delicious cooking smells, with coffee soon predominant, waft over the little camp. Monty sits in the shade of the compound, peaceful and poised, both withdrawn and alert, relaxed and yet visibly capable of mental activity if required. The compound assumes again an almost monastic calm. The staff go about their work without noise, and have the peace of mind which comes of being trusted. Monty's breakfast is brought to him where he sits, and a small table is brought along with it.

'Full Monty,' says the orderly.

'Thank you, corporal, thank you. Ah, what a beautiful morning!' he says, half to himself. 'An interlude of calm.'

He hears a car draw up outside the compound, but does not yet move. He has no sooner finished his breakfast, and is sitting back with his strong coffee, when De Guingand emerges from the office.

'Well, Freddie?' beams Monty.

De Guingand tries to keep the anxiety out of his face.

'A bit of a hitch, sir.'

'Come on then, Freddie, let's hear it.'

'Well, it appears that Gatehouse did go forward again with the tanks, but then felt compelled to withdraw again, because of further losses. It appears the chief of the Staffordshire Yeomanry went to him personally and begged him with tears in his eyes, to withdraw them, sir. Crews burning to death again, sir. Horrible.'

'Go on,' says Monty.

'Lumsden and Freyberg have made a little progress with the tanks, sir. However, down south the Free French have failed to take the Himeimat Ridge, and Horrocks has not managed to get beyond the second line of minefields.'

'Down south needn't matter at all at present, 'says Monty. 'But the Gatehouse situation is worrying. I wonder what I could have done to make myself clearer? It was an order!'

He stops, sits up straight, and for a few moments puts his head in his hands. De Guingand has never seen him shaken before.

'Take me to see Freyberg,' Monty says, 'we must go now.'

A few minutes later De Guingand and Monty are in the car, and arrive at Freyberg's HQ.

'I'm deeply, deeply sorry,' says Monty to Freyberg. 'You have done wonders, yet I can't get my British Armour to do their bit. But there's no point in your New Zealanders sitting about getting shot at, they must begin the crumbling operations today, with such armour as they have got. The Australians have done it … there is no need for yours to go forward, that's too difficult. They can retreat and work laterally, and take cover if the German tanks come in.'

'Very good, sir,' says Freyberg, 'I agree with you. We must do something or burst, sir.'

'I must speak to Gatehouse on the phone,' says Monty.

'We've been trying to get hold of him for some time, sir,' says Freyberg, 'Permanently unavailable, it seems.'

'I see,' says Monty, and the beady eyes look hard. 'I'll speak to Lumsden, then. He can contact Gatehouse and repeat my order.'

'Lumsden is also out of contact, sir' says Freyberg.

There is a pause.

'This is too much,' says Monty. 'It is a complete shambles.'

'Sorry sir,' says Freyberg.

'No need at all for you to be sorry, Freyberg. You have done wonders. But what on earth is going on?'

'I fear that Lumsden is a little afraid to lay down the law to Gatehouse, since he himself is equally cautious ... and feels equally at sea, sir.'

Monty takes a seat at last, and calms himself.

'Yes, the crumbling operations must begin today. Take your troops out of the front-line, Freyberg. Surrender ground if necessary. It is not forward ground that is of first importance just now. We must pull back and fight in the middle and near positions. But we must hold on to Mittereiya Ridge itself.'

'Perfectly clear, sir.'

'And we must abandon, in your sector, all plans of pushing in a south-westerly direction. Pull back and make north and north-west. And tell that blasted Gatehouse to defend Mittereiya Ridge from behind, when you can contact him. Pull out of all danger and make north. Perhaps I've been getting this all wrong, the capacity of our Armour ... We'll have to be a bit flexible, Freyberg, so long as the basic Plan is intact.'

They are both silent for a while. Freyberg does not dissent from these last statements, and the admission of possible error, but neither does he venture to agree with it.

'What is the trouble, do you think, Freyberg?'

'Must I say, sir?'

'I would appreciate your opinion, Freyberg.'

'Lack of skill with the Armoured Commanders, due to lack of training,' says Freyberg, uneasily aware that Monty has been in charge of training for many years.

Monty is silent.

'Gatehouse has admitted he is not easy with mobile battle, sir, nor with the integration of tanks and infantry and artillery.'

Monty goes on listening.

'And Lumsden is not even using his own artillery units, sir. Is not familiar with combined action of that sort.'

After a while Monty says quietly, 'It seems that all my emphasis on training has not been enough after all.'

A silence.

'I understand there was a lot of catching up to do, sir, what with disarmament right up to the mid-1930's on Britain's part,' says Freyberg.

'Yes, yes, yes,' says Monty quickly, 'but I did feel I had done just about enough.'

'There's also the mechanical inferiority of our tanks as tanks, sir,' says Freyberg.

'That I have heard many times, and perhaps I've taken insufficient account of it. Therefore we must adapt, taking full account of our weaknesses … '

'Of course, sir,' says Freyberg.

'We must hold the line here in the centre and in the south, but with reduced forces, Freyberg. The whole emphasis must shift further north, and yet the crumbling operation must go on today, in spite of our difficulties. You have been most helpful, Freyberg. I must hasten back to my Chief of Staff and put him abreast of our plans. Thank you, Freyberg.'

'Goodbye sir.'

Once back at TAC HQ, Monty gives De Guingard an account of his change of mind. Alexander and McCreevy have departed. Then De Guingard says, 'I must put you in the picture on another matter, sir. The great Rommel himself had arrived in Africa only today; he missed the first day and a half. I expect he is shocked at the effects of our bombing on his Tanks and Big Guns. But no doubt he can gather the strength for a counter-blow.'

'No doubt. We need to get Bill Williams' views on this.'

The Liaison Officers are up and about. Monty calls them all to a

Conference in his Map Caravan, together with the Intelligence Officer, Bill Williams. They pile in, and Monty says, 'Can you all see and hear?' as he points to a map on the wall.

'Now, I know I haven't yet heard from you, but I've been pretty well briefed on the situation, and it is not a happy one. What do you think, Bill?'

Major Bill Williams is at the front alongside Monty.

'It is deeply worrying in some ways, sir, for apart from the Australians and some Highlanders, our Infantry and Armour has hardly performed in these vital first two days. Rommel is back with his Panzer Army, and I fear he is planning a massive counter-blow to crush us before we have recovered sufficiently. He must be aware of our problems alongside Mitereiya Ridge, and perhaps he will attack there, where we are most exposed at the moment. And I fear, and intercepted Intelligence is pointing to the likelihood that his attack will come tomorrow, the 26th. We must steel ourselves to resist an onslaught.'

Bill Williams lets all this sink in, and then looks at Monty.

Monty looks at the Liaison Officers.

'Does Bill's analysis more or less agree with what you have seen on the ground?'

'Hard to say,' says John Poston. 'We see little sign of what Bill is warning of, but we do see some disaster and loss of morale on our part, sir. It is certainly worrying.'

'Bill, what are the strengths of our position, if any?'

Bill Williams picks up a map-stick and points at the map.

'The chief strength of our position is that Rommel is still not sure about Horrocks in the South. He is very likely thinking that our main blow will still come from there. Rommel has half his tanks down there, and is possibly frightened to bring them further north at the moment, in case of the possibility of our striking a massive blow down there. Our deception plan is working.'

Bill Williams pauses, for this to sink in.

'This of course we all know, and we also know that our bombing has done huge damage to his Tank strength. If he wants to strike us a massive blow, he will have to concentrate his Armour, either bringing up Tanks from the south, or sending

Tanks from the north down there, or to our Central position around Mitereiya Ridge. If he were to concentrate his Armour at Mitereiya Ridge tomorrow, he might blow a hole in us. That is our main worry at present. It would make sense for this to be done ... so long as he does not weaken his strength too much in the north, where the Australians are doing well. He mustn't lose the Coast Road.'

'Let me stop you there, for a moment,' says Monty, and goes on:

'What might be the effect on Rommel of switching our forces from the Centre, our New Zealanders mainly, and bringing them further north? At the same time defending the Ridge itself with Tanks and Artillery and enough Infantry to withstand a large attack ...'

'It would put him even more in two minds,' says Bill Williams. 'On the one hand, he might consider it another feint, with our real blow still to come from Horrocks in the south ... in which case he would not move much of his Armour northwards. On the other hand, he might think it is to be our main blow, in which case he would need to get his Armour up from the south as quickly as possible.'

Bill Williams pauses for effect, and then delivers his own main blow.

'What Rommel knows he <u>cannot</u> do is to bring most of his Armour up from the south to counter our main attack, and then send it back again if Horrocks after all lets loose in the south.'

'Not enough time, you mean?' says John Poston.

'No,' says Bill Williams, 'Not enough fuel. That is the rub for Rommel. Our Air Force has just sunk two of his huge oil tankers. We are gradually gaining dominance in the Mediterranean, though poor old Malta is at death's door. If we were to lose Malta, it would be another story. But they are holding out ... And on the question of fuel supplies, we hold the whip hand at the moment. Rommel, because of his fuel shortages, will have to think very carefully where to strike. It is this which inclines one to hope he will not take the rest of his Armour southwards or even centrewards, but will economize on fuel by striking more to the north, bringing up his Armour from the south only when he is reasonably certain that we will not after all attack there. If he were to go south with a mass of Armour, he has not the fuel capability to bring it all north again if things go wrong. And he cannot of course afford to lost control of his ports and oil terminals.'

'Thank you very much, Bill, very illuminating, and it makes our position not quite as bad as I had been thinking,' says Monty. 'We have gained the initiative by launching a massive attack, and it is just a matter of not losing that initiative through the tank weaknesses we have been suffering. We must at all costs keep this initiative, and keeping Rommel guessing is the key to that. We will therefore shift our axis from a south-western offensive based around Mitereiya Ridge here in the Centre, to an axis and an offensive further north, aiming to take the feature Kidney Ridge, here, at the climax of our campaign.'

Monty points to Kidney Ridge, north of centre.

'We already have some Armour out here, it is just a matter of bringing in some more, and of getting a dug-in hull-down position in that whole area, with field guns and the rest. Then our Infantry can continue their crumbling of the German infantry and Rommel's tanks will be forced to attack us. Once we are dug-in, we will welcome his attacks. The more he attacks us there, the more pleased I shall be.

'Therefore, we must move infantry and some Armour from the Mitereiya Ridge position northwards, while at the same time not allowing Rommel to break through and cross the Ridge itself. We can put General Gatehouse in a defensive position there, with his tanks, which is his strength. Horrocks can move some of his forces a little northwards, to plug the gaps ... but must basically stay put for the present, to maintain the deception in the south. Is that clear, gentlemen?'

'Crystal clear, as always,' says De Guingard, to general murmurs of assent and appreciation. 'I will get this to our Commanders post-haste, and all Liaison Officers will from now on tailor their observations to this change of plan.'

'Time for lunch, gentlemen, and you are all welcome,' says

Monty. 'Even Rommel has to stop for lunch, gentlemen. I have been studying his face carefully, and it has recently divulged that secret. I hope soon to find out if he is also required to make use of the thunder-box!'

This reference to the camp lavatory for officers has them all laughing as they move out of the Map Caravan, and towards the Mess Tent.

25 October afternoon.

The New Zealand infantry begin their pull-back from forward positions. Gatehouse's tanks man the Mitereiya Ridge on the safer side. The New Zealand infantry begin their fighting and 'crumbling' behind the Ridge, and in a northerly direction. This is a bitter struggle, but preferable to being exposed targets in the previous positions.

The Highland infantry further north, and the Australian infantry in the far north, intensify their 'crumbling' operations. This time, for all the Allied infantry, it is not simply a question of 'passing through', but of subduing and destroying the Axis infantry and field guns. Allied field guns and the deadly mortars are brought in. When these have done their work, so-called 'mopping-up' operations begin. This is the work of infantry in hand-to-hand conflict with those remaining alive in the Axis dugouts. Under smokescreens, the Allied infantry seek out the Axis positions where there is still life, and with hand-grenades, and then pistols and bayonets, finish off the survivors, again taking no prisoners at this stage. This is work that only the infantry can do, and only the infantry are required to do. For all the other arms, the word 'fighting' is hardly the right word. For them, it is really a question of machines and mathematics. The PBI, or 'poor bloody infantry', do all the dirty work that involves getting actually dirty and covered in blood, and hearing the screams of the wounded and dying. It is grim and terrible, and many members of the other arms are not at all sure they could do it themselves.

When Rommel realizes that this is now going on on a large scale, later in the day, he begins to mobilize his armour for an attack on the Allied infantry. However, he is not yet ready to call up Panzer divisions from the south, for Horrocks is still attacking in that area, and Rommel is still not sure that he can rule out the south as the focus of the main Allied offensive to come.

As night falls on the 25th, Rommel's position is weakened, in that his troops are not trained for night-fighting and movements, whereas Monty's are. The movement of Allied troops north continues therefore, after dark, and the infantry attacks on Axis positions also continues.

Chapter 20 - Victory

26th October

The change of plan is being authorized, understood and implemented at all levels. The Allied infantry assault on Axis forward positions continues all day, as the Panzers also come into operation. At the same time more of their armour and anti-tank guns are able to get forward, in the now crucial Kidney Ridge area, north of centre, and are able to protect their infantry against Rommel's Panzer attacks well enough, though with considerable losses.

When night comes, yet more Allied armour and anti-tank guns will come forward, and the digging-in process will continue. An air of greater confidence has already begun to spread through the 8th Army.

At 6.00 pm, Monty makes a decision that is entirely his own. On the 27th he will rest the New Zealand infantry units and some of the Highland and Australian units that have been heavily involved in the fighting, and bring in fresh units. A passing through and exchange will take place, the exhausted and bloodied fighters will pass to the rear, and spend two or three days bathing in the sea, well out of danger behind the lines.

27th October

During the night of the 26th-27th, Rommel at last decides that the Allied strength in the south with Horrocks was after all a feint, and he orders up many of the Panzer Divisions from there, including the crack 21 Panzer Division, for the fight around Kidney Ridge. But by the time these arrive, the Allied tanks and anti-tank guns and field guns are securely dug in, and present a massive defensive front. The Panzers, however, attack it, and attempt to break through, in order to save their infantry further forward, from annihilation.

Monty is now in his element. The main shape of the Plan has been preserved, and he is overjoyed to see the Panzers breaking themselves on the Allied defensive wall. The mood in the 8th

Army becomes one of exhilaration, and especially among those infantry units being rested. They are able to recuperate while knowing that they will be used again a few days later in what is planned as the Allied breakthrough. There is a return to that willingness to fight, a <u>fighting</u> to be allowed to fight, that existed in the week or so before the battle of Al Alamein began.

The Allies even go forward a little on their defensive front, and gain a toehold on Kidney Ridge itself. The Allied armour is beginning to redeem itself. Not every Axis gun is an 88 mm gun, they discover, especially as the heavy bombing, and artillery barrage, have reduced the numbers of these deadly weapons. If there is still bitterness in the Commonwealth infantry about the 'betrayal' by British armour, there is correspondingly a huge revival in the admiration for that best of all Britishers, Monty himself. Monty is becoming a demi-god, and is enjoying every second of it. He can actually sense the wave of admiration that sweeps over the 8th Army towards himself. He knows this is wonderful in more than a personal sense, and is far more than an experience of palpable gratification. He knows that this can be used for his Army to perform almost superhuman tasks. He knows also that the physical fitness and endurance he has trained the infantry for, will now come into its own. They will all go an extra mile now, with hope inside them, and a sense of impending glory for themselves. And mixed up with this is a growing love for Monty himself.

Monty now begins a few tentative forays in a large Staff car, towards the front line, standing up and waving while the troops recognize him and give him thunderous cheers. They put arms round each other while they shout, and tears are shed. Death itself becomes of no great account for each man facing it for himself, while this tremendous atmosphere exists. It is felt that the love which exists now will travel through to them in the face of death, the experience of death, and in the hinterlands beyond death. Shame becomes the fear, not death. To have acquitted oneself badly at the crucial time is now the fear, and the unthinkable thing. It is now obvious that one not must, but will, risk one's own life to deliver a comrade from fatal danger. That is the new law of this new mode of existence. The cold ice-block of primitive, elemental egoic fear in the guts has been dissolved.

Those who had thought it impossible now find it happening within themselves. When they think of home, they shed some secret tears again, but even home, and safety, and comfort, and relief and a renewed love and appreciation of the homely things and people, even these do not compare at the moment with the flood of renewed being, in which love and sacrifice and possible death are no longer terrible. The thought of returning home at last, safe and sound and loved, is hardly a greater joy than the thought of being loved and remembered, and loved yet again for the task they have done, for the tribulation they have brought upon themselves, for the ultimate sacrifice that they might have to make.

Surely those at home can know this feeling that they are experiencing out here. Surely this wonderful thing will reach them, just as the love sent from home reaches the soldiers themselves, silently and without the usual means of transmission. Letters and gifts are vital to them, but what the letters cannot say the soldiers can yet feel. It is an outpouring of love, and their own letters home cannot quite convey it.

It is a love of men for home, and a love of those at home for men at the front. It is still more than this. It has become a love of the task, a willingness to suffer and die for the task and for one's fellows in the task. It is also a love for one's Chief Commander, Monty himself. They will die also for Monty, because of his love for them. A love of Monty for his men. Does Monty actually love them, they ask themselves? If not, where in fact is this atmosphere of love coming from? Is it just hope and gladness that the battle can now be won? It is all that, but it is more than that. This little man, with all his sharpness, and simple almost banal phrases, and his obvious satisfaction with himself and desire for yet more glory and self-gratification, is after all most concerned for them. To save their lives if possible, but also to send his real love with and beyond the arena of death and dying, where they might indeed have to meet their earthly end this day or the next. The dry little man with his dry humour and insignificant bearing, his lack of obvious glamour and heroic looks, must indeed be a hero of some other kind, for he is the conduit for a reservoir of deep emotion. He is no demagogue. He does not work on them and rouse them up. They are not receiving the kind of inflation that will deflate later and leave them bitter and sad, like the impulses of sexual lust that some know only too well in their periods of leave and, in Monty's term, 'horizontal refreshment.' It is seen as amazing that he understands that need as well, and understands its imperative nature for some of them, and probably knows in his own way somehow its anti-climax as well, yet is willing to condone it for their sakes. Condoning the need even while perceiving the illusion. An indulgent parent, a seer, a wise man ... and an inexhaustible fount of love, it would seem.

When he arrives standing up in his car, stops and speaks to them, those who are thoughtful and look carefully see at last that it is in the eyes that the power is carried, not in the words, and certainly not in the undistinguished face as a whole, with its sharp ferrety look. And those who have been inspected on parade by Monty in the past remember above all the shock of his eyes suddenly making contact with their own, after a prelude of swift up and down glances at their body and bearing. It was more than eye-contact, it was a compact, there and then for every individual, the same for everyone, but different for everyone, as all truly personal things are. Some had cause to think it an illusion, as the ferret-fox eyes impression faded, but on seeing Monty again, the strong initial impression is revived. The power in the eyes casts a glamour over his words, his Speech-Day hackneyed sentiments about 'pulling together', 'working as a team', and so on. The glamour over-reaches his bearing and his ferrety face, his beret, and his staff car. Everything about him and around him is loved because he himself is loved.

Officers who rather resent his ego, and experience his blundering tactlessness from time to time, consider he will have all the faults of the egocentric, such as thinking only of himself ultimately, therefore blotting out all impressions of themselves and their personalities. But these receive a great shock when weeks or months later, in contact with him, he remembers everything about them. They begin to feel he can see so deeply into them that he knows even their secrets. Both officers and other ranks come to believe that Monty always knows what they are up to. He is a presiding super-ego to the entire Army, but a kindly super-ego, and one founded in love and genuine concern for their well-being. So if he is an egocentric, he is certainly a strange unique kind of egocentric. And if he is vain, he at the same time knows how to put his vanity to work, transforming it into an energy that goes out and energizes others. It acts in him as gratitude for the admiration and love he has received, and it is therefore a warm, outgoing vanity. It goes cold only if and when it has no outlet in command and authority. And if he is a fanatic, that judgement goes ill with his flashes of wonderful humour. There is talk of a wife he must have at home, who must be a wonderful woman, one of those who are always behind the success of great men. But nothing is known about her, nothing is divulged. There is even a rumour that he is a widower, but nothing certain is known. Monty stands above all ordinary causation anyway. Nothing or no one could account for his oddity, and for his greatness. He is like the therapist who will mirror everything the patient feels, who will seem to be like him in every way, yet is totally different, and subject to the same weaknesses and temptations, even while understanding them. While there is this mystery about him, there is a mystique and the transmission of power.

All this is going on in men's minds and feelings while the crucial battle is being fought on the 27th of October.

Back at TAC HQ Monty gives orders for the Australians to push even further north. At the same time, the order to rest some of the New Zealanders and some of the Australians and Highlanders, and put in fresh troops is being implemented.

There is no loss of momentum, but something of a shock for the new infantry units as they take over the lateral 'crumbling' operations in their various sectors. Casualties on both sides have been heavy, and the dead and the wounded are thick on the ground. The RAMC and the Friends Ambulance Unit move in at this changeover, and stretcher the wounded away, trying to comfort where possible, and being aware of the mine-lanes.

Sappers and infantry are still at work clearing mines for the lateral push. The fight is therefore both meticulously careful and ferocious. As Allied troops come upon the dugouts they have rained mortar-fire on and hurled grenades into, they have to overcome the shock of the bloody mess in there, the blown-off limbs, the copious blood still flowing, the desperate terror of the limping survivors. As these see the bayonet lifted and descending, they lift piteous hands and try to grasp and deflect the hideous blade, crying out 'Ah no,' or 'Nein, nein'. Sometimes they succeed in grasping it, and their hands are sliced and bleeding as they attempt to push it aside. At last the blade wins the battle, and the appalling screams shatter the air, and the attacker tries to scream even louder so as not to register the effects of what he has done. Sometimes his victim will continue to cling to the blade after it has entered his gut, reluctant to let it be withdrawn. The attacker has to stand then on the body and pull hard, noting to himself amidst this horror that in future he will aim the blade higher, and merely jab and wound rather than try to see through the business of killing.

Once the more or less active survivors have been dealt with in this way, those deemed beyond recovery are finished off with a pistol shot to the head. The troops then lie low, take breath, and prepare themselves for the next assault.

Those lucky ones withdrawn from the battle and now bathing in the delicious sea can, if they like, regard their immersion as both bliss and recreation and as partial absolution from the sin of war and killing. Some of the padres will have suggested this to them, and will have told them of the medieval clerical practice of absolving soldiers in a cleansing ceremony.

Some others will think that all the waters of the Mediterranean will not sweeten their hands, that have done such deeds. They will not know the word 'incarnadine', but may well be conscious of blood everywhere, and sense their own bodies as polluting the great sea. These will be forced, with the help of some padre, to reflect on the larger issues yet again, and be 'persuaded' of the rightness of their actions. They may remember Monty's injunctions against hate, and reflect on the kindness and wisdom in the depth of his eyes, eyes that seem to know the worst, while affirming the best. For the civilian conscript who has ended up in the infantry, and is now finding out what that really means, the presence and example of Monty is a lifeline, a route to preserving his own sanity. None of the other commanders seem able to reach down into the soul in quite that way.

In this way, and in many other ways, Monty's stature increases as the battle unfolds, each hour and each day. As he shows himself to the troops in battle, or to those behind the lines, or to those resting and bathing, each appearance becomes a positive confirmation of what has been felt before, an experience of solid worth, and of solid truth.. And the troops' experience of battle, especially those soldiers who were civilians, conscripts and volunteers, enables them to appreciate the honest sobriety of Monty's demeanour and of his words. The very banality of his speeches becomes a virtue. Words like 'honour', and 'comrades', phrases like 'working together', and 'the common cause', regain an original freshness. There is after all no need to elaborate when old tired words have recovered their energy, and shine in the darkness of war like new coins. Monty has rubbed the dirt and grime and tiredness off them, as a service for others. It is felt that in his own simplicity, these words had never lost their shine in the first place. He is like a vivid artist showing the world what the world looks like to him. And, even more importantly, showing what they look like, and how important they are to him, and how important in themselves.

Such is the atmosphere as the sun sets on the 27th of October. Rommel is being deprived of his massive counter-blow. The Allied defensive line stays firm, Mobile Panzers cannot break it, but rather break themselves on it. Big guns are themselves out-gunned, and meanwhile the Axis infantry is being destroyed behind it. The Allies also suffer very heavy casualties there, but every Allied soldier knows that with each day the enemy infantry will grow weaker, as they are denied new ammunition and other supplies.

The feeling on the night of the 27th of October among the Allies is one of immense optimism and satisfaction. The little man may be right after all. 'Knock Rommel for Six!' 'There cannot be any doubt about it.' 'He is definitely a nuisance.' 'We will deliver him a great crack, and then we will be done with him.' These seemingly glib little phrases echo in the mind, and acquire density.

In Rommel's camp, confidence is not so strong. The Panzer units from the south are not long in action before it is felt necessary to divert some from the Kidney Ridge area to the north, where the sudden Australian diversion towards the coast has created alarms. Rommel's breakthrough should have come today. If it does not come tomorrow, he will begin to worry.

Meanwhile the Australians have taken the important Hill 28, a feature north of Kidney Ridge, and therefore hold the initiative in that area. And the Allied artillery and bombing raids do not cease. Equipment is shattered, and the nerves of Rommel's fighting troops are also beginning to be shattered. There is no rest, day or night, no let-up.

28th October

John Poston has given Monty his latest verbal report.

'Thank you, John, go and get some sleep,' says Monty. 'I have some new ideas to ponder over, in conjunction with your report.'

Monty goes to bed in his caravan, and props himself up there, sipping a large mug of tea. At about 7am he emerges, and is served another 'Full Monty' breakfast in the courtyard, in the shade. The atmosphere is peaceful again. It is hard to believe there is a war on, except for the noise of the bombers going out yet again. But it is now as though dronings and bangs and crashes are part of the distant background of monastic life, as though the Kitchen Brothers are being a little noisy in their work ... nothing more.

Monty is sipping strong coffee as De Guingand comes out of the office towards him.

'Good morning, sir!' says De Guingand.

'Morning Freddie,' says Monty.

'What now, then, sir? More of the same?'

'In some areas, yes. Destruction of Rommel's infantry in our area must go on, of course. I want even more Australians to move northwards. We must aim for Sidi el Rahman at the coast, which will frighten Rommel, and we must be in a position soon to intercept their supply lines. That will be our breakthrough area, up in the north. We will need more of Horrocks' troops from further south to reinforce the New Zealanders, as we give another batch of these poor buggers a two-day rest. And we need Horrocks to cover the areas south of Kidney Ridge, so that Rommel cannot break through on our flank.'

'Understood, sir,' says De Guingand.

'Also, I'm thinking of giving our tanks a rest, as we will need the best of them in a few days, to follow up the break-through.'

'Resting the tanks, sir?' says De Guingand, not quite believing his ears. 'Can we afford to do so, sir? They've been doing a terrific job holding the defensive line, sir.'

'Yes, they have indeed,' says Monty. 'But, as we now know, they are not good at combined operations with infantry and artillery, and I am not confident, therefore, that they will be effective in the first stage of the breakthrough. For that we will use our infantry in the first instance, followed by fast armoured cars which will race through to their supply lines, and followed last by our Corps de Chasse, led, unfortunately, by Lumsden, which will then exploit the breakthrough. Tanks will therefore come last, Freddie, not first.'

'I see the pattern, sir. But will our defensive line hold?'

'Rommel will today have to divert more of his Panzer Force northwards, to meet the Australian threat. Even the Panzers still arriving from the south will have to go north. Rommel will be concluding by now, or soon, that the north and the coast is to be our breakthrough area, and there we must break him!'

'Well, he might ... or he might not,' ventures De Guingand.

'He can't afford to lose control of his Coast Line, whether he thinks we will break through there or not ... He will reinforce the north today, and our defensive line behind Kidney Ridge will hold ... In any case, we will not withdraw the tanks till after dark tonight.'

'Very good, sir,' says Freddie.

He withdraws. Monty finishes his coffee, and goes into his Map Caravan for a few minutes, where he studies the portrait of Rommel on the wall.

'Cunning fox or not,' he says, aloud, to it. 'You are being driven to earth.' Then he leaves the caravan and goes across to his office.

At Rommel's headquarters the orders are given to send some of the best Panzer Units to the north, to break the Australians' defensive line, and halt their infantry surge. He is confident he can do this while continuing to batter and weaken the Allied defensive line around and beyond Kidney Ridge. But the Allied shelling and bombing is remorseless, and a great loss of morale is even now happening.

During this day the spirits of the Allied forces remain high, in spite of high casualties, because there continues to be a stalemate on the front line, which is a useful stalemate from their point of view. They have told Rommel off, and their bombers and artillery, they hear, are beginning to wear down the capacity for endurance of Rommel's men. It is just a matter, therefore, of hanging on for a few more days, and the victory should be theirs. An immense fortitude is built up in the Allied troops, even as it begins to crumble in the enemy. Things are visibly in balance, but invisibly beginning to swing.

After dark, most of the tanks are withdrawn, and go back to the rest area. The big guns and field guns and the infantry stay on their defensive line, while the destruction of Axis infantry in the bloody, desperate battle goes on mainly behind them.

Monty visits some units again, standing up in his car, and the effect is as before. It is hard to think of snowballs in that desert, but the men certainly feel the effect as of a snowball growing larger by the hour. As the cold night swiftly arrives, and the hard stars are icily burning, the thought of victory also grows larger and larger in their minds.

29th October

The Australians have been making good progress in the north, and a certain desperation enters the minds of Axis troops and commanders. They can slow the advance in the north, but find themselves unable to break the defensive line. Some of the best Panzers and the best guns and infantry will have to remain here, rather than delivering a massive crippling blow elsewhere. Meanwhile they begin to feel themselves in danger around Kidney Ridge. Rommel himself is unwell, unable to sleep properly, and losing his calm and his relish for the battle.

Does Monty know this, as he stares again t the portrait in the Map Caravan at 7.30 this morning, after his meeting with John Poston, and his cup of tea as usual, (at six thirty, in bed, thinking and studying the reports)? Certainly a number of people who know him will attest to some psychic ability in him. His swift diagnosis of situations, and his frightening capacity to see instantly into character and capability, are sometimes evident. And there is the common perception, as has been said, that Monty always knows what you are thinking and doing. This is alarming, if a man feels he is not thinking and doing very well, though there is also the encouraging feeling that he can help you out of that slough of despond. The thought of Monty is worrying, but to latch onto the strength and calmness of Monty is to find release and revival. This extraordinary mental transfer is going on all the time, somewhere, in someone. No one malingers in the sick bay any more. There is a new readiness to fight, on the one hand, On the other, if one _is_ malingering, through a temporary weakness of mind or character, Monty will know, and orders for action, or even for your arrest will come through.

London Perspective

But in London, and in Whitehall, in the minds of Churchill and others, Monty and his capacities are not held in such awe. And today there is a crisis, one involving a judgment on Monty's own judgment. Anthony Eden, the Foreign Minister, has got wind of the fact that Monty has been withdrawing whole units of infantry, and now even the tanks, from the battle. He has conveyed this to

Churchill, together with his fears that this is the beginning of a retreat ... or, at the very least, a failure to press home our advantage at a sensitive stage of the battle.

Churchill, naturally, in his permanently overwrought state, in his anguish and near-desperation, is driven to anger. He calls Alanbrooke over to see him, and gives vent to his thoughts and feelings.

'What on earth is your Monty up to now, Alanbrooke?' Monty is always his Monty when things go wrong. Churchill will not yet take his share of responsibility for the appointment. This particular foible of Churchill's is what most gets up Alanbrooke's nose. But he remains silent and thinks it wise to let Churchill have his full rant.

'What is your Monty doing now, Alanbrooke? He has done practically nothing of any significance for the last three days, just sitting there and taking punishment. And now I hear he is actually withdrawing units from the fighting line! What in heavens name is going on? Is this the beginning of another defeat, for God's sake? Why did Monty tell us all he would break through in seven days, if he fights a half-hearted battle, and then, pronto on the seventh day itself, begins to retreat?' Churchill pauses for a few moments, and holds his head in his hands. Alanbrooke senses that he hasn't finished, and stays silent. At length Churchill withdraws his hands, and shows a face with signs of tears on it.

'Haven't we got a single general in our army who can win a single battle, Alanbrooke? Haven't we? And think of my position, Alanbrooke! The House of Commons on my back again ... and ... and worse than that. What am I going to say to the Commonwealth Prime Ministers, when they find that their gallant soldiers have died in their thousands to save our great country, which is no longer a gallant country, Alanbrooke, which can't even fight a battle to save our own throats from the knife, which cannot respond to the gallantry of our Commonwealth cousins-in-arms? It is shameful, Alanbrooke! I will die of shame. I will be shoved out, and you will be shoved out, and how will you like that, Alanbrooke? ... I said, 'How will you like that, Alanbrooke? ... Are you dumb or something, Alanbrooke?'

'Sorry sir, I thought you might have more to say.'

'More to say!' Churchill breaks in, 'I think I have made myself pretty clear, just for once!'

'I understand your difficulties, sir, but I think …'

'It is not my difficulty, Alanbrooke, that is of the essence … we may not like it, but we two are quite dispensable, Alanbrooke … I was wrong to put our difficulty at the forefront. It is our country's difficulty … our country's shame … our country's …'

'Please hear me out, Prime Minister! Please hear me out.'

'Certainly, Alanbrooke, certainly,' says Churchill, seeming to shrink like Toad of Toad Hall deflating.

'First of all, sir, I gather you have received your information from our Foreign Secretary?'

'That's true,' says Churchill, flaring up again. 'Surely I am entitled to gather my information from wherever I think fit? Am I Prime Minister and Defence Secretary, or am I not?'

'Certainly sir ... but it is not advisable to draw firm conclusions from a Foreign Secretary hundreds of miles from the front, who is himself drawing hasty conclusions on insufficient information, sir.'

'Insufficient, did you say, Alanbrooke? Did Montgomery or did he not say that he would break through and bring this battle to an end in seven days?'

'No sir, he did not.'

'Then what in the name of thunder did he say?'

'He gave twelve or thirteen days as the probable length of the battle, sir … we are now approaching the breakthrough phase …'

'And at the breakthrough phase he begins to withdraw his infantry and tanks! What am I to make of that, Alanbrooke?'

'You should not allow these premature and incomplete reports to upset your equilibrium, Prime Minister. For all you say about our dispensability, we cannot possibly do without you, sir … To be invalided out, sir rather than dismissed …'

'In Heaven's name, are you now calling me an invalid?' roars Churchill.

'Just a timely warning, sir, no more than that.'

Churchill is breathing hard, and Alanbrooke is barely

controlling his own temper.

'We are both tired and out of sorts, sir,' says Alanbrooke at last. 'For the sake of our country, we must try to stay calm.'

'You are right, Alanbrooke. But I must have this thing explained to me, or I cannot rest. We have a Chief of Staffs' meeting at 12.30. Eden will be there. So will good old Attlee. And so will Oliver Lyttelton. Oh, and General Smuts as well. You like him a lot, I gather.'

'He verges on greatness, sir, like yourself.'

'Like myself, Alanbrooke, eh … Huh! Greatness eh? Huh! Can't say I feel 'great' this morning ... as the Americans say. Can't say I've enjoyed much respect from you this morning, Alanbrooke … if this is greatness, huh! If this is what greatness entails, Alanbrooke … '

'Please calm down, sir, and shake hands. We're in this together, sir, if indeed we are in the soup.'

'Truth in that, Alanbrooke … How do you like the Silk Road, the Golden Road to Samarkand, Alanbrooke? I dream of it all the time … ' says Churchill as they shake hands.

'Just petrol fumes these days, I fear, sir,' says Alanbrooke. 'I'll be back at 12.30, sir.'

29th October

Chief of Staffs' Meeting 12.30   All are gathered round a table in Churchill's domain. Churchill himself begins proceedings.

'I've been considerably worried, gentlemen, by reports from the Alamein front. But I will call upon our Foreign Secretary, Mr Eden, to expand on this for us.'

'Thank you Prime Minister,' responds Eden,' Certainly I am seriously worried myself, when I hear reports that units of our army are being pulled out of battle at precisely the moment when we were hoping they would break through and give us a decisive victory. It is deeply disappointing, gentlemen, to have to suspect that our promising offensive is in fact petering out. It is not only the withdrawal of units, now, gentlemen. It is the fact that for the last three days, since we initially broke in, we seem to have done nothing. Much trust was placed in our new Army Commander, Montgomery, and also his chief, General Alexander. And yet both of them have really seemed to be losing their grip … our thought was of a stiff telegram to them both, gentlemen, in this considerably desperate situation.'

'Er, no,' Churchill interrupts, 'I have thought better of that, Mr Eden. Some form of communication, some plea for elucidation, and some indication of our worries at home – that would be sufficient, I'm sure. And I sent such a message last night. But thank you, Mr Eden, for voicing your strong concern. I will now ask General Alanbrooke to comment, as one in close touch with both Alex and Monty, and one knowing their minds not a little.'

'Thank you Prime Minister,' says Alanbrooke. 'I feel I need to say at once that Mr Eden's conclusion is almost certainly wrong, in that his knowledge of the last three days is superficial …' Alanbrooke registers, but ignores, a sharp movement from Eden at the word 'superficial'.

'I have to say,' he begins again, with barely concealed anger, 'that not to know that the last three days have been a successful containment of the most ferocious Panzer attacks on our forward positions, is simply not to understand the situation. If Mr Eden does not know this, he should not be airing his opinions, and attempting to put pressure on our commanders out there. We are on the verge of undermining our commanders at precisely the moment of victory. I, for one, will not allow this to happen, and I stake my position and my career on that,' says Alanbrooke, pausing, and looking straight at Eden, and then at Churchill.

'That's all very well,' says Churchill, 'but why is Montgomery withdrawing his infantry and tank units at this critical moment, then?'

'I think Mr Eden, as a former Staff Officer in the Great War, should understand this very well. It is surely standard practice to withdraw and rest units in preparation precisely for the next offensive blow – which should take place two or three days from now. In any case, it is a principle of Montgomery's to rest all units after two or three days in battle at all times. It is part of his philosophy of warfare, as he has often made clear … to those who have been listening,' he adds, with some acidity. 'For myself, Montgomery's withdrawal of units indicates, therefore, that we are not far from the critical hammer-blow … and of course he will be replacing the withdrawn units with fresh units as we speak. It is good news, it is just the news we should welcome. Why are we so jittery, so ready to believe the worst?'

Alanbrookes's contribution is digested in silence for a while. Churchill then turns to the venerable General Smuts and asks him for his opinion.

General Smuts smiles gently, and then says, 'I have not had the opportunity to speak to General Alanbrooke, but the points he has made about tactics are perfectly valid, and I have no problem in agreeing with them in their entirety … Also, I have great confidence in him, and if he has confidence in Alexander and Montgomery, then so have I. So far as I can see myself, they are the best military team we have had so far in this war. I think we should calm down, gentlemen, and let matters proceed as planned and allowed for.'

This intervention may not please Eden's vanity, but it brings balm to Alanbrooke, who visibly relaxes, and to Churchill, who feels his intense worries untangling themselves to some extent. Oliver Lytletton voices the concerns of the Commonwealth Prime Ministers, while at the same time averring that there need after all be no worries on their behalf.

The meeting ends in a good atmosphere, and as they rise to go, Alanbrooke takes General Smuts by the hand, and then thanks him deeply. A slightly awkward Anthony Eden tries to be genial, but his smile is somewhat marred by spiritual indigestion, as he inwardly reflects that this occasion would add to the impression of his having a highly strung and somewhat neurotic nature. He avoids Churchill's glance, but attempts at least to make it up with Alanbrooke.

'Sorry, Alanbrooke, if I've cried 'Wolf'. Just worry, really, nothing personal intended!'

'Say no more, Mr Eden. There are lots of nerves at the moment, and understandably. But we should keep to what we really know, and not allow bogeymen to grow in our minds.'

'If hopes are dupes, fears may be liars,' quotes Churchill as he cottons on to this conversation, and then goes on to say, 'I sent a revised telegram to Alexander and Montgomery, just a note to the effect that the American Torch landings in North Africa are to take place on the 8th of November, and hoping, just hoping, Alanbrooke, that some progress at Alamein can be made before that date ... to give our American friends a pleasant gift, that's all.'

'Splendid, Prime Minister. I can assure you that there will be good news from Alamein several days before that,' says Alanbrooke. He wants to add, 'with or without your telegram,' but manages to catch himself in time.

'Well, we all hope so, Alanbrooke. Goodbye, and good luck to us all.'

They all leave and disperse to their place of duty.

29th October 9 am. Monty's TAC again.

Monty is still in his Map Caravan. De Guingand brings him Churchill's revised telegram, which Monty reads in his presence.

'Fine, Freddie, fine, nothing to worry about there. Torch landing 8th November ... good. Churchill's a bit optimistic about French co-operation, but no matter.'

De Guingand returns to the Office, and shortly after this a quiet and luxurious staff car draws up, containing Alexander, his deputy McCreery, and a civil servant, Casey, all from Cairo. They are a little battered, having yesterday been subjected to Churchill's doubts and to his wrath. They know the crisis has passed, but are anxious to change the break-out plan in the way De Guingand has already suggested to Monty. De Guingand explains that he has himself put it to Monty, and that Monty is happy with the plan as is. De Guingand is again prepared to leave it at that, but the team from Cairo are not happy to do so.

'What's the urgency?' De Guingand asks.

'Churchill is the urgency,' says Alexander, 'we have had his rough tongue for hours.'

'I thought things had settled,' says De Guingand.

'Well, yes and no,' says Alexander. 'His revised telegram is moderate in tone ... but he really does want things speeded up now, and to strike at the Italian tanks from Kidney Ridge seems to us a good idea, in the circumstances.'

'Monty is keen on destroying more of Rommel's Panzers, even if the whole battle takes a day or two longer,' says De Guingand.

'As an ex-tank-man myself,' says McCreery, 'I think a change in plan is essential. We can destroy the Italian armour quickly, and then capture or destroy the Panzers later.'

'It's all a bit academic,' says De Guingand, 'I don't know why you have come all the way from Cairo to press this point. It is a good idea, but it isn't crucial, we are not going to lose the battle through not implementing it!'

There is a silence, until Casey suddenly says, 'Very well. I shall send a cable to Churchill saying again that things are not going well here ... then we shall see if it is 'academic' or not.'

'Oh no you won't!' shouts De Guingand. 'Oh no you won't! I presume, then, that it was you, you meddling damned fool, who started to worry Churchill in the first place! If you send that cable now, I will see you sacked, and drummed out of political life forever. You are a damned meddling fool, and you are wasting our time here, and are proving a poison pen in Cairo. How dare you presume to run our campaign here, you confounded man, you unadulterated idiot!'

'Neither Alexander nor McCreery not the office staff have seen De Guingand so angered.

'Sorry, De Guingand,' says Alexander. 'We are all getting a bit overwrought the last few days. Casey will not send any such cable, I will see to that.'

Casey sits down in a corner and nurses his wounds.

McCreery intervenes. 'May I not speak to Monty personally, Freddie, and try to persuade him?' he asks gently.

'No, you may not,' says De Guingand, in danger of flaring up again. 'Monty does not ... ' He checks himself. 'It will not work.'

'You don't need to conceal from me that Monty doesn't like me, Freddie,' says McCreery, laughing. 'I know that well enough. He's not one to conceal his dislikes, as you know.'

'Then why do you think you could persuade him with your

quiet little chat? You are not the one to soft-soap him,' says De Guingand.

'But perhaps you are?' says Alexander sweetly.

'Perhaps I am,' replies De Guingand.

'Will you do it, then?' asks Alexander.

'Perhaps I will try again,' says De Guingand. 'If I can persuade him it is his own idea, that will be the most effective way. But I will not attempt it now, with all of you here. You must pack up, all of you, and take your way back to Cairo, and leave us in peace. Then I will choose my time.'

'You are a good fellow, Freddie, and we'll leave it to you,' says Alexander, putting an arm round De Guingand's shoulder.

'Go quietly, please,' says De Guingand, 'It is better that Monty doesn't know you have been here.'

And they go quietly, as the chauffeur quietly purrs off in the de-luxe car.

Bill Williams and others rise to their feet, and embrace De Guingand, laughing and whooping.

'That's the way to deal with 'em, Freddie!'says Bill.

'Bit risky!' says De Guingand, 'Lucky Alexander is a good chap. Otherwise … Did you notice I'd stopped calling him 'Sir'? A stickler would have had me for that.'

'You are too precious here for that kind of nonsense,' says Bill again, 'Anyway, thank God you dealt with that fellow Casey … what a puffed up little nincompoop!'

'I sensed suddenly he had been poisoning Churchill's mind, and he more or less confessed it. Anyway, back to work.'

Peace settles down on TAC HQ again, with Monty still in his Map Caravan, and the rest at their tasks. As 11 o'clock approaches, De Guingand slips out of the office and knocks at the caravan door.

'Come in, Freddie. I've nearly finished here. Did I hear a car, and some sort of shouting match?'

'I don't think so, sir,' says De Guingand.

'Strange,' says Monty.

'Strange indeed,' says De Guingand. 'However, to business. I trust you have been thinking a little about that proposed change of plan since we last spoke, sir?'

'Was I supposed to think any more about it, Freddie?'

'Well, no, not strictly, sir … I just thought that perhaps I tried to rush you earlier. I shouldn't have woken you at 5 o'clock. The new intelligence could have waited, sir. But now you've had more leisure, sir, I just wondered …'

'I've been very glad of the leisure, Freddie … and pretty glad to have been out of that shouting match, too!'

De Guingand doesn't know what to say.

'Did I catch that rat Casey's voice, Freddie?' says Monty at last.

'Well, yes sir, you did!'

'And that skunk McCreery? Wasn't he there as well?'

'Well, yes, sir, he was,' De Guingand admits.

'And did I catch the voice of good old Alexander pouring oil on troubled waters?' asks Monty again.

'That also is true, sir.'

'And did not Freddie raise his good baritone voice to a fine crescendo, such as is usually heard only in La Scala, Milan, and other such places?'

De Guingand laughs uproariously, and thumps his fist on Monty's table.

'I've been fighting for you, sir. Fighting to preserve your peace and quiet.'

'I know you have, Freddie, I know you have. And I thank you for it. You kept those two creatures Casey and McCreery from spoiling my morning. I cannot thank you enough. I'm surprised Alexander lent himself to their silly schemes, however … What a stupid waste of his time, driving from Cairo at this juncture!'

'I agree,' says De Guingand, 'I agree. And just to press a little scheme that hardly matters one way or the other … Coming all that way!'

'But you have just come all the way from the office to press it upon me, Freddie,' says Monty.

'Not to press it, sir, just to find out if you have given it any more of your thought, sir. I have made my point now, sir, and will return to the office, if you don't mind, sir?'

'Mind? Certainly not. Urgent work for all of us now. Peace …

and careful attention to detail ... a quiet spirit ... and good meals. I'll see you at lunch, Freddie.'

'Right sir. Cheerio! See you at lunch, sir,' says De Guingand, and walks down the caravan steps, and into the compound.

'Oh Freddie!' comes Monty's voice from within.

'Sir!' shouts De Guingand.

'I've changed my mind about the plan, Freddie. I've decided to change it after all.'

'Ah!' says De Guingand weakly, and trying not to burst with laughter.

'Well, aren't you pleased?' shouts Monty, 'I don't hear much rejoicing out there, Freddie, are you skipping about like a lamb, or not?' Monty is still shouting.

'No, sir, I am not,' shouts back De Guingand. 'It is not so important, sir.'

'Dashed ungrateful of you, I must say. Well, it was Churchill's telegram that did it, Freddie … Churchill's telegram … not those blighters from Cairo!' Monty shouts.

'I understand, sir!' shouts De Guingand.

'Nor you, Freddie,' Monty continues. 'Understand that?'

'Yes sir … see you at lunch, sir.'

29th October

The men of the 8th Army are as far from the military politics and wrangles of the day as from Sirius, the Dog-Star. They are experiencing exhilaration as the struggle appears to be going their way. The smell of a great victory is in the air. Those who were fearful have mostly lost their fear, partly because of the atmosphere of success, but mainly because of the feeling that began a few days before, and grows more potent with each day – that of their own importance, whether or not they themselves survive the battle. They learn that to have a high self-esteem, which is reinforced by comrades, and by successful grappling with difficulties, is precisely what is needed in order to feel dispensable and unafraid. One's worth has been averred 'on high', in such a way that one can believe it – and being surrounded by comrades in the same state creates a mighty force of faith and

Often it seems that one's comrades are transfigured. Rough bodies and faces, as in Stanley Spencer's paintings of the Great War, acquire beauty, with a special light coming from them. Each man can feel the admiration coming from others. Such admiration is now unrestrained, with a common male inhibition removed. A sensation of being admired is actually registered, and adds to each man's being. And such love of women as each of the soldiers has experienced so far, can seem excelled by this new experience.

The vigorous Australians and some New Zealanders have increased the volume and speed of their attacks towards the north. It is being reported that Rommel has sent more Panzer regiments to assist his defence there, so that the Axis assault on the Allied positions around Kidney Ridge has weakened in intensity, to a degree that is beginning to be felt. It is no longer expected that a huge Panzer attack will soon be tried in this area, with the intent to actually break through. For as the Axis armour continues to come forward, it is destroyed in sufficient numbers to make a more powerful assault later considerably less likely. Those at the Front can see this, and feel it.

Meanwhile the infantry battle goes on, mainly behind the armour and gun front-line. In the north, the Australian infantry has destroyed Axis infantry by going forward, as further Allied armour swings into their defence. The Australian casualties are extremely high, but no complaints come from that quarter. Their morale and self-esteem is as high as it can ever be, without degenerating into fanaticism. They had their own natural high spirits and optimism, but Monty's spirit has also become part of them. They have taken Monty to their hearts, and fight for him as much as for anyone of anything else.

When the German Panzers in the north mount a large counter-attack against the Australians, there is some concern in Cairo, and at Monty's TAC HQ. There is an approach to Monty about the new and dangerous situation, as the Allied tank strength there is not great. But Monty expresses his full confidence in General Morshead and the Australian guns and infantry. Monty's confidence is repaid as the Australians see off the Panzer attacks, and destroy a large number of tanks.

The Australian resistance is also extremely useful in helping to conceal from Rommel where the Allied attempted breakthrough will occur. Allied success in the north, and nearness to the coast, strongly suggest that the Allies will make the breakthrough there – a good guess, since Monty had, up to the last moment, planned to do just that.

Soon after speaking to De Guingand at 11am, Monty holds a TAC HQ conference to describe the change of plan, and the timing of the breakthrough. 'Supercharge Freyberg is to be Commander, with further support from Horrocks' troops (13 Corps). The troops that have been rested are to take part. It will be a thrust westwards, taking full control of Kidney Ridge, and then further west to Tel-el-Agaggir on the Rahmand Track, the enemy supply line. Once a hole is broken, armoured cars will go forward. It is proposed to launch the first attack on the evening of the 30th.

Cairo is informed by TAC that Monty has accepted the change of plan, and in London, Churchill, Alanbrooke and others in the picture, wait with considerable anxiety and suppressed exhilaration for the final chapter in this section of the Book to unfold.

'How did you do it, De Guingand?' asks General Alexander from Cairo. 'What a clever, charming fellow you are! You were quite right to send us packing, De Guingand, quite right. Did you succeed in persuading him it was his own idea?'

'He didn't need persuading, sir, He had already changed his mind while we were in the office, and it seems he heard ... or intuited, I think ... every word we said!'

'How hilarious, De Guingand! Well, good luck. And Churchill will be pleased, and the pressure from London is off, thank heavens,'

'For the time being, sir,' says De Guingand.

'As you say, for the time being. 'The time being' is all the time there is at the moment, I'm afraid. Until we are on top. Goodbye again, De Guingand ... and I think you will need a rest after this battle is over. Will Monty agree with that?'

'He will if I ask him, sir.'

'Then ask him, De Guingand, ask him. I will support you.'

'I'm feeling pretty fine just now, sir.'

'But when the immediate crisis is over, you will collapse. We don't want you being permanently ill, De Guingand, so we will rest you!'

'Thank you very much, sir ... and goodbye.'

30th October TAC HQ: It is planned that late that night and into the morning of the 31st, the Australians will launch yet another attack on the northern positions, and aim to reach the sea. This is to be followed, soon afterwards, in the latter part of the night and around dawn, by the 'Supercharge' breakthrough from Kidney Ridge by Freyberg's New Zealand units, Horrocks' South Africans and Indians, and a Highland division. It is therefore hoped that on the 31st of October, during the day, and certainly by the evening, the enemy's back will be broken.

31st October

Late at night on the 30th, the Australians launch their attack in the north, which is again very successful. But in the early hours of the morning there is a serious hitch. Freyberg, finding some of the infantry tired, and the artillery still needing instruction on how to support the Australians in the north and then switch to the New Zealanders in the Kidney Ridge area, asks for another twentyfour hours before launching his attack. To add to the confusion, General Lumsden is being obstructive, and probably sulking because the plan was to use the infantry, in Freyberg's attack, before bringing in Lumsden's tanks. He knows he is being judged 'unreliable' by Monty, and resents it, still feeling that his disobeying of Monty's orders earlier in the battle had had good cause. Lumsden is now delaying the assembly of the New Zealand troops by refusing to move his tanks. De Guingand contacts Lumsden, and orders him to co-operate. Monty, out of respect for Freyberg, agrees to a delay of twentyfour hours.

But the situation becomes tense and uncertain, for after the military success of the most recent Australian attack, Rommel has mounted a ferocious Panzer counter-attack on them, and they again suffer heavy casualties. There is now no hope of a breakthrough to the sea, and, worse than that, while Freyberg's 'Supercharge' is on hold, there is a danger that the Panzers will pass the Australians' left flank, and make for the sea themselves, further east, pinning the Australians down in that area, and separating them from the 'Supercharge' forces.

It might even be that 'Supercharge' could not now go ahead at all, but that several more days of defensive battle will have to ensue before it is safe to release it. Monty and his TAC HQ staff fear that by that time both the energy of troops and the state of supplies will be inadequate for a triumphant conclusion. Had Lumsden and his armour been up to the job, the situation could have been different, of course.

There are some tense hours, and for Lumsden, the sack is looming. The weakness of British armour has nearly lost the Allies the breakthrough and the victory they need.

1st November

Monty is up nearly all night, as are De Guingand, Bill Williams and others at TAC HQ, but they manage not to panic. The Australians hold the Panzer counter-attack magnificently, again with heavy casualties, and the guns make further serious inroads into the strength of the Panzers. This heroically tenacious defence by the Australians is clearly the key to the rest of the battle, as Monty recognizes.

All through the day of the 1st of November, Rommel is confident that he can hold off the Allied breakthrough long enough for the Allied troops to be too tired to carry it through adequately when the time comes. Rommel's Panzers and infantry are still full of spirit and fight like tigers to turn defence into dominance. During this time Monty sits down and writes three letters.

2nd November 1am:

Montgomery writes in his diary: 'Our attack went in under a

creeping barrage on a front of 4000 yards, fired by over 300 25-pounders ... the attack was a complete success.'

Rommel, however, is still thinking that the breakthrough would come in the north, and it is only at about 6am that he orders Africa Corps Panzers to defend against the fresh attack and breakthrough. On the other hand, the British tanks are again slow, as Montgomery records in his diary entry for 6am: '1st Armoured Division was late, and did not get up there before daylight. The enemy launched heavy counter-attacks against the north flank of the area of penetration. Very heavy fighting developed and went on all day. 1st Armoured Division slowly gained ground and took heavy toll of the enemy tanks and anti-tank guns, while not suffering too much themselves.'

It is Brigadier Currie's 9th Armoured Brigade which takes the brunt of Rommel's counter-attacks, at this stage, having reached Tell-el-Aqaqqir before dawn. Lumsden's 1st Armoured Brigade lags behind and indeed shelters behind it. Currie's Brigade by this time is so shattered that it has to withdraw from battle, and there is consequently insufficient good armour to exploit the breakthrough fully.

By 7am, Rommel is mobilizing the whole of Africa Corps for a huge counter-attack in the breakthrough area. Rommel's message is intercepted, at 9.11am, and sent straight to Leese and Lumsden, who now succeed in bringing up their armour and a large quantity of anti-tank guns and other artillery. There follows a massive onslaught on Rommel's best armour that lasts all morning, and all that afternoon. Rommel, at 4.30pm announces to his Staff that he is now fighting a rearguard action only, and that preparations for a retreat to Fulia should be put in place. By the evening, half of Africa Corps' tanks have been put out of action.

Monty still has in reserve two armoured Divisions, the 10th and the 7th. At 6.15pm, infantry, followed by these tank Divisions strike south-west, to get well behind German lines and by-pass the Africa Corps at the same time. Shortly after this, Rommel contacts Von Thoma, commander of the Africa Corps, and asks him his view of the situation. Von Thoma confesses it hopeless, and Rommel finally authorizes a retreat.

At 7.50pm, Rommel radios his admission of defeat to the German High Command. He then sits down and writes a letter to his wife.

From this time on, Monty was a national hero, and was seen together with Churchill on posters, in magazines and films. And yet Alamein was only the first of his triumphs.

'THE END OF THE BEGINNING'

Lightning Source UK Ltd.
Milton Keynes UK
UKOW02f0351210616

276753UK00003B/68/P